RUNNING THE COUNTRY

David Coates

Hodder & Stoughton

in association with

The Open
University

This book is a component of the Open University course D212 Running the Country. Details of this and other Open University courses are available from the Central Enquiry Service, The Open University, PO Box 200, Milton Keynes, MK7 2YZ, United Kingdom, Tel: 0908 653231.

British Library Cataloguing in Publication Data

Coates, David

  Running the country

  I. Title

  330.9

  ISBN 0-340-56781-3

First published 1991

Edited, designed and typeset by The Open University

Printed in Great Britain for the educational publishing division of Hodder & Stoughton Ltd, Mill Road, Dunton Green, Sevenoaks, Kent by Thomson Litho Ltd, East Kilbride.

2860C/d212sbi1.1

CONTENTS

ACKNOWLEDGEMENTS

This book was written with the guidance and help of an Open University Course Team chaired by Richard Maidment and administered by Christina Janoszka. I would like to thank Richard and Christina for their original invitation to undertake this task, and for the encouragement and assistance they subsequently provided. I have a debt too to the other members of the Course Team, who gave their time and expertise to the improvement of this manuscript: to Frank Boyle, Tom Burden, Jennifer Frances, Peter Hamilton, Rosalind Levačić, Tom Ling, Jeremy Mitchell, Norma Sherratt, Elaine Storkey and Grahame Thompson. Stephen Clift supervised the transformation of my text into this printed and published form, after Anne Hunt, Mary Dicker and Gloria Channing had produced what seemed to me (and no doubt even more to them) an endless series of drafts.

My debt to all of them is enormous. If there is strength and value in what follows, it is more a product of their efforts than of mine. I suspect that the only parts of this text to which I can unambiguously lay claim are the contentious bits which slipped through their careful scrutiny. The Running the Country Course Team were a tough lot to work for. I know their thoroughness made me write with greater clarity and precision than I would otherwise have done. I simply hope that all their comments, and my responses to them, have now combined to produce a book which is worthy of your time and attention. If they have, then this enormous collective effort will have been worthwhile.

David Coates
Leeds
June 1991

Grateful acknowledgement is made to the following sources for permission to reproduce material in this book:

TABLES

Tables 1.1 and 1.2: McCormick, B.J. (1988) *The World Economy: Patterns of Growth and Change*, Philip Allan Publishers; Table 1.3: Castles, S. and Kosack, G. (1973) *Immigrant Workers and Class Structure in Western Europe*, Oxford University Press; Table 1.4: Cox, A. (1982) *Politics, Policy and the European Recession*, © Andrew Cox 1982, reproduced by permission of Macmillan Ltd and St Martin's Press Inc.; Table 1.5: OECD (1983) *Economic Outlook*, December 1983, Organization for Economic Co-operation and Development; Table 1.6: GATT (1982) *International Trade 1981–2*, Geneva; Table 1.7: OECD (1979) *The Impact of the Newly Industrializing Countries on Production and Trade in Manufacture*, Organization for Economic Co-operation and Development, 1979, 1984; Table 1.8: Szeftel, M. (1984) *World Development Report 1984*, The World Bank; Table 1.9(a): UNCTNC (1983) *Transnational Corporations in World Development: Third Survey*, New York, United Nations and UNCTNC (1978) *Transnational Corporations in World Development: a Re-examination*, New York, United Nations; Table 1.9(b): UNCTNC (1981) *Transnational Banks: Operations, Strategies and Their Effects in Developing Countries*, New York, United Nations; Table

2.1: Reddaway, W.B. (1983) 'Problems and prospects for the UK economy', *Economic Record,* vol.59, Economic Society of Australia; Table 2.2: Central Statistical Office (1987) *UK Balance of Payments,* reproduced with the permission of the Controller of Her Majesty's Stationery Office; Table 2.3: (1968) *Census of Production: Industry Analyses,* reproduced with the permission of the Controller of Her Majesty's Stationery Office; Table 2.4: (top) Gough, I. (1979) *The Political Economy of the Welfare State,* Macmillan, (bottom) Department of Employment, *British Labour Statistics: Historical Abstract 1886–1968,* reproduced with the permission of the Controller of Her Majesty's Stationery Office; Table 2.5: Buck, N.H. (1988) 'Service industries and local labour markets: towards an anatomy of service job loss', *Urban Studies,* vol.25, pp.319–32; Table 2.6: Martin, R. (1989) 'Regional imbalance as consequence and constraint in national economic renewal', in Green, F. (ed.) *The Restructuring of the UK Economy,* Harvester Wheatsheaf; Table 2.7: Toporowski, J. (1989) 'The financial system and capital accumulation in the 1980s', in Green, F. (ed.) *The Restructuring of the UK Economy,* Harvester Wheatsheaf; Table 2.8: Halsey, A.H. (1988) *British Social Trends Since 1900,* Macmillan Ltd and Sheridan House Inc.; Tables 2.9, 3.5 and 3.10: Reid, I. and Strata, E. (1989) *Sex Differences in Britain,* Gower; Table 2.10: *The National Economic Review,* May 1987, reproduced by permission of the National Institute of Economic and Social Research; Table 2.11: Smith, D. (1990) 'Work still needed to close productivity gap', *The Sunday Times,* 2 September 1990, Times Newspapers Ltd and the Nomura Research Institute; Tables 2.12 and 5.1: Martin, R. (1988) 'Industrial capitalism in transition: the contemporary reorganization of the British space-economy', in Massey, D. and Allen, J. (eds) *Uneven Development: Cities and Regions in Transition,* Hodder & Stoughton Ltd; Table 3.1: Urry, J. (1985) 'The class structure', in Coates, D., Johnston, G. and Bush, R. (eds) *A Socialist Anatomy of Britain,* Blackwell Publishers; Table 3.2: Noble, T. (1975) *Modern Britain: Structure and Change,* B.T. Batsford Ltd; Table 3.3: Scott, J., 'The British upper class', *Directory of Directors,* Reed Information Services; Table 3.4: Beresford, P. (1990) 'Britain's rich', *The Sunday Times Magazine,* 8 April 1990, © Times Newspapers Ltd 1990; Table 3.6: Central Statistical Office (1986) *Social Trends,* reproduced with the permission of the Controller of Her Majesty's Stationery Office; Table 3.7: Brown (1984) *Black and White Britain,* Gower; Table 3.8: Hudson, R. and Williams, A.M. (1989) *Divided Britain,* reproduced by permission of Pinter Publishers Ltd. All rights reserved; Table 4.3: Savage, S.P. and Robins, L. (1990) *Public Policy under Thatcher,* Macmillan London Ltd; Table 4.4: Denver, D. (1989) *Elections and Voting Behaviour in Britain,* Simon & Schuster, © David Denver 1989; Table A.1: from *Global Shift: Industrial Change in a Turbulent World,* by Peter Dicken. Copyright © 1986 by Peter Dicken. Reprinted by permission of Harper Collins Publishers Inc.; Table A.2: Rostow, W. (1961) *Stages of Economic Growth,* Cambridge University Press.

FIGURES

Figures 2.2 and 3.3: Hudson, R. and Williams, A.M. (1989) *Divided Britain,* reproduced by permission of Pinter Publishers Ltd. All rights reserved; Figure 2.3: Atkinson, J. (1984) 'Manpower strategies for flexible organizations', *Personnel Management,* August 1984, Personnel Publications; Figure 3.1: 'Share ownership in the UK by age and sex', *The Times,* 5 November 1988, © Times Newspapers Ltd 1990; Figure 3.2: 'The growth of poverty in the 1980s', *The Independent on Sunday,* 29 July 1990; Figure A.1: World Bank (1983) *World Development Report 1983,* New York; Figure A.2: 'Chart of the stages of economic growth' (1961), courtesy of *The Economist.*

PHOTOGRAPHS

pp.16 and 126, Topham; pp.23 and 60, Ford Photograph Library; p.26, Nicholas Lee, Cambridge; p.38, BZW; p.44, World Health Organization/Jean Mohr; p.49, Mansell Collection; p.62, Volvo; p.87, Neil Libbert/Network; p.89, Access; pp.96 and 148, Press Association/Topham; p.109, Downing Street Press Office/Photo Stephen Berkhauer; p.119, Andrew Yeadon; pp.130 and 166, Pacemaker Press; p.136, Associated Press/Topham; p.141, Labour Party Photograph Library; p.157, John Sturrock/Network; p.170, European Parliament.

Cover: front, Olympia & York Canary Wharf Ltd; background, ICI Chemicals Photo Library.

ABBREVIATIONS

BBC	British Broadcasting Corporation
CBI	Confederation of British Industry
CDU	Christian Democratic Union
COPPSO	Conference of Professional and Public Service Organizations
CPAG	Child Poverty Action Group
EC	European Community
EEC	European Economic Community
GATT	General Agreement on Tariffs and Trade
GCHQ	Government Communications Headquarters
GDP	Gross Domestic Product
GEC	General Electric Company
GLC	Greater London Council
GNP	Gross National Product
ICI	Imperial Chemical Industries
IMF	International Monetary Fund
IRA	Irish Republican Army
IT	Information Technology
MSC	Manpower Services Commission
NATO	North Atlantic Treaty Organization
NEB	National Enterprise Board
NEDC	National Economic Development Council
NHS	National Health Service
NIC	Newly Industrializing Country
OECD	Organization for Economic Co-operation and Development
Quango	Quasi-autonomous non-governmental organization
RAF	Royal Air Force
RUC	Royal Ulster Constabulary
SDP	Social Democratic Party
TUC	Trades Union Congress
UDI	Unilateral Declaration of Independence
UVF	Ulster Volunteer Force

INTRODUCTION

This book has been drafted with a certain audience in mind. It has been written to assist the work of those many students who are in need of a broad introductory survey of UK life and society since 1945. It has been written for those who need to grasp quickly the major political, social and economic changes to which the UK has been subject since the end of the Second World War. What the book tries to supply is a *map* of major developments in the recent past, a map upon which students can later place a series of more detailed studies on the running of particular parts of UK society. The job of such a map is to provide essential background and context: and, by the signposting that it does, to help students to integrate their more detailed studies into a fuller and more coherent understanding of how the contemporary UK is run.

The title and concerns of this book are shared with an Open University course in the social sciences — this text provides background material for students taking that particular programme. But it is not directed at them alone. There are many courses in further and higher education for which such a general text can play a similar introductory role; and indeed there are many general readers who may appreciate an overview of the recent past of the kind presented here. So although the title and content of this book reflect Open University concerns, the book should be understood as complete in its own right, with its material and themes available for use as an introduction to many different ways of studying the character of the contemporary UK.

I am concerned here with the ways in which the contemporary UK is — and has recently — been *run*; and I will use the term 'run' to refer to a number of different but related things.

I will use it to refer in part to the mechanisms by which resources are allocated and sectors of social life co-ordinated. You will find the text reflecting regularly on the presence/absence of three different *modes of co-ordination*: market co-ordination, co-ordination by hierarchy, and co-ordination by networks. The precise nature of these three modes of co-ordination will be discussed in more detail later in this introduction. The text will explore the presence of each of them in specific areas of contemporary UK life; and it will use them to throw light on how different parts of UK economy and society operate and are operated.

So that will be one of the text's concerns: modes of co-ordination, ways of running a complex economy and society over nearly half a century. But the notion of 'running' involves more than the procedures by which the allocation of resources and the co-ordination of social life have occurred. It involves more substantive, less procedural, things as well. A second concern of the text will be with the *personnel of co-ordination*, with the runners and the run. The chapters which follow will regularly examine who actually does the running. If the UK is run by conscious decisions, we need to know who takes those decisions and by what right. If, on the other hand, much of contemporary life is the product of co-ordination without conscious decision-taking, if it is run by pilot-less processes of co-ordination, then we need to know who/what set those processes into operation, and who/what guarantees the conditions within which they operate undisturbed. In addition therefore to examining the differential impact of particular modes of co-ordination on the running of the contemporary UK, the text will have something to say about the co-ordination of modes.

An exploration of this kind — the telling of the story of the post-war UK through a concern with co-ordination and co-ordinators — also requires that the story itself be told. A major task of each chapter will be the documentation of *how the UK has actually been run*. Successive chapters will trace key developments in first the economic, then the social and cultural, and finally the political life of the contemporary UK. This 'telling of the story' will put the flesh on the bones of the analysis. It should enable us to see more clearly who is running the UK and through what mechanisms of co-ordination. It should enable us to see how successful that running has been — and it should, as it does so, enable us to locate *the dominant characteristics of the society* being 'run' in this way.

Books of this kind are always written for a purpose, and I hope that this purpose is now clear. It is that you should be left, when you have read this text, with a better sense of the four related things involved in the notion of 'running the country':

1   the *country*: the changing composition and dominant characteristics of UK society in the post-war period;

2   the *story*: the way UK society has been organized, integrated and led since 1945;

3   the *decision-makers*: the key institutions, social groups and individuals who have run the country through those years; and

4   the *modes of co-ordination*: the underlying criteria and mechanisms by which post-war developments have been held together and determined.

1   THE QUESTION OF APPROACH

As you can imagine, writing a book of this kind is a protracted and complex business, requiring unavoidable choices of framework and emphasis. Facts do not speak for themselves, nor stories emerge without story-tellers. Even the most simple and elementary history of a period is a product of choices made by the historian — about what to include and what not, what to emphasize and what to play down, what to treat as cause and what as effect. So as you read on, you need to be aware of the choices that have been made here. You also need to be aware of the consequences of those choices for the content of what follows, for the emphases and explanations it contains, and for the pattern of silence and omission with which it will be accompanied. The best way I can think of to generate that awareness as you begin is to contrast the design and organization of this text with the underlying structures of a number of other texts which recently have attempted to cover some or all of the same ground.

When I set out to write this book I gathered around me a number of other books for guidance and for comfort. On the desk at the moment are Kenneth Morgan's much acclaimed *The People's Peace: British History 1945–1989,* David Childs's *Britain Since 1945: a Political History,* Chris Cook and John Ramsden's *Trends in British Politics Since 1945,* and Arthur Marwick's *British Society Since 1945.* These are just four of a number of texts surveying the post-war UK experience from different angles and in different ways. Each of them is distinct in its content and approach; and each varies in the degree to which it is explicit about the approach and structure it is using. Morgan and Childs are relatively silent about the framework and emphasis they have chosen to adopt; but in fact each focuses narrowly on public and political events. They tell the story of the UK since 1945 largely in terms of politicians, political parties and the activities of governments. By implication, if not by design, they play down the importance of economic, social and cultural change in the post-war UK, and treat politics as an activity largely driven by itself. Cook and Ramsden, and Arthur Marwick, do more. There are essays in the Cook and Ramsden volume on economic debates, on trade unionism, on nationalization; but always within a focused preoccupation with national political life. Of the four, it is Marwick who spreads his canvass widest, exploring economic change, social developments, geographical and cultural shifts as well as political developments. It is Marwick too who is most explicit about the theoretical choices underpinning his approach, insisting that there are as many valid approaches as there are 'ways … of skinning a cat' (Marwick, 1990, p.7), and laying out in his first chapter four themes (of national decline, recent national revival, growing social freedom and the question of tolerance and consensus) around which to organize his narrative.

As you will see as you read on, I have drawn on all four of these works without being at all content with their overall focus and framework. Any analysis of 'running the country' has to examine the character and role of national political institutions and personalities, as the works of Childs and Morgan do, but it has to look at many other things as well. So the focus of this book has to be much wider than theirs, and it cannot rely, as they do, on a simple chronology of national political events to give shape to the sequence of its chapters. They are largely content to narrate. Here we must also explain: and explanations require a more developed and explicit theoretical framework than they deploy. But in probing both wider and deeper, as we will do here, the need for shape, coherence and order in the telling of the tale becomes even greater. The tale could be told as a series of discrete histories (one on economic change, one on political change …) of the kind offered by Cook and Ramsden. That at least would give the study the width of coverage it requires. It could even be organized thematically, on the Marwick model. That would give what follows a coherence more discursive approaches lack. But the problem with any discrete approach is that the linkages between the chapters is invariably buried and lost — it certainly is in the Cook and Ramsden volume — and the thematic structure (as laid out by Marwick at least) is in the end idiosyncratic and arbitrary in its choice of concerns. We need some more coherent and credible way of finding organizing foci than simply picking them out of the air; and we need some systematic way of tracing the interconnections between different aspects of contemporary social change. We need, that is, to build our story around recognizable, distinct and defensible bodies of social theory in ways that many other studies of the post-war UK do not.

I have chosen to make use here — in what I hope you will find is a light and unobtrusive way — of a particular body of recent Marxist economic and social theory: regulationist theory. You do not have to know any Marxist theory to read what follows, and you will not know any theory as such by the time your reading is over. This is not a book of social theory, but one informed by a particular theory: and all you require — to read it with value — is an awareness of the general character of the theoretical framework by which it is informed. Like all varieties of Marxist theory, regulationist theory treats the way the economy is organized as the ultimate determinant of other forms of social, cultural and political change: and it insists on linking all aspects of social life together, as part of a recognizable system of relationships that can be labelled, discussed and analysed as one whole unit. As you will see as you read on, this particular approach to an understanding of contemporary life treats the post-war period as one distinguished from earlier times by the predominant 'regime of accumulation' (the way production and consumption are organized) within it; and then treats the economy understood in that way as the context within which to situate social change, political developments, and the whole complex of dominant cultures and ideas. Regulationist theory gives what follows both its vocabulary of analysis (a concern with capitalism, with social classes, and with patterns of domination and subordination) and its particular agenda of explanation (starting first with the economic, then dealing with the social and the cultural, and only finally with the state). In this way, and because this book is informed by a particular set of theoretical concerns, we will arrive at the agenda of a Morgan or a Childs last, and only after taking a line of march that is distinct and different from that of a Cook and Ramsden, or a Marwick.

I offer you this interpretation of how the UK is run because I remain convinced of its superiority over other available interpretations. But that is my decision, taken after years of study and reflection, and it is important that I write in a way which leaves you free to come to a similar moment of decision, or indeed to come to a decision of a different kind. I know that any telling of the tale requires the imposition of a structure, but I have no wish to impose my structure on you — and certainly no wish to do so unannounced. Yet there is no space here to survey in detail all the alternative approaches available, and to explain why regulationist theory seems the best way in to me. That, after all, would require a very different and far more theoretical book. So all I can do is to draw your attention to the underlying framework of what follows, and signpost alternative approaches to which you can turn. And all I can do — in addition — is to keep the impact of my particular approach as limited and as light as I possibly can on the text to come, and to indicate in footnotes (as I will) those relatively few moments when you need to be most on your guard — those moments when my particular approach is having a very powerful and direct impact on what you are being asked to read and absorb. Otherwise what I have tried to do is to draft a text that is as theoretically-uncontentious as I can make it, to leave you with a body of information that you might now — or later — choose to reinterpret in other ways.

I emphasize this so you can be aware as you read on that the route you are being asked to follow is a particular one. I emphasize it too as a reminder that other readings of the experience of the post-war UK are available to you if this one seems incomplete or unpersuasive. The twin dangers of a Marxist approach are always reductionism and over-systemization. There is always a tendency in Marxist scholarship to reduce everything back to determination by economic factors, and to fail to give sufficient weight to the autonomous and non-economic generation of social, cultural and political change. There is always the associated danger of tying everything up too neatly — of giving the impression that everything feeds off everything else and that there is one underlying logic at work — one ultimate explanatory trajectory — if only you dig deep enough. That is why Marxism as a body of theory has so strong an appeal to those trained in economic science and to those with a penchant for the tidy — two serious social flaws that I at least have in abundance. But it is also why such an approach has its uses as a preliminary route to understanding. It gives you a coherent and integrated picture of post-war change in the UK which — once you have grasped it — can then be progressively refined and relaxed: to let in more autonomous forms of explanation and more complex cross-cutting patterns of cause and effect. A sophisticated Marxist analysis of contemporary life is a good place from which to begin the pursuit of understanding, I always think, even if it is not always necessarily the best place to end.

2 MODELS OF CO-ORDINATION

There is one other way out of this dilemma of competing organizing frameworks — and that is not to confront it at all. This particular escape route is not always a respectable one to take, particularly if you find yourself in more philosophically-minded and theoretically-rigorous academic circles. But if you pick your friends with greater care, you can always put off this debate on organizing frameworks by concentrating instead on lower-order, more middle-level theoretical issues — especially if you can find ones that require attention by scholars from all theoretical backgrounds. Such a set of middle-range theoretical issues are available to us here — a set of issues concerned with models of co-ordination, with ways of allocating resources in the running of the contemporary UK. So it will be possible to read what follows simply with this level of concerns in mind, and to leave bigger questions — of 'regimes of accumulation' and the like — unexamined and unexplored. And for that reason, I need to alert you in this introduction to what is at stake at this middle level of theory, and to make clear the role that these models of co-ordination will play in the argument to come.

Models of co-ordination will be used in this text to round out your understanding of the way the UK has been run since 1945. By the time your reading is complete, you should have a clearer sense of the *country* being run: its changing composition and dominant characteristics in the post-war period. You should have a sense of how the country has been run: of the *story* of how the UK has been organized, integrated and led since 1945. You should be clearer too on *who* does the running: on what are the key institutions, groups and individuals who have taken the big decisions on the nature of UK life. And you should also have a greater sense of the *modes of co-ordination* underlying the running of the post-war UK.

For across the chapters you will see an argument develop about the changing weight of markets, hierarchies and networks as co-ordinators of life in the UK since 1945, and about the differential impact of each on the various sectors of UK existence: on its economy, its social structure, its cultural systems and its state. You will meet an argument about the growing role of *hierarchies* as co-ordinators of economic and political life, a role enhanced by the spread of bureaucracy and the growth of monopolies. You will meet an argument about the importance of *networks* as co-ordinators of private relationships (in the sphere of family and friends) and as lubricators of the interplay of bureaucracies — with the running of the contemporary UK facilitated by the existence of informal social linkages between key figures in both private corporate hierarchies and the bureaucracies of the state. And overwhelmingly you will meet an argument about the fall and rise of *markets* as co-ordinators of activity within the economy. You will find the whole post-war story treated as one preoccupied with the degree to which governments should/should not, and did/did not, attempt to manage markets.

Now to assess the adequacy of all this, you need to go into your reading equipped with a clear sense of what is involved in each type of co-ordination. You need to be aware of the characteristic mechanisms, outcomes, strengths and weaknesses of each. So though no one type of co-ordinating device exists in practice in pure and isolated form, let us pretend for a moment that these models of co-ordination can be isolated and studied alone, in order to indicate their dominant and defining individual characteristics.

2.1 MARKET CO-ORDINATION

The market acts as a co-ordinating mechanism by using prices to transmit information between agents keen to engage in exchange. It invites a self-interested response by those agents, rationally pursuing private goals within a shared framework of rules which set limits on legitimate modes of behaviour and which specify the rights (particularly the property rights) of the participants concerned. It is a mode of co-ordination characterized by (a) the absence of any central directing agency, (b) the associated de-centralization of decision-taking by atomized and formally equal social actors, (c) the absence of explicit coercion in the process of co-ordination, and (d) a dependence on the existence of strong rules guaranteeing property rights, ease of access and the absence of monopoly privilege and other restraints on trade. The characteristic outcome of market co-ordination is a *sale/purchase*.

The strength of the market as a co-ordinating device has long been that specified by Adam Smith: namely that when in a market an individual seeks

> his own advantage ... and not that of the society ... he is, in this as in many other cases, led by an invisible hand to promote an end which was no part of his intention. Nor is it always the worse for the society that it was not part of it. By pursuing his own interest he frequently promotes that of the society more effectively than when he really intends to promote it.
>
> (Smith, 1776, Book 4, Chapter 2)

A market as a mechanism of co-ordination is what Hayek has called a *catallaxy* — 'a network of many economies, firms, households etc. ... not a deliberately made organization but ... a product of spontaneous growth [which] because it has no common purpose of its own, enables a great variety of individual purposes to be fulfilled' (Barry, 1979, p.45).

Advocates of the market as the dominant mode of co-ordination emphasize its capacity to stimulate efficiency and innovation in production. They stress its ability to co-ordinate, without conscious human intervention, the literally millions of individual decisions made in a complex economy; and they point to the greater equality and freedom enjoyed within it by individual producers and consumers, when set against the degrees of individual equality and freedom achievable within other major mechanisms of co-ordination. Critics of markets as co-ordinating devices emphasize the degree of insecurity they generate for producers, and the waste and inefficiency associated with the *ex post* co-ordination of buyers and sellers in market exchange. They point to the propensity of markets to degenerate into monopoly and inequality, their insensitivity to externalities of a non-pecuniary kind, and the disproportionate sensitivity of markets to the needs of those with purchasing power, at the cost of ignoring the needs of those without. Critics of markets also tend to be uneasy with the individualism and competitiveness engendered by regular participation in market exchange.

2.2   CO-ORDINATION BY HIERARCHY

Hierarchies act as co-ordinating mechanisms by combining clear vertical lines of command with strict horizontal specialization of tasks. The characteristic institution for hierarchical co-ordination is the modern bureaucracy. Hierarchical co-ordination is characterized by (a) centralized decision-making, (b) the implementation of centrally-made decisions by lower levels of functionally-integrated and formally unequal social actors, (c) clear sanctions — of demotion and dismissal, for those in breach of centrally specified rules, and (d) universally understood procedures for the taking and implementing of decisions. The characteristic outcome of co-ordination by hierarchy is a *ruling*.

The classic specification and defence of hierarchical co-ordination — to set against that of the market by Smith and Hayek — is Max Weber's. Bureaucratic organization, according to Weber

> is characterized by: hierarchy (each official has a clearly defined competence within a hierarchical division of labour, and is answerable for its performance to a superior); continuity (the office constitutes a full-time salaried occupation, with a career structure that offers the prospect of regular advancement); impersonality (the work is conducted according to prescribed rules, without arbitrariness or favouritism, and a written record is kept of each transaction); expertise (officials are selected according to merit, are trained for their function, and control access to the knowledge stored in the files).

> (Beetham, 1987, pp.11–12)

It was Weber's view at least that the 'bureaucratic type of administrative organization is, from a purely technical point of view, capable of attaining the highest degree of efficiency ... it is superior to any other form in precision, in stability, in the stringency of its discipline, and in its reliability' (ibid., p.14). Advocates of co-ordination by hierarchy emphasize its capacity to mobilize vast numbers of resources for the achievement of agreed ends, and the capacity of those ends to be collectively and not just individually specified. Advocates also emphasize the ability of hierarchical co-ordination to be done *ex ante* rather than *ex post*, to include in its calculations non-monetary and non-individual criteria and concerns (social justice, environmental protection, producer security and so on), and thereby to be able to provide a range of public goods that no market system could satisfactorily generate.

Critics of co-ordination by hierarchy tend to stress the adverse effects of bureaucracy on individual initiative and efficiency, and the propensity of hierarchical co-ordination to degenerate into corruption and privilege. Hierarchies are both difficult to control and prone to develop goals of their own. Critics emphasize too the inability of central decision-makers to gather the sheer volume and detail of knowledge necessary to co-ordinate the activities of millions, and the associated threats to the freedoms of individual producers and consumers associated with too great a dependence on this mode of co-ordination.

2.3 NETWORK CO-ORDINATION

This is a model of co-ordination which emphasizes the importance of negotiating outcomes from functionally/socially related individuals or groups. It is a mode of co-ordination that can have both institutional and informal manifestations: in tripartite economic bodies, in 'old boy' networks, in informal social connections lubricated by shared membership of clubs, and so on. In networks (a) the co-ordination of social life and the allocation of resources is settled through explicit processes of negotiation, bargaining and compromise, (b) the actors involved are linked to each other in some way — either by participation in shared circuits of production or politics, or by shared involvement in social circles of some kind, (c) no one actor is in a position to exercise direct coercion on another, but sanctions are still involved — sanctions of social disapproval, exclusion or withdrawal, and (d) network co-ordination requires a shared set of interests and understandings between the parties, and an agreement to abide by the settlements voluntarily arrived at. The characteristic outcome of network co-ordination is an *agreement*.

Advocates of networking as a mode of co-ordination see it as more sensitive to individual requirements than either price systems or bureaucracies. They see network co-ordination as capable of generating wider degrees of popular support for decisions taken than is common in either of the other two major modes of co-ordination discussed here; and emphasize the contribution made by networking to social stability, harmony, consensus and order, and to the smooth performance in practice of co-ordination through markets and administration. Critics see in network co-ordination the dangers of particularism, oligarchy and privilege. Networking operates to reinforce and extend the immediate interests of the participants, at the cost of shutting off any automatic representation of long term interests, of excluded parties, and of universal norms.

2.4 · LOGICS OF CO-ORDINATION

It is the presence, distribution, interaction and changing importance of each of these three types of co-ordinating device that you should look for as you read the chapters which follow. You will find, I think, that different sectors of society rely more heavily than others on one particular mode of co-ordination: the economy on markets, social life on networks, and the state on hierarchical structures of various kinds. But you will find too that no one mode of co-ordination enjoys a monopoly of influence even in the sectors in which it is dominant. Hierarchical modes of co-ordination play a critical role even in the private sector of the economy. Networking helps to lubricate the activity of the state. Hierarchies and markets also help to co-ordinate aspects of social life.

You should see as well that over time the relative importance of particular modes of resource allocation varies both within and between particular parts of modern UK society; and that this is important because each mode of co-ordination has a recognizable set of consequences of its own. If you rely on markets as your chief means of resource allocation and social co-ordination, then you can expect competitiveness between individuals to intensify, in-equalities between them to open up, and certain kinds of efficiency in resource use to grow. If you rely on bureaucracies as resource allocators and social co-ordinators, then you can expect relationships of superiority and subordination between individuals to increase in importance, uniformity in treatment to expand, and certain kinds of inefficiencies in resource use to emerge. Networking tends to consolidate relationships of reciprocity and trust. It also allows particularism to creep into the allocation of social resources; and in allocative systems that rely heavily on networking, the efficiency of resource use tends to be given less importance than the consolidation of existing patterns of privilege and power. Markets left to themselves make societies efficient but atomistic. Hierarchies make them uniform but status conscious. Networks segment them into insider and outsider groups, but make them more co-operative in spirit and tone.

So the shift between modes of co-ordination is not just a technical issue. What is at stake is the character of the society that is being co-ordinated in particular ways. That is why particular mixes of modes of co-ordination have been canvassed by different political groups in the post-war UK. Modes of co-ordination and political projects go together: and you will need to watch for that linkage as you read the chapters to come. How to co-ordinate the UK, how to allocate resources between us all, is still the big political issue before us in the 1990s. To answer it satisfactorily — and to understand the nature of the choices we now face — we need a clear sense of how the society has been co-ordinated in the past, and with what consequences. The mapping of the past is an essential prerequisite to the shaping of the future: and it is the task of the chapters that follow to offer you just such a map.

3 THE ARGUMENT TO COME

The 'map' on offer here has four main parts: context, economy, society and state. The content of each is broadly as follows.

3.1 THE CONTEXT

Chapter 1 will document the changing international context within which the UK has been run since 1945 — an international context which has had the most profound effect on the internal character and development of the UK itself. This international context was until recently the most stable, and now has become the most volatile, of all the elements in the contemporary UK story: and we will need to provide you with a firm grasp of the sources of both the original stability and the recent change. To do that, we will need to demonstrate how, for nearly 30 years after World War II, the international context within which the UK was run was firmly set — and was not expected to alter. In those years, the world was divided into blocs of mutually antagonistic social, economic and political systems: into a *First World* of industrialized capitalist democracies, a *Second World* of centrally-planned state-socialist one-party states, and a *Third World* of under-developed economies and normally autocratic (often initially colonial) political systems — for whose loyalty the leading powers in the First and Second Worlds were perpetually in competition. Indeed, until the late 1980s at least, competition was a critical feature of the post-war international order of which the UK was so important a part. The East and the West competed on a series of fronts. They competed militarily, in a Cold War built around an escalating arms race which periodically threatened to spill over into something warmer. They competed for world leadership and Third World allies. They competed in space, in culture, in the claims they made about their records on human rights and scientific advance; and they competed on economic performance. Within the First World too, individual economies and nations jockeyed for positions of political influence and economic strength; though always here under the umbrella of US military leadership and economic superiority. For 40 years after the defeat of fascism in 1945, this competition between capitalist economies, and the wider conflict between capitalist and state-socialist systems, were the basic, stable and defining features of the UK's international context. Together, they constitute the first key element in the 'big international picture' that we need to survey in Chapter 1.

Some elements of that context have now changed, and some have not. What has changed most is the Cold War itself: with the rapid and unexpected collapse of the Soviet empire in Eastern Europe and the visible disintegration of Communist Party control inside the Soviet Union. The international order can now no longer be structured, as it has been since 1945, on competition between blocs. That competition is, to all intents and purposes, over. What has not changed, however, is the competition between economies within the capitalist bloc itself: though even here the world is not now as it once was. US economic dominance has gone. European and Japanese economic strength has grown. Multinational corporations now straddle national boundaries. A new international division of labour has created centres of industrial and financial power in parts of Asia and the Middle East. Whole new systems of organizing production have come and gone; and with their rise and fall US economic power has flowed and ebbed as well. Indeed it is one of the paradoxes of the UK's current international context that the very moment of US 'victory' in the Cold War has coincided with an increasingly effective challenge to US economic leadership inside the 'victorious' capitalist bloc. The 1990s is witnessing the creation of a new international political and economic order, to replace the settlement established under US leadership in 1945. That is why the rise and fall of US power, the recent re-emergence of German (and increasingly now more broadly European) economic and political influence, and the UK's attempt to find a new place for itself on this shifting international landscape, will constitute the second key element in the 'big international picture' to be surveyed in Chapter 1.

3.2 THE ECONOMY

Chapter 2 traces the key changes in the UK economy since 1945, and relates them to the changing international context within which the UK has been obliged to operate. It traces the pattern of economic and political decline experienced by the UK in the post-war years; and shows how the slowness of UK governments to readjust to their reduced circumstances actually impeded necessary processes of economic modernization. The 'lost opportunity' of the 1950s was obscured for a while by the UK's participation in the general prosperity of the long post-war boom; but economic weaknesses evident by the early 1960s have preoccupied public life ever since. Chapter 2 shows how the insertion of the UK economy into the international order, and the UK's failure to modernize its industrial base, has left economic life here dominated by a particular economic geography, a particular pattern of industrial ownership, and the increasing subordination of key elements of UK industry and finance to global processes and to foreign control.

Chapter 2 also traces internal constraints on those who would run/reform the UK economy. It charts the rise of working class industrial power in key sections of UK manufacturing industry in the 1950s and 1960s, it documents the very different distribution of power and experience inside the work processes of the public sector, and shows how militancy in the public sector and dwindling competitiveness in the private combined to provoke extensive government-led industrial restructuring in the 1980s. That restructuring was accompanied, as had been the earlier period of rising working class industrial power, by major changes in patterns and levels of consumption. Chapter 2 charts those changes, and shows how they have culminated in the emerging economic crisis of the 1990s: one dominated by supply-side problems in the manufacturing base of the economy, by inflation and by deficits on the balance of payments.

3.3 THE SOCIETY

Chapter 3 looks at those who run the UK economy and society, and at those who are run by them. It examines the sources of privilege and power in the post-war UK, showing how those sources were put in place over a long period, and how carefully they are still tended in order to guarantee the transmission of privilege between generations. The chapter then looks in detail at the groups of men and women who have enjoyed privilege and exercised power since 1945, treating them as a propertied class built around the ownership and management of productive capital, and spilling out into a network of 'the great and the good' who have run (and continue to run) most of the major social and cultural institutions in the contemporary UK. The chapter also looks at the forces shaping the more limited degrees of influence and more modest standards of life experienced by the rest of us: and charts how those standards and experiences have changed since 1945. In particular, it examines the continuing role of class, gender and ethnicity as determinants of social power in the contemporary world.

Chapter 3 also considers to what degree, and by what mechanisms, UK society in the post-war period can be said to have run itself. It does that by examining the impact of a particular cluster of ideas. It argues that the dominant culture in the post-war UK has included — among its key elements — particular views on the inevitability and desirability of a capitalist way of organizing economic and social life, a particular understanding of the neutrality and integrity of the legal system, and a particular understanding of the nation and its interests. The chapter also examines the degree of resistance to this dominant culture, and traces the patterns of change within it since 1945 — resistance and change that have also been important determinants of the way in which the UK has been run in the past, and will be run in the immediate future.

3.4 THE STATE

Chapter 4 is concerned with the reaction of successive UK governments to the pattern of economic and social changes imposed upon them since 1945. It charts the retreat of the UK state from its immediate post-war role as a world power: examining the loss of Empire, the dwindling significance of the UK as a military force, and the shift in UK governing preoccupations from America to Europe. Chapter 4 links these changes to a growing awareness in UK governing circles of the need for economic modernization; and looks in detail at the two dominant economic 'solutions' canvassed by different UK governments since 1945 — one 'social democratic' in character, the other 'neo-liberal'.

This changing international role for the UK state, and these competing projects for economic reconstruction, have had important consequences for the structure of the UK state — for the way it attempts to run UK economy and society — and for the pattern of political attitudes and loyalties that the state has attracted to itself in the post-war period. Chapter 4 charts these too. It looks at the rise and fall of a quasi-corporatist state in the post-war UK, and at the recent emergence of a less corporatist, more centralized liberal state. It also records the way in which popular views have changed to such things as public ownership, state economic management, market forces and party loyalty; and examines the extent to which the 'rolling back of the state' in the UK in the 1980s has been matched by changing popular attitudes to the role of markets, hierarchies and networks as allocators of scarce resources.

3.5 CONCLUSION

Chapter 5 is a chapter of questions — questions about the future running of the UK, questions whose shape reflects the central arguments of the chapters that have gone before. The big question left by the first chapter's discussion of the UK's international context is the way the UK will be run in the 1990s from *within* an increasingly integrated European community. The big question left by the second chapter is the extent to which continuing economic weaknesses within the UK will reduce the capacity of UK decision-makers to exploit to the full the opportunities opened up by European integration. Chapter 3 leaves us with questions of social cohesion and control in the troubled context of the 1990s, and Chapter 4 with the nature of the political projects competing for our loyalty in these troubled times. At stake in those political projects will be different mixes of markets, hierarchies and networks as modes of resource allocation: and in that way Chapter 5 will end, as this introduction began, by exploring the mechanisms of social co-ordination under which we will all live out the end of this century and enter into the next.

CHAPTER 1:   THE CONTEXT

In any analysis of how the UK is run, the first question to be settled is 'where is the analysis to begin?' The structure of any argument is invariably part of the argument itself. If we begin our analysis of the running of the UK by examining local material — concentrating initially on developments within the UK — then we give a clear signal about where we believe sovereignty and power to lie. The very structure of the argument suggests that power lies here in the UK, that the parameters within which the UK is run are to be found primarily within its own borders. But in truth they are not: which is why our analysis of local UK institutions and processes must wait until later chapters. The key constraints on the freedom of action of those who would run the UK come in the first instance from beyond the UK. They come from the wider *global* order, and from the UK's place within it: which is why we need to look at that global order first.

The *global* imposes itself on the *local* in the running of the UK in a number of important ways. Time and again, as we will see throughout the text, the possibilities and options available to local decision-makers are affected by the UK's involvement with other economies and societies. The freedom of action of major UK institutions and leaders is restricted by the power and interests of those foreign systems. Indeed many of the institutions which we think of as characteristically 'ours' can in truth only be fully understood when seen as part of global institutions which impose their own requirements on what are, in effect, their UK 'subsidiaries'. So there is a global *context* and background to the way the UK is run, there are global *constraints* on what happens here, and global forces are themselves in part *constitutive* of key elements of contemporary UK life and society. That is why any analysis of the UK needs to begin by placing the UK in its wider context, and by examining the co-ordinating principles and dominant characteristics of the wider international order.

Three characteristics in particular seem important here. The first is the way in which, until 1990 at least, the international order was divided into competing political and economic blocs: capitalist on the one side, state-socialist on the other. The second is the way in which, in that divided world, the UK played so key a role inside one of the blocs. The third is the way in which those blocs are now beginning to disintegrate, that a new international order is beginning to emerge. So if we are to grasp how the UK has been run hitherto, and if we are to see the forces emerging to shape its context of action in the 1990s, we will need a clear picture of the blocs, their trajectories and their disintegration. In particular we will need to understand the character of the bloc of capitalist economies and liberal democratic states to which the UK has — and continues — to belong. The consolidation of that understanding is the task of this chapter.

There are really two ways of achieving that understanding. One is to take the long view, to see the post-war experience of the UK as merely the most recent moment in the centuries-long rise and fall of economic and political systems. The other is to close in on the post-war years alone: to look in detail at the performance and development of the bloc of capitalist economies and liberal democratic states of which the UK is a part. Limitations of time, and the particular concerns we have here, make that second option the necessary one, and therefore the one that we will follow. But it is a pity to miss out the long view entirely; and your understanding of post-war developments will improve if you situate them in a longer time frame. That is why the Appendix exists. There you will find a discussion of capitalism as one mode of production and of state-socialism as another: and a brief explanation of the way in which the post-war system of mutually-antagonistic liberal democratic and one-party states emerged. You do not have to read the Appendix to follow the story of this chapter: but it is there, as more general background, if your interests take you in that direction.

1   THE INITIAL CHARACTER OF THE POST-WAR INTERNATIONAL ORDER

Let us now take the shorter view: and attempt to characterize the nature of the post-war international order as it emerged in the years after 1945. One way of doing that is to concentrate attention on two of its outstanding features: the way the capitalist part of the divided world order was organized around US power; and the way in which the core capitalist countries — once organized in this way — were able to enjoy unprecedented and sustained periods of economic growth and prosperity. To grasp the context in which the UK was run in the first 25 years of post-war peace, we need to understand something about the role of the USA, and something about the nature and causes of the prosperity which spread out from America to other leading capitalist nations.

1.1   AMERICAN POWER

The United States emerged from World War II as the one fully-modernized and non war-damaged industrial economy. 'At the end of the war the USA controlled some 70% of the world's gold and foreign exchange reserves, and more than 40% of its industrial output', at a time when 'Europe and Japan had been devastated by war and the Third World was still locked into colonial servitude and contained less than one per cent of the world's industrial capacity' (Brett, 1985, p.63). In 1945, the USA alone was in a position quickly to generate the food stuffs, capital goods and flows of money vital to the reconstruction of war-torn Europe. Moreover, its soldiers were distributed across vast swathes of Western Europe and the Far East, and its ruling groups were determined to use their economic dominance and military power to keep world markets open to US goods — as they had not been between the wars. In 1945 the threat to US markets no longer came from right-wing nationalism, which had been trounced in the war, and at least temporarily discredited by its association with fascism. The threat now came from the Left, from resistance movements led by communists. As the post-war years began it was communism, not fascism, which stood in the way of US power.

American troops marching through London, September 1942

US economic and military power was used in the immediate post-war period to sustain a particular settlement in Western Europe and Japan. That settlement had both a political and an economic dimension.

Politically, US pressure was directed to the weakening of the communist presence in Western Europe. The United States accepted the division of Europe between the Soviet Union and the West agreed at Yalta in 1943, and used its military power to put down local communist attempts to shift that division, most notably in Greece between 1944 and 1948. US money funded the reconstruction of broad Christian Democratic political forces (and in places, moderate social democratic ones too) as popularly-based parties of the Centre capable of withstanding the mass appeal of communism. US backing was given to McCarthyite purges of the Left: from governments (in France and Italy in the 1940s) and from vast swathes of public life (trade unions, universities, the media …) in the early 1950s. Older (even pro-Nazi) capitalist groups were quietly rehabilitated in the late 1940s and early 1950s, and strong labour movements were effectively broken by employer and government campaigns in Japan, France and Italy. And the United States supported UK moves to create a military alliance against the Soviet Union (NATO) in 1949. The political base of the post-war settlement was the *Cold War;*[*] and that cold war justified the retention in Western Europe and the

---

[*] The origins of the Cold War are a matter of immense controversy. Who started it? What interests did it serve? For an overview of the debate, see Halliday (1983) and Cox (1990). Cox argues — convincingly in my view — that the Cold War was US generated and Soviet reinforced: begun as a defensive US response to a fear of loss of control in Europe, and quickly reinforced by Soviet defensive moves against what it saw as US aggressive intentions. On this, see Cox (1990, p.29).

Far East of large numbers of US troops for over 40 years after the end of the world war which had put them there in the first place.

Economically, the formal structures of the new post-war order were initiated in 1944 in negotiations at Bretton Woods in New Hampshire. The US government was well aware that force alone would not be enough to block the spread of support for communism or to keep Western European and Asian markets open to US goods. Only the revival of Western European economies, and the spread of their prosperity more evenly between their peoples than had hitherto been the case, could in the end dull the appeal of anti-capitalist forces. So US planners successfully imposed — both on other governments and on an initially sceptical US Congress and people — a new international economic order based on the dollar.

In the settlements negotiated at Bretton Woods, a new system of regulated currencies was agreed for the post-war years. All currencies were given a fixed exchange rate against the dollar, and all governments were charged — as their first priority — with the pursuit of economic policies to sustain that exchange rate. These exchange rates and policies were supervised by a new international financial agency dominated by the United States and based in Washington — the IMF — from whom loans were available *in extremis* for governments which were finding it difficult to maintain the parities of their currencies, and with whom it would be possible for those governments to negotiate currency devaluations. Successive US governments also worked to keep world markets open to the entry of US goods and capital, by participating in rounds of negotiations in GATT (the General Agreement on Tariffs and Trade) established in 1947. 'The GATT rules [were] primarily designed to encourage non-discrimination between countries and the progressive reduction in tariffs' (Brett, 1985, p.77). A US-managed trade bloc was thus put in place, using the dollar as its unit of exchange.

In return the United States agreed to provide other members of the bloc with the dollars they needed. American administrations did this by loaning vast numbers of dollars to sympathetic Western European governments — in Marshall Aid — to enable them to buy US goods for their own economic reconstruction. They also agreed to keep large numbers of troops in Western Europe, whose presence deterred both the Soviets and local communist forces, and whose financing ensured a steady flow of US funds into the economies so protected. And the United States allowed the export of US capital to facilitate the economic reconstruction of potentially competitor industrial economies. In consequence, the United States ran major balance of payments deficits from 1952; deficits paid for in dollars whose release into the international economy then lubricated world trade. The dollar, that is, fuelled an unprecedented period of economic growth in a system protected by NATO, opened up by GATT, and supervised by the IMF.

But though the United States ran a balance of payments deficit through the 1950s and 1960s, it did not run a deficit on its balance of trade. It spent more than it earned abroad on maintaining its soldiers, on lending dollars, and on exporting capital. But the superiority of its agrarian and manufacturing sectors (based on its greater labour productivity) meant that through the 1950s and 1960s many of those dollars were used by European and Japanese consumers to buy US capital goods and consumer products. Indeed it was to be precisely when the US lost its lead in productivity and trade that the system ran into crisis in the early 1970s. In the meantime it was US industrial supremacy which underpinned the long boom of the post-war years, and it was US military technology in particular that fuelled industrial change.

For after 1940 the United States forged a massive military-industrial complex, and whole regional economies inside the United States (particularly in the new South and in California) developed to service the demands of the US government for ever more sophisticated and extensive military hardware. In the end that pattern of economic and regional change within the United States would also contribute to the diminution of American-based international economic prosperity; but in the 1950s and 1960s its impact was precisely the reverse. 'In the post-war decades … military industries … functioned in the US just as cotton did in the industrial revolution in Britain, as the "leading sector" … stimulating the boom in electronics [and] research and development' (Thompson, 1980, p.17). The military-industrial complex provided the cutting edge of the new productivity, and acted as the motor of economic growth in the United States, growth which then spilled out into the entire capitalist bloc.

American power also oversaw a particular balance of forces between Third World and First World producers. Prosperity in the West was fuelled by processes of unequal exchange between the Third World and the First. In the post-war years, Third World economies were locked into international capitalist trading patterns primarily as suppliers of cheap raw materials and other primary products. The colonial controls enjoyed by certain Western European powers were used in the 1940s and 1950s to ensure such integration; and to attract a supply of cheap migrant labour to Europe to ease the labour shortages which emerged there as industrial growth continued unabated. The United States relied on less overtly political means to incorporate Third World economies: lending money and supporting authoritarian governments to ensure a cheap and reliable supply of the inputs needed by Western industry. Empires fell in the post-war years, as movements for political independence won power in India, Pakistan, Indo-China and eventually Africa too: but the subordination of Third World economies to international market forces remained intact well into the post-colonial period. Only in Indo-China did liberation from empire threaten to take the area out of the ambit of Western power and influence; and there of course, the Americans were to fight (and lose) their own colonial battle — in Vietnam — in the 1960s. Elsewhere — in the immediate post-war period — the political and economic writ of the United States and its NATO allies ran largely unchallenged.

SUMMARY

- US political and economic power was a key feature of the post-war international order.

- Politically, US power was used to defeat internal and external obstacles to a capitalist restructuring of Western Europe and Japan. The Cold War was central to post-war prosperity: both as an ideology, and through the centrality of military-industrial spending to economic growth and innovation.

> • Economically, the US 'empire' was consolidated by a system of fixed exchange rates, a generous supply of dollars, and the opening of trade to US goods. It worked economically because (and to the degree that) the US economy was more productive and efficient than other economies in the capitalist bloc.

1.2 GROWING PROSPERITY

If American power was one overwhelming feature of the international context in which the UK was run after 1945, economic prosperity was the other. Between 1948 and 1973 the advanced capitalist economies experienced a quite unprecedented period of unbroken economic growth, and that growth has continued since 1973 in an equally spectacular but less stable way. 'By 1973 output in the advanced capitalist countries was 180% higher than in 1950 … *More was produced in that quarter century than in the previous three-quarters*' (Armstrong *et al.*, 1984, p.167). Between 1948 and 1971 the volume of world trade grew at an annual average percentage rate of 7.3 per cent, and between 1971 and 1980 of 5.8 per cent. The comparable figure for the 1913–38 period was only 0.4 per cent and for the years 1890–1913 only 3.7 per cent (McCormick, 1988, p.19).

Table 1.1   Economic growth in the USA, Japan and the EEC, 1953–85 (annual percentage increase in GDP)

	1953–62	1963–9	1970–80	1981–5
USA	3.0	4.4	3.1	3.0
Japan	8.7	11.3	5.4	3.9
EEC		4.6	3.3	1.3
West Germany	6.6	4.5	3.2	1.4
France	5.1	5.4	3.6	1.2
UK	2.9	3.1	1.3	1.9
Italy	6.0	5.4	4.0	0.9

Source: McCormick (1988, p.175).

These rates of economic growth were quite remarkable, and had an enormous impact on virtually all aspects of post-war social life. After all, 'with growth on that scale output doubles every ten years.' While they were maintained, with population growth of 1 per cent, 'each generation could expect to be roughly twice as well off as its parents and four times as well off as its grandparents' (Armstrong *et al.*, 1984, pp.167–8). Such a set of expectations was quite literally without precedent. And the change here was qualitative as well as quantitative. People did not simply consume more than their predecessors. They also consumed revolutionary new products. Think what we have now come to take for granted, that only a generation ago would have been literally unimaginable. By 1969, for example, 'millions of people were able to watch on colour television as the first human set foot on the moon' (ibid., p.168). Achievements and equipment which would have seemed quite magical in 1945 were by then commonplace and ever more generally available.

This pattern of growth was unprecedented in at least three ways.

- It was unprecedented for capitalist economies to experience largely unbroken periods of growth of this length. There had been periods of expansion in the past, but never long enough for a whole generation to be able to bathe in the expectation of *steadily rising* living standards.

- It was unprecedented too for economic growth to generate such generalized levels of affluence through societies as a whole. In the past, economic growth had added to the wealth of the few without qualitatively altering (except in marginal ways) the living standards of the bulk of the producing classes. This was not the case after 1945. The bulk of what was produced from that date was goods and services which added to the quality of life for the vast majority of the populations of the advanced capitalist countries, who in consequence came to experience an unprecedented *level of material affluence*.

- It was unprecedented in a third sense too: in that it was based on a spectacular and sustained increase in the productivity of labour. Labour productivity in the 1950s and 1960s grew so quickly that it effectively doubled every ten years in Japan, every fifteen years in the EEC, and every 30 in the UK and USA. It was in the post-war years that the heavy dependence on manual labour — on actual human muscle power and sweat — to produce the bulk of what was consumed gave way to the extensive mechanization of main productive processes. In the core industries of the post-war Western economies, a labour process based on skilled craftsmen and unskilled toilers gave way to one based on machine production and semi-skilled machine operators. Generalized post-war prosperity, that is, was based on the greater labour productivity released by ways of organizing production often referred to as *Fordism.*[*]

---

[*] It is here that 'regulationist theory' is making its first and most decisive impact on the way the material you are reading is being presented. There is a vigorous debate in the academic literature on the appropriateness and meaning of Fordism as a term, and of regulationist theory as an approach. (For that debate, see C. Smith (1990) and Clarke (1990).) Those who use the term Fordism with greatest facility actually make it cover a number of distinguishable things:

1 a new and particular way of organizing the actual production of goods — especially in the automobile industry (hence the term);

2 associated alterations in the organization of classes and consumption (the arrival of a new semi-skilled machine-minding working class enjoying unprecedented levels of personal consumption);

3 a new role for the state — managing the economy to ensure full employment, and providing a range of basic welfare services — a state often referred to as a Keynesian welfare state; and

4 the key role of the United States as co-ordinator and axis of the whole system.

Table 1.2 Growth rates of real output per worker employed (% per annum), 1873–1986

	UK	USA	France	W. Germany	Italy	Japan
1873–99	1.2	1.9	1.3	1.5	0.3	1.1
1899–1913	0.5	1.3	1.6	1.5	2.5	1.8
1913–24	0.3	1.7	0.8	−0.9	−0.1	3.2
1924–37	1.0	1.4	1.4	3.0	1.8	2.7
1937–51	1.0	2.3	1.7	1.0	1.4	−1.3
1951–64	2.3	2.5	4.3	5.1	5.6	7.6
1964–73	2.6	1.6	4.6	4.4	5.0	8.4
1973–79	1.2	−0.2	2.8	2.9	1.8	2.9
1979–86	1.8	0.6	1.6	1.7	1.2	2.8

Source: McCormick (1988, p.208).

It is possible to conflate all four, and to talk of something called 'global Fordism'. Henk Overbeek, for example, has written that 'the Fordist stage of development of capitalism can ... be characterized as Fordism when considered at the level of the organization of production, as the era of the Keynesian welfare state when looked at from the level of society and state, and as the *Pax Americana* when looked at from the perspective of the overall organization of the capitalist world system' (Overbeek, 1990, p.87). And he is not alone in using the term Fordism in this umbrella sense.

However, not everyone is so sure about the wisdom of so global a sweep, or so sanguine about the value of the term at all. Critics point to two broad dangers which those using the term 'Fordism' need to avoid.

1 The danger of over-generalizing. It is not the case that all sectors of any one major capitalist economy organized themselves on Fordist lines, or that such organization was the only source of rising productivity in the post-war Western economies. Nor was it the case that all successful Western economies in the post-war period adopted Keynesian welfare policies. Fordism in production, and Keynesianism at the level of the state, did not always go together.

2 The danger of implying the existence of a post-Fordist accumulation regime of equal uniformity and importance — the danger of implying that Fordism has now gone and has been replaced by something else.

I see the dangers, but find the term useful even so. The question of what, if anything, is happening in the contemporary economy is a fascinating one to explore. It is very important that we tackle it at the end of the book — so that one of the pieces of the jigsaw of public life in the 1990s will become clear. Fordism is a useful foil to use when exploring that. But it is also important — as I hope the chapter shows — as a guide to how economic life in the West has been organized hitherto. Fordism in its narrow sense — as a way of organizing production — *is* evident in key sectors of economy after economy in the advanced capitalist world. Fordism in its wider sense seems to be an increasing feature of the majority of advanced capitalist countries too from the 1970s. There are important national variations in the time of arrival, and degree of exposure, to Fordism in this wider sense; and we need to be sensitive to that. But we do need a term to capture the character of the core industries of the long post-war boom: and until someone invents a better one it seems to me that Fordism will do as that term.

For living standards to rise on the scale of the post-war years, two things are always necessary: an enhanced supply of goods and services, and the capacity of more and more people to buy them. Generalized affluence requires rising *productivity/output* and *rising consumer demand*. Fordism provided both. As we have just noted, Fordism here has both a narrow and a wider meaning. It refers to a particular way of organizing production. It can also stretch out to include a more generalized set of social and political conditions which enable the potential of the new methods of production to be realized to the full. The Fordist character of the post-war economic order in the most affluent and developed of the Western capitalist countries can then be captured in two related lists of points: the first on the organization of production, the second on the conditions surrounding it.

The organization of production:

1   the development of mass production — based on assembly line/continuous flow production processes;

2   the use of machine-paced, semi-skilled labour rather than skilled craft labour and unskilled labour;

3   managerial concern with the scientific organization of work in the enterprise as a whole;

4   an emphasis on marginal product differentiation, inbuilt obsolescence and advertising to encourage mass demand;

5   the consolidation of collective bargaining over wage rates.

The conditions surrounding production:

1   the predominance of mass consumption of standardized mass-produced commodities and/or the collective consumption of goods and services provided by the state;

2   the central role of private and public credit in maintaining levels of consumer demand and full employment;

3   an increased role for the state, facilitating the supply of goods and guaranteeing demand levels necessary for their purchase;

4   the development of the welfare state to establish a minimum social wage and to generalize mass-consumption norms.

(Adapted from Jessop, 1988, pp.4–5.)

Fordism — understood in this way — is really a particular 'regime of accumulation', one based upon *mass* production and *mass* consumption for the first time in capitalist history. At its heart were industries making large quantities of standardized goods by bringing together semi-skilled labour and assembly line production systems. In a Fordist 'accumulation regime' it is not necessary for every industry to be organized in this way, or for every aspect of mass production to be based on assembly line techniques. On the contrary, even in a period of Fordism, significant sectors of industrial output can — and do — continue to be organized on non-Fordist lines: in small batch production and in small companies with only a limited capital base. The main point — in this new Fordist world — is that mass production industries become dominant in the economy as a whole. They become the key ones generating

One face of Fordism: cars awaiting export at Harwich

> a virtuous circle of growth based on mass production, rising produc-
> tivity based on economies of scale, rising incomes linked to produc-
> tivity, increased mass demand due to rising wages, increased profits
> based on full utilization of capacity, and increased investment in
> improved mass production equipment and techniques. Not every
> branch of the economy must be dominated by Fordist production
> techniques for this mode of growth to be realized: it is sufficient that
> the leading sectors are Fordist. Indeed, if the expansion of Fordist
> mass production is to find a mass market, there must be matching
> growth in the production of other types of goods (such as electricity,
> steel, oil, road building, and housing) and services (such as retailing,
> consumer credit, and the servicing of consumer durables).

(Jessop, 1988, p.6)

Such Fordist systems of industrial production — with long large-scale runs
of standardized products, mechanized tasks, managerial control of the
labour process, and flow line production — spread through the economies
of the advanced capitalist world in the 1950s and 1960s. New industries consolidated themselves as major employers, accumulators of capital, and
generators of output. Industries such as vehicle construction, pharmaceuticals, light engineering and electronics came to provide larger and larger percentages of GNP, and to push into a subordinate role the 'leading industries'
of the earlier waves of capitalist expansion. The centrality of coal, cotton,
shipbuilding and railways to the core economies of the capitalist West gave
way to the centrality of cars, chemicals and light engineering. And as they
did so, their arrival brought semi-automated production systems into the
centre of modern manufacturing, and enabled labour productivity there to

grow steadily throughout the 1950s and 1960s. This is how one recent commentator has characterized the evolution of industry in the world economy since 1945.

> The post-war era has been characterized by the rapid growth of a bunch of 'new' industries based on new technological possibilities that emerged during the previous twenty years or more ... The industries that emerged on a significant scale during the 1940s and 1950s — electronics, synthetic materials, solid-state devices, petrochemicals, agro-chemicals, composite materials and pharmaceuticals — created rapidly growing new markets. At the same time there was a rapid growth in demand for capital equipment, often of a new kind. The wealth generated by the emergence of these new technology-based industries caused an associated boom in demand for consumer durables, leading to the rapid growth of the automobile and consumer white goods industries.

> (Rothwell, 1982: cited in Dicken, 1986, p.20)

If we are to grasp the way in which post-war prosperity depended on a very particular constellation of forces, we would do well to realize that Fordism was not simply a post-war phenomenon. After all, Henry Ford had designed his automated production system for the Model T Ford a generation before; and the United States had enjoyed a Fordist boom of rising living standards and buoyant output in the 1920s. But that boom had collapsed in the USA in 1929; and the collapse there had helped to trigger the rise of fascism in Europe in the 1930s. Pre-war Fordism had been short-lived and unstable. Industry had possessed the capacity to generate a *supply* on Fordist lines, but had lacked the *demand* to absorb the output so generated. The defeat of the organized labour movement in the United States in the 1920s had blocked the development of a broadly-based and affluent market for the mass-produced goods of the first Fordist era; and the fierce protectionist battles of the 1930s had prevented foreign markets from acting as an outlet for US surpluses (Davis, 1987, *passim*). Prosperity was more sustained after 1945 because the balance of forces surrounding Fordism was significantly different, and more favourable to the generalized spread of successful mass production. There was a different international distribution of power between nation states (with the US in the ascendancy, as we have just seen), and a different internal balance of class forces. The roots of post-war prosperity lie here too, and not just in the Fordist nature of production itself.

What blocked successful Fordism in the United States in the 1920s was the lack of purchasing power of the organized working class — broken as wage bargainers in a series of bitter industrial disputes in the early 1920s. By 1945 the balance of class forces within the Unites States, and within the majority of the major European capitalist countries, was very different. The rise and militancy of industrial unionism in the United States in the New Deal days of the 1930s, and the entrenchment of union power in the full employment conditions of World War II, had left US industry covered by collective agreements that tied wage rises to productivity and output. As US output soared in the 1940s and 1950s, so too did the purchasing power of at least the white male sector of the American working class. Similar shifts in class power occurred in parts of Western Europe too. In the United Kingdom, a government commitment to full employment was the price ruling groups had to pay for the popular mobilization against fascism between 1939 and 1945. In other Western European states, sustained growth also eventually left labour scarce and jobs plentiful. Against this background of full employment, working class self-confidence grew. Labour shortages and trade union organization combined to keep wages rising in line with productivity across the core economies of the capitalist bloc (first in the USA, the UK and Scandinavia, and later in West Germany, France, Italy and Japan); and in this way helped to sustain levels of consumer demand vital to the continued expansion of Fordist-based production systems.

The inter-war years had made clear just how difficult it was to create the conditions of mass prosperity in the capitalist West, and how finely balanced had to be the interplay of capital, labour and the state if profits and wages were to rise together. If labour was too well organized, profits would plummet. If wages were too low, sales would stagnate. The successful accumulation of capital required plentiful supplies of labour and plentiful supplies of consumers at one and the same time. That is why post-war prosperity came to depend on more than the emergence of well-organized core workers (whose wages kept demand buoyant). It also came to rely on a ready supply of less well-organized workers, whose presence kept wage costs down and productivity high. Three sources of such 'cheaper labour' became available to the new industries of the capitalist bloc in the post-war period. *Rural populations* provided much of the initial labour force of both the Japanese and Italian 'economic miracles'; and displaced persons from Eastern Europe played a similar role for the West German economy. Changing social attitudes to gender roles, family and marriage released more and more *women* into the employed labour force in the post-war period. And labour moved from Third World economies to First World ones in unprecedented numbers. *Labour migration* was a vital contributory factor to sustained economic growth in advanced capitalist countries after 1945, labour migration which occurred on a scale matched only by the nineteenth century influx of the European peasantry into the United States. Thirty seven million

Table 1.3 Immigrants in Western Europe in 1970

	Immigrants (thousands)	Total population (thousands)	Immigrants as percentage of total population
Austria	68	7,323	0.9
Belgium	679	9,581	7.1
France	3,177	49,866	6.4
West Germany	2,977	62,000	4.8
Great Britain	2,603	52,304	5.0
Luxembourg	28	335	8.3
Netherlands	72	12,597	0.6
Sweden	173	7,869	2.2
Switzerland	972	6,071	16.0
Total	10,749	207,946	5.2

Source: Castles and Kosack (1973, p.4).

people moved into the USA, and 15 million into Western Europe, between 1945 and 1975: pouring out of former colonies, out of the southern United States and Latin America, and out of the Middle East, to provide a cheap unskilled labour force for rapid industrial expansion.

A new role for government was also central to this successful fusion of mass production systems and working class spending power. Pre-war economic orthodoxies across Western Europe had been predominantly *liberal* in character: arguing that governments helped economic growth best by governing least, by letting private enterprise act alone to create markets and jobs, and by keeping government spending and wage levels as low as possible. By 1936 economists influenced by the writings of John Maynard Keynes were arguing that such government restraints ate away at levels of consumption necessary for economic growth. By the mid 1930s Keynesian economists were saying instead that what was wanted was a New Deal in which governments spent money, fuelling investment and demand by running deficits on the public accounts to keep private accounts in surplus.

This kind of thinking had a major impact on post-war government policy in countries as disparate as the UK, Austria and Sweden — though in truth not all Western economies in the post-war years reached prosperity the Keynesian way. In fact, 'neither West Germany nor Japan followed Keynesian policies in their major periods of economic expansion, adopting instead orthodox fiscal and monetary policies' (Hirst and Zeitlin, 1991, p.8). So there are definite variations of national experience here: in the timing,

John Maynard Keynes, 1883–1946

character and scale of government economic management. But what is common to the entire post-war period and to the major Western economies is the increasing importance to each of them of the economic policies adopted by governments.

Governments in a number of Western European countries took into public ownership basic public utilities that could no longer be run profitably by private capital. Governments in all advanced capitalist countries expanded their employment of teachers, social workers, doctors and nurses — effectively absorbing the labour released from the private manufacturing sector by the growth of productivity there — whilst in the process providing new and extensive welfare, education and training facilities to the employed labour force. And increasingly over the post-war period, democratically elected governments began to regulate their own levels of spending, their taxation policies and investment plans, their monetary controls and credit restrictions, to keep aggregate levels of demand in their economies high enough to absorb the entire output of their highly productive manufacturing sectors. In this way politicians won popular support and re-election, electorates experienced steadily rising living standards, and companies were able to realize the profits they needed to finance further rounds of industrial investment and economic expansion.

Let us be clear too on the modes of co-ordination at play in this period of American dominance and Fordist methods of production. Over-ridingly, economic prosperity in the post-war years was based on the spread of *market* processes of exchange. The reduction in tariff barriers, the increasingly international movement of goods and capital, and the growing involvement of more and more people in high and expanding levels of consumer spending — all these were vital elements of the post-war prosperity. But that prosperity was not based on market mechanisms of allocation alone. It was based rather on a system of highly regulated market processes, one in which market exchange went on within complex *networks* of rules and institutions. These networks both surrounded and underpinned the entire bloc. The bloc was protected, at its edges, by a military network based on NATO and other alliance systems. It was organized internally through an economic network laid down at Bretton Woods, extended through the GATT and supervised by the IMF. And it was underpinned at its base by networks of collective agreements between employers and workers which kept working class purchasing power rising in line with output. The whole system worked because networks regulated market exchange; and the whole system worked too only because its productive core was organized on increasingly *hierarchical* lines. Big multinational companies emerged in this period. So too did extensive state bureaucracies and welfare systems. Neither inside the Fordist production system of the big firms nor inside the state was allocation organized on market lines: *inside* the main institutions operating in the market, resources were allocated not by price but by managerial order. Fordism worked through a fusion of market, network and hierarchy. And it stopped working, or at least stopped working as well, when that fusion lost its internal balance. It stopped working, as we will now see, amid difficulties created for market forms of co-ordination by the sheer weight of the networks and hierarchies built up in the years of prosperity. The UK was run, up to 1973, in a world dominated in part by the success of Fordism. It has been run since in a world dominated by the fact that, of late, Fordism has worked less well.

SUMMARY

- The core economies of the capitalist bloc experienced an unprecedented period of growth and prosperity between 1948 and 1973.

- One basis of that prosperity was Fordism. As a system of production, Fordism is best seen as assembly-line production of standardized consumer goods. It spread through the economies of the advanced capitalist countries between 1948 and 1973, bringing new industries into prominence, and new styles of life to the broad mass of the populations in those societies.

- Fordism had this impact only because of a favourable set of social and political circumstances: a change in the balance of social forces produced by different national mixtures of full employment and trade union organization, labour migration and government spending.

2 THE RESTRUCTURING OF THE POST-WAR ORDER

I hope you can now see the complex ways in which US power and Fordist regimes of accumulation interacted to create generalized prosperity in the capitalist bloc: that you can now understand how, between them, American power and Fordist ways of organizing production generated nearly 30 years of political stability and economic progress. Thirty years is a long time. Things that persist for that long come increasingly to be taken for granted, come to be seen as inherently permanent; and certainly the UK was run between 1945 and 1973 on the premise that American power and growing affluence were with us into the indefinite future. In a real sense, as we will see later, the UK was *too* easy to run in those years because of its insertion into so benign and settled an international order. UK policy-makers were shielded by the international climate from facing up to the things they needed to do if UK economic power and political influence was to be maintained in the tougher times to come. Difficult choices on social and economic reform were delayed because those tougher times were not anticipated, because the need for major structural reform within the UK was neither recognized nor seized. Running the country has become more difficult in the last 20 years partly because those tough choices were not faced and resolved early enough; and partly because of the growing fragility of both American power and Fordist accumulation regimes. We will look at the UK's 'lost opportunity of the 1950s' in the next chapter. Now, as a preliminary to that, we need to trace the increasing fragility of US economic leadership and the emerging limits of the mass production systems put in place in advanced capitalist countries in the years of the long post-war boom. We need to understand how and why the international order has now changed, and how those changes have conspired to make the UK's failures of policy in the 1950s suddenly and belatedly so costly to us all.

2.1 THE DECLINE OF US ECONOMIC POWER

The first signs of trouble — of the changing basis of international prosperity — came into view as early as the mid 1960s. By then the recovery of the West German and Japanese economies, and the 'economic miracles' of France and Italy — recoveries made possible only by the availability of US dollars, capital and know-how — had already begun to erode the gap between US manufacturing productivity and the productivity of other leading capitalist industrial nations. A 25 year growth period lubricated by persistent deficits on the US balance of *payments* was by then beginning to be undermined by the emergence of a deficit on the US balance of *trade*. In 1971, for the first time this century, America's trade balance went into deficit — imports exceeding exports to the value of $2.7 billion — and it stayed in deficit (except for 1973 and 1975) throughout the 1970s. Importers of manufactured goods within the capitalist bloc no longer looked automatically to the United States for the goods they bought; and no longer required dollars to buy them. Demand grew instead for other leading currencies: for the Deutschmark, the yen and the franc; and dollars accumulated in the vaults of the central banks of each major European capitalist power. In 1972, for the first time since the war, the West German economy exported more manufactured goods than did the USA; and by then, in any case, the Americans were heavily involved in the Vietnam War. The financing of that war added enormously to the size of the US deficit on its balance of payments. Dwindling US competitiveness combined with escalating US military spending to accelerate the flow of dollars entering the international system, dollars which by then could find recipients only at a lower rate of exchange. In 1971 the US government was forced to devalue the dollar, and so to abandon the whole system of fixed exchange rates which since 1944 had provided a stable financial framework for the expansion of world trade.

The 'fall of the dollar' in 1971 then opened a period of rising prices and unemployment. The reappearance of European and Japanese industrial growth had already affected inflation rates before 1971 as the competition of industrial economies for scarce Third World commodities began to inflate their price, and alter the terms of trade between the First World and the Third. The collapse of the Bretton Woods system then accentuated that inflationary surge. Governments were suddenly able (and for electoral reasons, were keen) to let local levels of demand rise, trade gaps to open and currencies to devalue to cope with the shortfall in foreign currency: at the cost of rising import prices to the home consumer. The Yom Kippur War, and the fourfold increase in oil prices in 1974 that followed, then added the final touches to the inflationary crisis.

Table 1.4 Inflation in the 1970s (% changes from previous year)

	1970	1971	1972	1973	1974	1975	1976	1977	1978	1979
Total	5.6	5.3	4.8	7.9	13.6	11.4	8.5	8.7	7.0	8.5
W. Germany	3.4	5.3	5.5	6.9	7.0	6.0	4.5	3.7	2.7	4.1
Sweden	7.0	7.4	6.0	6.7	9.9	9.8	10.3	11.4	10.0	7.2
Netherlands	3.6	7.5	7.8	8.0	9.6	10.2	8.8	6.4	4.1	4.2
France	4.8	5.5	6.2	7.3	13.7	11.8	9.6	9.4	9.3	10.7
Britain	6.4	9.4	7.1	9.2	16.0	24.2	16.5	15.8	8.7	12.0
Italy	5.0	4.8	5.7	10.8	19.1	17.0	16.8	17.0	12.1	14.8
Spain	5.7	8.3	8.3	11.4	15.7	16.9	17.7	24.5	19.8	15.7

Source: Cox (1982, p.15).

It was an inflationary crisis, moreover, which precipitated widespread retrenchment by all Western European governments, faced as they were with balance of payments deficits that had suddenly opened up to as much as 4–5 per cent of GNP. Governments slammed on the brakes — raised taxes and cut spending — to prevent a further erosion of their balance of payments. In 1975 the capitalist world economy stumbled. For the first time since 1948, world trade did not grow; and for the first time in a generation Western governments found themselves facing the prospect of inflation and unemployment rising together. Indeed the first major indication that something was going seriously wrong in the Western capitalist economies in the 1970s was the *stagflation* which suddenly swept the entire bloc in 1974–5. Table 1.5 shows the persistence of unemployment as well as inflation in the advanced capitalist countries well into the 1980s.

Table 1.5 Unemployment rates, 1973–83[1] (percentages of work-force per annum)

	Advanced capitalist countries	USA	Japan	EEC
1973	3.4	4.8	1.3	3.0
1975	5.5	8.3	1.9	4.5
1980	5.6	7.0	2.0	6.0
1981	6.5	7.5	2.2	8.0
1982	7.9	9.5	2.4	9.3
1983[2]	8.4	9.8	2.7	10.1

[1] Adjusted by OECD to secure comparability between countries.
[2] First nine months.

Source: Harrison and Bavar (1987, p.57).

The immediate response to these more difficult conditions was an intensification of international competition. Large multinational corporations competed for a greater share of what — in the 1970s — was a more sluggishly growing world market. As Table 1.6 makes clear,

> between 1973 and 1983 growth rates were half or even less than half of those prevailing between 1963 and 1973. After 1973, annual growth rates became extremely variable. In 1975 both manufacturing production and trade *declined*; a situation unknown for nearly forty years. There was a sharp — but short-lived — recovery in 1976 but by 1980 and 1981 world manufacturing production was virtually static. Exports, though more resilient, were still at less than half the annual rates of the 1960s. Quite evidently, boom had been transformed into slump.
>
> (Dicken, 1986, pp.18–19)

Table 1.6   Annual growth rates of world manufacturing production and exports, 1963–81 (percentage change)

	1963–73	1973–81	1974	1975	1976	1977	1978	1979	1980	1981
Production	7	3.5	3	−1.5	8	5	4.5	5	1	1
Exports	11	5	8.5	−4.5	13	5	5	5	4.5	4.5

Source: Dicken (1986, p.19).

In the more competitive climate generated by difficult trading conditions, the strong swallowed the weak; and a gap opened between those economies whose productive systems were already extensively modernized and labour intensive and those which were not. US industry (and, as we will see in the next chapter, UK industry as well) proved particularly vulnerable to this competition. US manufacturers had for too long been protected from the full rigours of world competition by the sheer size of the internal US market and by the 'cost plus' purchasing procedures of the US military. In 1960 US labour costs were three times higher than those in Europe and ten times those in Japan; and that gap only narrowed, but did not go away, in the two decades that followed (Armstrong *et al.*, 1984, p.220). Even a series of competitive devaluations by US governments could not prevent the progressive domination of US internal markets by more efficient foreign competitors. As Parboni put it:

> The devaluation of the dollar — or rather, the various devaluations that occurred through the seventies — did serve to halt the American economy's loss of competitivity, as is demonstrated by the halt in the decline of the US share of world manufactured exports. Nevertheless, the improvement in American competitivity was not transformed into an increase in industrial accumulation or an acceleration of the growth of industrial productivity. The United States thus appears to be suffering from some of the problems that have long racked the British economy: slow growth of industrial productivity, insufficient accumulation in industry compared with

competing countries, mounting weight of the service sector in the national income — in a word, de-industrialization.

(Parboni, 1981, p.9)

The hold of US manufacturers — not simply on foreign markets but also on the internal US market — was seriously eroded in the 1970s and 1980s by the arrival of Japanese and West German competition. As late as 1966 'the total value of North American manufacturing production was higher than that of Western Europe and Japan combined. Since 1975 however it has been lower than that of Western Europe alone' (Parboni, 1981, p.7). Whole 'rust belts' opened up in the United States, as old industries collapsed and as US capital shifted abroad. The revival of military spending in the Reagan years enabled new high-tech industries to flourish in the US south and west; but by then the hold of US-based producers on their own internal consumer goods markets had been seriously dented. We can see this diminution of US manufacturing dominance in Table 1.7 which shows figures on the changing pattern of manufacturing within the core capitalist countries between 1963 and 1981.

Table 1.7   Shifts within the core: manufacturing change, 1963–81

	World rank		Share of world manufacturing output (%)		Average annual rate of change (%)	
	1963	1980	1963	1980	1960–70	1970–81
USA	1	1	40.3	29.4	5.3	2.9
West Germany	2	3	9.7	12.4	5.4	2.1
UK	3	6	6.5	3.8	3.3	−0.5
France	4	4	6.3	7.0	7.8	3.2
Japan	5	2	5.5	15.7	13.6	6.5
Italy	6	5	3.4	4.5	8.0	3.7
Canada	7	8	3.0	2.4	6.8	3.5
Share of world total			74.7	75.2		

Source: Dicken (1986, p.28).

2.2   THE RISE OF NEW CENTRES OF ECONOMIC POWER

What has replaced total US dominance of world manufacturing output in part are new centres of industrial power *within* the major capitalist economies themselves. Table 1.7 makes clear the rising force of West German and Japanese manufactures; and the figures, though striking, do not tell the entire tale. It is hard to overstate the impact of Japanese industry in particular on the management thinking and consumer patterns of the rest of the advanced capitalist world in the last decade. The entry of Japanese goods into the US home market in the years after Vietnam destroyed the easy internal monopoly hitherto enjoyed by the large US-based companies. Japanese banks came to be key financiers of the US deficit on the balance of payments: and Japanese production techniques and management styles became *the* model to which all aspiring industrialists were referred for inspiration and guidance. As the American economic star waned after 1971, the Japanese rose even faster and higher than the German; to give Asia the cutting edge on industrial performance as the 1990s begin.

US dominance of world manufacturing has been eroded too by the tentative beginnings of a new international division of labour. Industrialization has spread out: into southern and Eastern Europe, into parts of Latin America and into South East Asia. Export-oriented manufacturing has flourished recently in parts of Europe (Spain, Portugal, Greece and Eastern Europe) and in the Third World (South Korea, Hong Kong, Singapore, Taiwan, Brazil, Mexico, Argentina and the Philippines). Much of this new manufacturing activity is still controlled from the core. 'About one-third of manufacturing exports from newly industrializing countries [NICs] takes place under the wings of the multinational corporations. And an EEC estimate for *all* developing countries puts the figure even higher, at 45%' (Hoogvelt, 1987, p.73). But even so, a significant change is occurring, in at least part of what were formally peripheral providers of primary produce to core industrializing nations. We can see that in the way in which the share of peripheral economies in the total volume of manufactured exports has risen from 6 per cent in 1960 to 12.6 per cent two decades later: and in the way in which, of that 12.6 per cent, 7.3 per cent came from the eight Third World countries and 2.7 per cent from the four European NICs mentioned above (ibid., p.70).

This is not to say, however, that the basic relationships within the system between core and periphery (between First World and Third) have altered out of all recognition. They have not. Power has shifted *within* the core — away from the United States — rather than *out* of the core altogether. But new forms of First World dominance over the Third World have also come to prominence. Much of the Third World is now linked to the First through relationships of debt. A major debt crisis stalks the wings of the international system, waiting to be precipitated by the default on payments of a large Third World borrower. This 'debt crisis' has been created by the changing patterns of lending and borrowing which accompanied the down-turn in world trade, and the rising oil prices, of the mid 1970s. One significant initial response to the shift in terms of trade between 1965 and 1973 was the adoption of ambitious programmes of industrial development by those Third World governments who suddenly found themselves in possession of greater flows of foreign currency (especially oil money) and credit-worthiness. Western European banks, short of domestic borrowers in the tighter economic conditions of the 1970s, lent generously to such Third World developers. But Third World export earnings proved more ephemeral than the bankers had hoped, as a second major Western recession (in 1980–1) reduced world demand for Third World products and altered the ratio of debt interest to export earnings for most Third World borrowers. By 1983 there were 32 countries in which the servicing of debt (the simple paying of the annual interest charge) absorbed more than 15 per cent of their total export earnings, 32 countries in which the burden of foreign debt was eating into local living standards. We can see something of this crisis in the First World — when a major bank writes off large chunks of its profits (as the

Midland Bank did in 1989) to cover unpaid Third World loans. But the impact of the debt crisis has been as nothing in the industrialized core economies when set against the austerity, poverty and political repression which it has fuelled in the non-industrialized countries of the periphery.

Table 1.8 Servicing of external public debt as a proportion of total exports (percentages debt servicing/exports for 1983 unless otherwise noted)

Countries where debt service is more than 20% of exports

Costa Rica 50.6	Ivory Coast 31.0	Yemen PDR 25.1	Burma 22 (1981)
Morocco 38.2	Bolivia 30.5	Argentina 24	Colombia 21.3
Mexico 35.9	Turkey 28.9	Dominican Republic 22.7	Kenya 20.6
Algeria 33.1	Brazil 28.7	Tunisia 22.3	Congo 20.5
Ecuador 32.5	Pakistan 28.1	Uganda 22.3 (1981)	Malawi 20.3
Zimbabwe 31.6	Egypt 27.5	Guinea 22.2	

Countries where debt service is more than 15% of exports

Uruguay 19.8	Chile 18.3	Togo 16.8	Jamaica 15.4
Peru 19.6	Nicaragua 18.3	Afghanistan 16.2 (1980)	Philippines 15.4
Nigeria 18.6			

Countries where debt service is more than 10% of exports

Venezuela 15.0	Yemen Arab Republic 13.9	Sri Lanka 11.9	Jordan 11.2
Honduras 14.9	Senegal 13.7 (1982)	Guatemala 11.7	Papua New Guinea 11.2
Paraguay 14.9	Somalia 13.1	Ethiopia 11.5	Sudan 11.2
Bangladesh 14.7	Indonesia 12.8	Central African Republic 11.3	Zaire 10.9 (1982)
Ghana 14.2	Zambia 12.6	Syria 11.3	India 10.3
Cameroon 13.9	South Korea 12.3	Thailand 11.3	Mauritania 10.1

Countries where debt service is more than 5% of exports

Madagascar 7.4 (1980)	Liberia 6.6	Mali 6.1	Tanzania 5.1
Sierra Leone 7.2	El Salvador 6.4 (1982)	Malaysia 5.9	Haiti 5.0
Panama 6.8			

Source: Szeftel (1987, p.92).

Nevertheless, though First World domination of the Third remains intact, economic power has shifted within the First World itself. As we have seen, at the corporate level — and in the sphere of consumer goods in particular — US-based manufacturing capital lost its pre-eminence in the 1970s and 1980s. It became just one player among many struggling for competitive advantage. At the level of national economies and trading blocs, that competition intensified too. The 25 years of unbroken economic growth achieved by the capitalist bloc after 1948 had been based on a diminution of barriers to trade. Successive GATT rounds had opened more and more markets to US goods (and as they came on stream, to West German and Japanese ones too). Prosperity and freer trade went together. But in the 1970s the emphasis changed. Japan continued to sustain powerful administrative and legal barriers against easy foreign entry to its internal market (and came under increasing pressure, as its trade balance went into ever greater surplus, to take those barriers down). Within Europe, the EC expanded its membership from six in 1958 to nine in 1973 and to twelve in 1981; and sustained powerful tariff walls against predominantly agrarian producers (including those in the USA and the Commonwealth). There are now important and competing regional centres of economic power within the capitalist bloc. Europe is one. Japan is another. The USA is simply a third: and it is the rise of Japanese and *European* power, more than anything else, which is now altering the international context within which the UK is to be run.

2.3   GROWING ECONOMIC INTERDEPENDENCE

So I hope you can see that the collapse of the Bretton Woods system of fixed exchange rates in 1971, and more importantly the shifting distribution of power between economies which precipitated the collapse, created a quite different framework for international economic activity in the capitalist bloc in the 1970s and 1980s from that which had predominated in the two decades before. Yet even in those first two post-war decades, the revival of European and Japanese industry had had a profound effect on patterns of trade and prices. Even then the growth of trade *between* leading capitalist countries had increasingly locked industrial economies together. In the 1950s, the internal trade of the industrial countries in manufactured products 'constituted about 25 per cent of total world trade. In 1963 it had increased to about 30 per cent and in 1973, the year before the oil price-rise, to 38 per cent. By 1980 the industrialized countries [had come to] account for 82 per cent of world exports of manufactured products — and of that almost 72 per cent is their trade with each other.' (Anell, 1981, p.66.) As a result, over the post-war period as a whole, each advanced capitalist country became ever more dependent for its economic success on levels of demand in the others. That is why the 1950s pattern (of separate national trade cycles) had by 1966 been replaced by a common pattern of expansion and contraction in the system as a whole. In the 1950s it had been possible for the West German trade cycle to be out of line with, say, that of the UK. West Germany in recession could expand by exporting to the UK in boom, and vice versa. After 1966 such 'de-linking' became increasingly difficult to achieve.

Table 1.9 'Vital statistics' of the top transnational corporations

(a) Manufacturing (1980)

Corporation	Country of origin	Total sales ($ million)	Foreign content as a percentage of	
			assets	employment
General Motors	USA	57,728	12	31
Ford Motor Co.	USA	37,086	40	58
IBM	USA	26,213	46	43
General Electric	USA	25,523	28	29
Unilever	UK/ Netherlands	24,161	36	48
ITT	USA	23,819	33	53
Renault	France	18,958		24
Philips	Netherlands	18,377	26	79
Volkswagen	West Germany	18,313		38
Siemens	West Germany	17,583		32
Peugeot-Citroën	France	16,825	15	22
BASF	West Germany	16,499		25
Hoechst	West Germany	16,458		46
Bayer	West Germany	15,858	44	44
Nestlé	Switzerland	14,608		54
Tenneco	USA	13,488	25	
ICI	UK	13,295		41
Matsushita Elec.	Japan	12,860		53
United Technologies	USA	12,399	21	32
Proctor & Gamble	USA	11,416	19	33
Dow Chemical Co.	USA	10,626	49	39
St Gobain	France	10,291	61	53
Union Carbide	USA	9,994	31	46
Eastman Kodak	USA	9,734	24	35
Caterpillar Tractor	USA	8,598	40	24

(b) Banking (1975)

Bank	Home country	Total assets ($ billion)	Foreign affiliates Developed Countries	Developing Countries	total
Bank America Corp.	USA	94.9	85	174	259
Citicorp	USA	87.1	67	167	234
Deutsche Bank	West Germany	80.3	28	37	65
Banque Nationale de Paris	France	78.2	37	60	97
Crédit Lyonnais S.A.	France	74.1	26	38	64
Societé Générale S.A.	France	66.9	29	32	61
Dai-Ichi Kangyo Bank	Japan	73.3	17	16	33
Dresdner Bank A.G.	West Germany	61.6	29	37	66
Chase Manhatten Corp.	USA	61.2	59	128	187
Fuji Bank Ltd.	Japan	61.2	17	19	36
Sumitomo Bank Ltd.	Japan	63.6	18	13	31
Mitsubishi Bank Ltd.	Japan	62.7	16	16	32
Sanwa Bank Ltd.	Japan	61.6	17	18	35
Westdeutsche Landesbank	West Germany	51.3	18	5	23
Banco do Brasil S.A.	Brazil	49.1	24	23	47
Industrial Bank of Japan	Japan	53.3	22	23	45
Barclays Bank Ltd.	UK	48.7	71	123	194
Commerzbank A.G.	West Germany	48.4	35	31	66
National Westminster	UK	45.3	25	5	30
Tokai Bank Ltd.	Japan	45.9	14	7	21
Mitsui Bank Ltd.	Japan	44.1	16	16	32
Taiyo-Kobe Bank Ltd.	Japan	42.0	10	5	15
Manufacturers Hanover	USA	40.6	27	28	55
Swiss Bank Corp.	Switzerland	39.1	27	22	49
Algemene Bank Nederland	Netherlands	38.8	52	65	117

Source: Dicken (1986, pp.56, 87).

Delinking was difficult partly because by then advanced capitalist economies were linked to each other by more than trade. They were also linked by the presence in each of them of the same multinational companies and banks. Two decades of prosperity had a profound effect on company structures as well as on national economic autonomy. The availability of large world markets that could be fully exploited only by economies of scale

37

fuelled the growth of multinational corporations. By the 1960s a new economic institution was beginning to occupy the attention of Western European governments — the US-based transnational company. The American version would be joined in the 1970s and 1980s by Japanese and Western European-based multinational concerns. Such large companies were not new. What was new was their number, scope and centrality to the economies of the capitalist bloc. 'In the nineteenth century transnational companies [had been] involved mainly in the extractive industries and in agricultural commodities: financial flows tended to pass through specialist financial houses. In the post-war period multinational companies have become increasingly important in manufacturing (especially cars and electronics) and even in banking' (McCormick, 1988, p.9). By the 1970s such companies were major players in the growth industries and leading sectors of the long post-war boom; and their presence there altered the terms on which individual economies could be run. Western governments had started the post-war period with considerable degrees of national economic autonomy, and with the capacity to exercise direct political control over their predominantly locally-based and controlled industrial and banking institutions. By the 1970s and 1980s much of that government power had effectively gone.

But delinking was also difficult because of the increasing *regional and global integration* of the entire economic exercise: not just ownership and trade, but also production and exchange. By 1990 key consumer goods — automobiles and electronic equipment — were often generated by production systems of an international kind: with a carburettor built here, sparking plugs there, and so on. By 1990 we have evidence, that is, of the emergence of global systems of production in certain key industries. We also have evidence of far

The equity floor of BZW in the 1980s

more extensive degrees of import penetration across national boundaries. Global production may be a feature of only a few industries, but global exchange is now a feature of virtually all.

For today 'the world is an economic unit in quite a different fashion' to any earlier period. This is evident to all of us as we shop on any UK high street, or settle to watch the evening news. 'Transport costs have been reduced so dramatically that almost the whole commodity market — the only major exception being some parts of food production — is subject to international competition.' (Anell, 1981, p.61.) As never before, every major industrial sector faces international competition in its domestic market. Revolutions in communications have turned capital markets into entirely global entities; and national boundaries and cultures are now submerged by satellite media. There is a serious tension here between the local and the global. In the years of US dominance (in the 1950s and 1960s) industrial economies were reconstituted within core national states. The years of US economic decline that followed have been accompanied by an increasing international integration of economic processes which has seriously eroded the autonomy of those national political structures. It is not just that the major national players have shifted position in the international economic order within which the UK is run. It is also that — in economic life at least — the boundaries of the UK are so perforated by international economic flows that it is increasingly difficult to see where the UK economy stops and the rest of the world economy begins.

2.4   THE COLLAPSE OF THE COLD WAR

As we saw earlier, the ideology and military spending associated with the Cold War, and the division of the world into blocs, played an important part in establishing post-war Western prosperity. The ideology of anti-communism legitimated American leadership and military presence in Western Europe. It legitimated moves in the late 1940s and early 1950s to break the power of trade unions and communist parties, not only in Western Europe, but also in Japan, and to head off (by military action if necessary) the winning of power by left-wing forces in Latin America and South East Asia (Cox, 1990, pp.29–30). Military spending fuelled economic expansion both directly and indirectly. The maintenance of US forces abroad brought much needed dollars into the international system; and the research and development associated with the US military-industrial complex fuelled new technologies for civil production as well. The existence of a bloc of states under US leadership during the Cold War, with its own internal institutions (GATT, IMF and NATO), provided financial security, military protection and an integrated set of markets for economic expansion.

But to a degree, as we have also seen, the Cold War was dysfunctional to the longevity of Western prosperity, at least to a system of prosperity based on US economic leadership. Soft military contracts from the US government helped to undermine the competitiveness of US industry. 'High military spending held back development of non-military industry in the USA, producing lower productivity growth and slower economic growth than its major competitors.' (Smith, 1987, p.156.) As Brett has it:

> During the 1950s and 1960s American defence expenditure was always significantly higher than that of its leading industrial competitors, and a large percentage of this was spent overseas ... Although this contributed significantly to the health of its arms industry, its overall effect on the relative strength of the domestic economy was certainly negative, tying up very large numbers of workers and huge amounts of raw materials and sophisticated capital equipment in unproductive activities which contributed nothing to the modernization of the social and economic infrastructure, or to the strengthening of the productivity and competitiveness of the productive sector itself.
>
> (Brett, 1985, pp.119–20)

Moreover, as we have already seen, US military expenditure (especially in Vietnam in the 1960s) flooded the world with by then unwanted dollars, and speeded the collapse of the Bretton Woods arrangements. It also superimposed on the economic trade cycle a Cold War cycle of military spending, which brought its own attendant difficulties of funding and resource allocation. Military expenditure was high in the early 1950s, to contain North Korea, then fell in a period of détente. It was high in the 1960s and early 1970s, to contain North Vietnam, and then steadied in the early years of the Carter administration. It soared again in the New Cold War days of the Reagan administration; then fell in the early 1990s as the Soviet Union itself began to disintegrate — as its credibility as a military threat began visibly to decline. In each expansion, parts of US industry flourished and retooled — particularly the high-tech industries of the US south and west; but in each expansion the relative competitiveness of the consumer goods industries of the US north-east weakened by comparison. In other words, the arms race had its own impact on the industrial structure and competitiveness of the US economy; and made its own contribution to the erosion of economic dominance on which American leadership in the Cold War had initially been based.

The Cold War was officially called off by the signing of the Treaty on Conventional Armed Forces in Europe in Paris in November 1990; and this, as well as the recent disintegration of Soviet control over its Eastern European empire, has now added a new uncertainty to the system of states and economies within which the UK is situated. In ideological terms, the collapse of Soviet power has strengthened the legitimacy of capitalism as a whole (and discredited the political credibility of left-wing forces), and holds out the prospect of new markets for multinational capital in all its forms (from hamburger houses in Moscow to heavy engineering). But at the same time it has put a large question mark over the military institutions and alliances of the capitalist bloc, and over the likely pattern of military expenditure in the 1990s. How will the West function if peace really does break out?

It is hard to judge these matters with any precision from the vantage point of the early 1990s. There is much uncertainty in the international order, with US military power and self-confidence enhanced — at least temporarily — by the Allied defeat of Iraq in the Persian Gulf. But it is at least possible that any permanent reduction in Cold War tension will hit US industry particularly hard, and speed up the diminution of US power and leadership in the capitalist bloc. It certainly must alter the balance of authority between the United States and the large (and increasingly self-confident) bloc of European states now poised to absorb Eastern Europe into their orbit. Eastern Europe is sufficiently unstable and economically under-developed to add to problems of capital accumulation in Europe as a whole to the end of the century; and prospects in the Soviet Union are still so uncertain that Western military spending will no doubt be sustained at high peace-time levels for a while. But the economic and political potential that Eastern Europe now offers to a revitalized Western European capitalism is such that it seems likely that the international order within which the UK will be run in the 1990s will be much more dominated by *European* states than — as in the immediate past — by the USA. A reunited Germany, at the head of an increasingly integrated European Community, seems to be the legacy left to policy-makers in the UK from the decline of both the Soviet and the American empires around whose conflict international economic and political life has been organized since 1945.

SUMMARY

- American dominance in output, trade and finance has diminished since 1971. Dollar devaluation that year effectively ended the Bretton Woods agreement. Since 1971 US pre-eminence in manufacturing has been effectively challenged by West German and Japanese companies.

- Power relationships have shifted within the core economies, and between the core and periphery. The 1980s have witnessed the emergence of a new international division of labour, and a serious debt crisis, in the Third World. US leadership of the core has been challenged by the rise of European and Japanese economic power. This is one reason why UK economic and political life in the 1990s will increasingly be dominated by developments in Europe rather than by developments in the United States.

- The bloc as a whole has become increasingly integrated in the last 20 years: by trade flows between advanced capitalist countries, by the emergence of multinational companies and banks, by shared problems of inflation and unemployment, by a common exposure to more sluggish growth patterns and intensified competition, and by the increasing international integration of production and exchange. This puts a big question mark over the ability of individual governments to control their own national economies.

> - The Cold War tension between East and West has been the basic framework of international relations in the post-war period. The financing of US military power had a complex (and probably adverse) effect on the ability of the United States to maintain its position of economic leadership in the capitalist bloc. As the Cold War declines in potency, it is *Europe* which is emerging again as a key centre of economic power and political influence on the world stage.

3 THE LIMITS OF FORDISM

International economic and political conditions have become less stable in the last 20 years in part because of the paradoxical consequences of US success. The visibly superior character of US-led capitalism (fed into the USSR in the 1980s through international satellite media systems) ate away at the internal stability of its Cold War Russian opponent; and helped to compound those internal economic and political contradictions within the USSR which brought the Soviet empire to its knees after 1985. Inside the capitalist bloc, equally important but less traumatic contradictions opened up because the USA had so successfully reconstituted Western European and Japanese capitalism. As we have seen, once they were reconstituted, the economic base of US leadership was quickly eroded. The competitiveness and innovative force of US manufacturing wilted as the energies of the US state were directed elsewhere: into policing the bloc as a whole (with its attendant military costs) and into running its own military-industrial complex (with adverse effects on US manufacturing productivity, wage costs and research and development). Stronger, more civilian-rooted competitor economies emerged, none strong enough to dislodge the US completely, but each powerful enough to challenge the American capacity to finance its balance of payments deficits indefinitely by the printing and export of dollars. At the level of *exchange* within the system — at the level of the circulation and financing of goods — the US writ no longer ran unchallenged. US goods were no longer the premier choice in the market; and because they were not, the willingness of foreign buyers and sellers to hold dollars was commensurately reduced.

But beneath this level of exchange, deeper problems of *production* began to emerge too, problems which affected the whole international capitalist system, and not just the relative strengths of particular national economies within it. Prosperity after 1945 had rested on the linked ability of industry to generate goods, workers to produce them, and consumers to buy them. From the 1970s the relationship between all three became more problematic.

As we have already had occasion to mention, the growing affluence of the 1950s and 1960s had rested ultimately on the *rising productivity of labour* — on fewer and fewer workers producing more and more goods — through their involvement in semi-automated systems of industrial production, in mass production assembly-line work of a Fordist kind. This post-war 'revolution' in productivity came first from *introducing* such production systems into first one sector of industry and then another; and then from *refining/speeding up* the work process in sectors already organized in this way. The initial impact of Fordist methods of assembly-line working on productivity was massive, and could be sustained just so long as sector after sector was reorganized on Fordist lines. But when that had been done — when we had completed the two/three seven-year trade cycles that it took to spread Fordism into each branch of industry capable of absorbing it — then the rate of growth of industrial productivity began to slow. It was just no longer possible to create new leaps in productivity by the introduction of semi-automated production systems. Instead — and until whole new technologies of production were generated — productivity gains became possible only through the reorganization of already-mechanized assembly lines, the intensification of management pressures on labour, and the speeding up of the work process.

Advanced capitalist countries varied in the degree to which (and the precise moment at which) this 'exhaustion of Fordism' started to show. It came first to those economies (the US in particular) where Fordism had been established the longest, and to those (like the UK) in which the balance of social forces around industry kept investment in modern technologies low and worker militancy high. But the slowing down of productivity growth was something experienced by the majority of the main capitalist economies in the 1970s: and it was certainly by then a pronounced feature of UK economic life. Indeed in the UK at least, by as early as the late 1960s, substantial productivity gains in industries long-established on Fordist lines could only be extracted by squeezing more and more work out of workers: and that, of course, produced worker resistance — the other face of the growing crisis of Fordism.

In this way too, economic success contained its own contradiction. The rapid expansion of industrial output and employment in the 1950s and 1960s ate away at the system's supplies of cheap and amenable labour: and it did so for two different but related reasons.

1   The actual sources of cheap labour began to dry up. Initially, as we saw earlier, new labour forces were plentiful. They were to be found among the displaced persons of war-torn Europe. They came from Eastern Europe until the Berlin Wall went up in 1961. They came from the peripheral economies of the Mediterranean and the colonies; and they came from the over-populated countryside of southern Europe and Japan. By the late 1960s much of this was changing. Eastern Europe was closed off, the countryside effectively de-populated, and core economies beset with the problems of absorbing ethnic minorities into their decaying inner cities. Married women too were drawn back into paid labour in the post-war years, in a quiet social revolution of profound importance. But women in a patriarchal culture are never a perfect reserve army of labour. They carry heavy domestic responsibilities as well; and for many of them, particularly those with children, part-time paid work was all they could manage. So even their arrival, and certainly the influx of migrant labour, did nothing to meet the system's need for full-time skilled manual and professional workers. It was on their efforts and

capacities that Fordism ultimately depended; and it was their scarcity which in the end helped to bring 'the golden age of Fordism' (Barbrook, 1990, p.28) to an end.

2   Moreover the application of machinery to production on Fordist lines shifted the balance of class power in industry. Small groups of workers found they could immobilize vast amounts of capital by industrial action. The absence of large-scale unemployment took away the most potent of managerial sanctions — dismissal. Instead — in the UK in particular — managers faced shortages of skilled workers, and were prepared to hold on to those they had by recognizing and negotiating with their unions and their shop stewards. A generation of workers emerged after 1945 used to full employment, used to rising living standards, and used to negotiating with local management for easier working conditions and for greater degrees of job control and pay. It was a generation who were prepared to use their industrial power: and Fordism ran into crisis when they did so. To varying degrees across the capitalist bloc in the early 1970s, firms found themselves caught between slowing rising productivity and rapidly rising working class militancy.

These symptoms of malaise in the Fordist regime of accumulation came to dominate the economic agenda of Western governments in the 1970s. Trapped between intensifying competition and confident labour movements, many major European industrial concerns ran into a profits crisis in the early 1970s (for the UK experience of this, see Glyn and Sutcliffe, 1972). A gap appeared, for the first time since the 1940s, between productivity growth and wage growth. This added an inflationary pressure to those already released into the system by rising commodity prices and falling exchange rates. Government spending suddenly became inflationary, as manufacturing output dipped. Low levels of productivity in the state sector (both in the manufacturing parts nationalized because they were uncompeti-

Late arrivals at the feast: migrant workers entering Switzerland in the 1970s

tive, and in the very labour-intensive welfare bureaucracies) kept public sector wage bills high, while manufacturing output on which those wages were to be spent was now growing more slowly. Governments found themselves facing a 'fiscal crisis of the state' (O'Connor, 1973). They simply had greater and greater problems financing their own expenditure and employment without adding to inflation.

As Fordist-based production systems ran into difficulties of slowing productivity and rising wage pressure in the 1970s, governments reared for a generation on the maxims of Keynesian economics suddenly found themselves in difficulty too. Governments could no longer spend their way out of recession, as they had done in the 1940s. They either kept spending high, at the cost of inflation and trade deficits — and saw jobs destroyed in their industrial base as local firms collapsed before stronger international competitors. (This was the experience of the Mitterand government in France in the early 1980s, and of Labour in power in the UK between 1974 and 1976.) Or they cut their own spending and pegged the wages of their own employees — at the cost of 'winters of discontent' and electoral rejection (viz. the Labour government in the UK after its 1976 'conversion to monetarism'). National patterns varied a little, of course, depending on the strength of a particular economy relative to the rest, and on the militancy of particular labour movements. But in general Keynesian-inspired governments kept in office by prosperity in the 1950s and 1960s lost power by the same route in the decade that followed: rejected because they could no longer guarantee the rising prosperity which their electorates had by then come to take for granted.

The politicians took the blame, as once they had taken the credit, and paid the price of living in new times. Other politicians — of a less Keynesian persuasion — took their place at the centres of power. The Carters and the Callaghans gave way to the Reagans and the Thatchers. Workers, unions, welfare spending, high taxation and industrial subsidies — all these were blamed too, and lost out accordingly. In effect politicians who had relied on *networks* of a political kind to manage capitalist markets, found themselves replaced by politicians determined to bring the *market* back as the key allocative device. The face of these two political projects, in the UK at least, will occupy us in Chapter 4. But what we need to hang on to now is the recognition that in reality the roots of our present economic difficulties lie, as they have always lain, far deeper than politicians and policies. They lie rather in the way in which the success of Fordism eroded its own pre-conditions, and brought inflation and large-scale unemployment back into the Western capitalist economies again. The 'regime of accumulation' on which post-war prosperity had been based had run up against its limits, with enormous consequences for government policy in the 1980s and for political options in the decades to come.

The economic consequences of the slowing down of productivity growth in the 1970s and early 1980s, and of the intensified international competition with which it was associated, have been considerable. They have inspired the pursuit of whole new technologies of industrial production, ones relying heavily on the use of fully-automated computer-driven machinery to speed the production of mass consumer goods. Computerization has also been deployed to increase the quality and differentiate the range of goods being produced, in an attempt to hold on to threatened consumer markets. More difficult producing and selling conditions have inspired managements in big industrial concerns to challenge the industrial power of their own work forces, to explore new methods of worker involvement in production and design, and to scale down the number and cost of the core of skilled workers on which their production systems rely. And the tougher economic climate of the 1980s led governments to re-examine their role, and to reassess their ability to deliver full employment, welfare provision and industrial aid. In other words, the growing difficulties of Fordist-based production in the 1970s and 1980s have raised the possibility that we might be moving into a new and different 'regime of accumulation' capable of underpinning capitalist prosperity and democratic politics in the 1990s and beyond.

As we saw earlier, at the international level, 'running the country' in the 1990s has to go on against a background of uncertainty and fundamental change: as the Cold War ends, and Eastern European communism disintegrates; and as US economic dominance gives way to rising Western European and Japanese power. And at the level of capitalist production — our other main line of march through this chapter — 'running the country' in the 1990s has to go on against the background of an equally potent uncertainty and change — this time associated with the growing problems of Fordist ways of organizing production in advanced capitalist countries. Whether, as a result, the UK will have to face some kind of a post-Fordist future — as well as a post-Cold War incorporation into a reorganized bloc of European states under German leadership — will therefore be one of the main questions to which we will return in the final pages of this book.

SUMMARY

- Post-war stability based on Fordist methods of production became less secure in the 1970s and 1980s as the rate of growth of productivity slowed and as the incidence of working class militancy rose.

- This had major consequences for the viability of governments basing their economic policies on Keynesian lines; and ushered in a new politics of market-based Conservatism.

- One question for the 1990s is the degree to which a new system of production is emerging, to offer new possibilities for economic growth and political control.

CHAPTER 2: THE ECONOMY

So far we have established two broad and inter-connected parameters within which the post-war UK has been run: one largely political and military, the other unambiguously economic. We have seen how the UK's post-war international context was shaped by first the establishment and much later the disintegration of a particular post-war order: one built on US leadership of a Western bloc of capitalist nations, and on a Cold War struggle between capitalism and communism. We have seen that Cold War rise and fall, and US dominance flow and ebb. We have also seen the grounding of post-war Western prosperity in a particular way of organizing key productive processes, and become aware of emerging difficulties in that 'regime of accumulation'. We have seen the spread and the limits of Fordism. What we need to do now is to focus on the UK's involvement in all of that — and make use of these inter-connected parameters to illuminate important developments in the economic, social and political life of the post-war UK. Social changes will occupy Chapter 3, political ones Chapter 4. Our focus in this chapter will be on the economy.

The rhythm of argument here — as we said at the start of Chapter 1 — is one that moves from the global to the local, and not in the opposite direction. For if we are to grasp both the options and the constraints that operate on those who run the contemporary UK, and if we want to understand how and why the UK has been run in a particular way since the war, we need to keep firmly before us this image of the UK as part of an international economic and political order. And not just part, but a key part. The UK economy, the UK currency, UK soldiers and empire, were all vital elements in the post-war reconstruction of the world order. The UK began the post-war period as senior ally to the United States in the design and policing of the non-communist world. It began the post-war years immersed in a *network* of international relationships dominated by the United States. It has ended the period as a middle-ranking Western European economic power without a distinct world role of its own. It is approaching the end of the century still seeking its own place in a new *network* of international relationships dominated by the rising power of Europe. The UK experienced much of the post-war period as one of decline: and all that follows here has to be set against that background. It has to be understood as part of the steady erosion of the UK as a world power, and as part of the various attempts made by those who run the UK to reverse that decline.

1 THE ROLE AND CHARACTER OF THE POST-WAR ECONOMY

1.1 THE CHANGING PLACE OF THE UK IN THE WORLD ORDER

As in Chapter 1, we face a choice of explanatory strategies as we try to capture the role and character of the post-war UK economy. We can focus, and indeed will have to, largely on the documentation of recent trends, so that you can emerge from your reading with reliable data on the present organization and recent history of economic life in the UK. But in doing so, it helps to set those trends in a greater span of time: to see post-war economic developments in the UK as part of a longer story of UK economic growth and decline. And that longer view is particularly important here because the roots of contemporary economic difficulties were laid down so long ago, and because the past has thrown forward such a shadow over contemporary UK institutions, attitudes and options. Here, as in so much of UK life, 'the legacy of past generations lies like a nightmare on the brain of the living' (Marx, 1852), and we need a sense of that legacy if we are to understand fully the shape of post-war economic activity in the UK, if we are to see who is able to run the economy, and if we are to see why they run it in a particular way.

It is not possible fully to understand the significance of the UK's diminished standing as a world economic and political power without remembering how starkly that contrasts with the UK's standing in the world a century before. By 1815 the UK had won one empire (in India and Canada) and lost another (in the United States). By 1850 its economy was 'the workshop of the world', the main (indeed then largely the only) source of manufactured goods and investment capital. By 1870 its manufacturers, trading networks and currency were playing much the same role as US manufacturers, banks and currency played after 1945: fuelling industrial development elsewhere by exporting capital goods and loans; and having sterling act as a reserve currency. Sterling was acceptable in exchange (literally 'as good as gold') across the emerging capitalist world in the nineteenth century in much the same way that the dollar has been since 1945. By 1914 indeed, the UK ruled one quarter of the globe — in the largest (and certainly the most scattered) empire the world has ever seen. All this from an island one third the size of Texas!

But as we have seen with the post-war American empire, imperial domination is a transient thing. It flows and then it ebbs, eaten away in part by the consequences of its own success. After 1870 UK capital helped, as US capital helped after 1945, to construct powerful industrial competitors, who in the end challenged and destroyed the dominance of the economy they initially emulated. Recent American slowness to modernize its industrial base has its parallel in UK reaction to the arrival of new technologies (based on electricity) and new competition (from Germany and the USA) in the 1890s. UK

The height of Empire: the Viceroy's state entry into Delhi, 1903

industry did not quickly adopt the new technology. Instead it retreated into the safer markets of the Empire; and failed to retain its industrial leadership on the world scale. Capital exports (and the income they generated) protected the balance of payments until liquidated to pay for two world wars; and the Empire (India especially) both buttressed UK pride and sustained traditional UK industries (especially cotton) until removed by political independence and transformed by partial Third World industrialization in the 1940s and 1950s. By then in any case the UK no longer had either the economic strength or the military capacity to play the world role it had developed for itself a century before. By 1945 UK politicians had to accept a supporting role to a new imperial power; and even that role played havoc, after 1945, with the internal readjustments necessary for industrial modernization.

The submersion of the UK in a network of international relationships dominated by the United States, and the dependence of UK governments on US aid and military support, was evident both in World War II, and in the political and economic settlements that emerged from it. In the negotiations at Bretton Woods in 1944, it was American proposals which were accepted, and the dollar which reigned supreme. UK proposals for a new international currency beyond the control of any one national government gave way to the reality of the economic and military power of the United States. Sterling emerged from Bretton Woods as a second reserve currency — acceptable as an international means of exchange in the sterling area based on the old Empire and Commonwealth, but no longer internationally regarded 'as good as gold'. Nor should this international unease with the reliability of sterling surprise us. For by the 1940s the UK too was heavily dependent on US loans, was as short of dollars as everyone else, and was quite simply economically and militarily incapable of holding onto the vast land masses occupied by UK troops in 1945. India, Ceylon and Burma were abandoned by 1948. UK power in Greece was replaced by American in 1946. The UK played a major role in Korea, at the US behest, in 1952 and 1953; but thereafter cut back its military commitments stage by stage. It was the Americans who used financial pressure to pull UK troops out of Egypt in 1956, and a Labour government after 1965 that pulled UK troops home from east of Suez. The United States was left to fight in Vietnam alone, as the UK concentrated on coping with (and retreating from) a series of smaller colonial wars (in Malaya, Kenya, Cyprus and Rhodesia). The UK retained a military presence in West Germany and Berlin into the 1990s, retained its formally independent nuclear deterrent, and kept its defence spending within NATO at a higher level per head of the population than any state other than the USA. But increasingly over the post-war years, the military role of the UK appeared anachronistic, a legacy of an era of economic and political dominance long since gone, one kept alive only to satisfy the vanity of UK ruling groups and only at a heavy internal cost.

The great power pretensions (and associated overseas military expenditure) of successive British governments in the early post-war years had a number of quite serious internal economic effects. As Stephen Blank put it, a key feature of Britain's economic problems in the post-war period lay in the 'attitudes, commitments and policies of Britain's top political leaders', in the way in which 'British governments after the war were committed ... to restore and protect Britain's international position' (Blank, 1985, pp.210, 217). The real failure of Attlee's Labour government lay here, in its inability to 'recognise the extent of their problems and instead to allow the apparently soft option presented by American assistance to be used to evade the need to take tough decisions on overseas defence commitments' (Brett, 1985, p.140).

More directly, military expenditure shaped patterns of research and development in the industrial sector, affected the allocation and effort of scientists and technologists there, and ate away at civilian modernization initiatives at critical moments of post-war reconstruction. This was particularly so in the early 1950s, when the redirection of investment into war production distorted the reconstruction of the engineering industry at a particularly important moment of economic revival. West Germany and Japan, after all, flourished in part because they lacked the distorting impact of military spending. Their engineering industries had to survive without military contracts, without the cost-plus cushioning of state arms-procurement programmes. 'What is demonstrably the case is that [between 1950 and 1966] Britain was spending four or five per cent more of its gross national product on defence than they were. In Japan and Germany almost all of this difference went into productive capital investment which, at compound interest, meant that their industry was able to overtake and surpass Britain's by the 1960s.' (Brett, 1985, p.140.) There was a real sense in which the countries that lost the war were better placed to win the peace.

But if the military spending associated with the UK's over-stretched world role was the most direct cause of the UK's post-war economic decline, it was not the major one; and arguably, decline would have happened even if excessive military expenditure had not. For in 1945 the UK's world role required more than simply the world-wide distribution of UK soldiers. It also required that sterling be made available — and be protected — as an acceptable reserve currency, stable in its exchange rate with the dollar. The initial rate set in 1944 quickly proved untenable. Sterling was devalued in 1949; but between then and 1967 (when devaluation came again) internal economic policy was geared to the protection of sterling and to the defence of the UK role as banker within the sterling area. Powerful City interests pressed successive governments to maintain a stable and high exchange rate, thereby keeping London as a key international financial centre; and politicians seemed to hold on to a high exchange rate as a token of their own international standing.

Industrial and labour interests were slow to see the danger that this represented to their long-term prosperity, cushioned in world markets as they were for a decade by the wartime dislocation of their German and Japanese competitors. But from the mid 1950s the 'cost' of maintaining sterling as a reserve currency became increasingly clear. From then, confidence in the pound could be maintained only by keeping the balance of payments in surplus; and that in its turn required the maintenance of high interest rates in London to dampen domestic levels of demand (for imports) and to hold speculative capital in sterling. Both immediate industrial modernization and longer term manufacturing investment were severely damaged by this 'stop go' policy geared to sterling's protection; so that an opportunity was lost in the 1950s to reconstitute the UK as Western Europe's leading industrial power.

The manufacturing base of the UK economy found itself instead locked into 'a vicious circle of slow growth, low investment and low productivity gains' (Aaronovitch *et al.*, 1981, p.165) falling further and further behind the 'virtuous' growth path of, particularly, its West German equivalent; where rapid growth fuelled high investment and persistent productivity gains. The contemporary running of the UK economy remains more difficult than it need be because that opportunity, once lost, never returned. UK industry could have established its own competitive edge while West Germany and Japan were still recovering from war and occupation: but the UK's 'economic miracle' did not occur. The world pretensions of its rulers, and the world role of its financial institutions, effectively shut that option down; and in doing so fixed the economic agenda of each post-war British government to date. The failure of the 1950s left the UK perennially obliged to *catch up* with stronger competitors; and left it faced with the dilemma of how to avoid adopting short-term crisis measures that would eat away at any long-term strategy of economic recovery. Locked into a vicious circle of 'low investment — low productivity — low competitiveness — low investment', the overwhelming problem for UK economic policy-makers in the last 30 years has been the same: how to break out into a cycle of 'virtuous' growth.

That, as we will see in Chapter 4, is something no British government to date has effectively managed to do; and in a way their failure need not surprise us. The entire weight of two centuries of UK history stand in the way of economic regeneration in the 1990s. There is much debate in the relevant literature about when, how, and why the UK went into economic decline (Coates and Hillard, 1985, *passim*). There is considerable disagreement among scholars in this field about whether that decline began in the 1890s (with the retreat into Empire) or only in the 'lost opportunity' of the 1940s and 1950s, and about whether this decline has been reversed by Thatcherite policies of economic reconstruction. There is also much discussion about whether whatever degree of economic decline has occurred is best explained — as here — in terms of City–state relations, or in terms of industry–trade union ones. Are the causes of decline, that is, best grasped by emphasizing the fusion of financial interests and imperial pretensions, or by stressing the strength of trade unionism and the weakness of the entrepreneurial spirit? As far as I can tell (and as will become more obvious later in this chapter and in Chapter 4) the long-established weakness of UK-based manufacturing industry still remains an important and dominant feature of contemporary economic life: and in that sense Conservative policies since 1979 have not 'worked' yet, and are unlikely to. For they have not tackled adequately a whole complex of social forces, institutions, attitudes and practices inherited from earlier periods of economic dominance and imperial glory. The UK economy is difficult to run now because of the presence within it of powerful legacies of the past, and there is still an important sense in which we are — even today — paying a price for the UK's quite unique experience of industrialization.

The UK industrialized first because its industrial and commercial middle class was particularly strong; and other social forces and institutions which elsewhere were central to industrialization here played only the most marginal of roles. Neither the state nor the banking networks were directly and heavily involved in the process. Nor was accumulation slowed — in the nineteenth century — by anything but the minimum of working class resistance. The *state* held the ring (and used its navy to win and retain open markets abroad). The *banks* lubricated exchange, and absorbed surplus savings; but the main nineteenth century job — of London-based banks at least — was to lend to foreigners (who then used the money to buy British goods). Nineteenth century *trade unions* were too weak to block rapid industrial change, and had only managed to establish a toe-hold among male skilled workers (and miners) by the end of the century. And neither the cultural values and political programmes of a pre-capitalist aristocracy, nor those of an anti-capitalist labour movement, were strong enough to prevent the consolidation of a *liberal capitalist popular culture* which identified industrial success with laissez-faire politics.

But the very social conditions and balance of social forces and institutions which underpinned nineteenth century UK industrial dominance also undermined the ability quickly to modernize productive techniques and restructure industrial output when international competition came. The modernizing agencies used elsewhere were otherwise engaged in the UK case. The UK *state* had no experience of, or enthusiasm for, industrial intervention. Its whole laissez-faire mentality turned something as modest as tariff reform into a major political hurdle, one that it took the Conservative Party 30 years — from 1902 to 1932 — to clear. Its élite *education system* was geared to the training of colonial administrators rather than industrial managers; and the nineteenth century retention of aristocratic domination of social and cultural life stopped the 'enterprise culture' of northern industrial capitalism from sweeping all before it. The *banking* networks were disproportionately involved in financing overseas (and competitor) systems of accumulation; and had a far less intimate involvement in local industrial investment than did banking networks in the USA, Germany and Japan.

So neither the state nor the financial sector were readily available as modernizing instruments for twentieth century UK industry, and whatever degree of *working class industrial strength* was consolidated (it was in fact precious little between the wars, but much more since) got in the way as well. The dominance of northern English/Scottish industrial capital over the commercial and financial élites of the English South East proved to be a one/two generation phenomenon at most. It was effectively gone by 1914 — to leave UK industry in the first half of the twentieth century locked in an increasingly anachronistic mould: suffering from under-investment, a lack of new industries, and a disproportionate dependence on industries in decline — and subject to political leadership that was preoccupied with financial concerns and the maintenance of an ambitious world role.[*] Through the inter-war years and up to the 1950s, *networks* of various kinds cushioned UK decision-makers from any direct confrontation with the market forces eroding UK industrial strength: social networks surrounding the inter-war state; international networks of a military and economic kind agreed in the 1940s; networks of imperial preference left over from the height of Empire; and new networks of collective bargaining and welfare provision put in place after 1945. Over many years these networks combined to block any state-directed or privately-initiated restructuring of the post-war UK economy. The seeds of the contemporary weakness of the UK economy were laid long ago, and it is their working out which has dominated the running of the economy since.

SUMMARY

- Post-war UK history has been over-shadowed by a retreat from Empire, and by the reluctant shedding of a world role no longer commensurate with the economic and military resources available to sustain it.

- The slowness of this readjustment to the UK's diminished power has had serious economic consequences, as an opportunity was lost in the 1950s to modernize UK industry. Economic policy since then has been dominated by attempts to 'catch up' with stronger competitors, to break out of a 'vicious cycle' of decline into a 'virtuous cycle' of growth.

- The long term roots of that economic weakness lie in the balance and character of social forces and institutions which surrounded early UK industrialization. The UK entered the twentieth century with no tradition of economic modernization by the state, by the banking system or even by the labour movement.

1.2 THE POST-WAR PERFORMANCE OF THE UK ECONOMY

There are two broad reasons why economic modernization on the scale that — in retrospect — was clearly required did not occur in the 1950s and 1960s in the UK. One, which we have emphasized already, was the preoccupation of politicians with the retention of the UK's world role, and the associated

---

[*] For two more detailed arguments on this line, from very different theoretical standpoints, see Anderson (1987) and Barnett (1984, 1986).

failure of other potential modernizing agents to compensate for that. The other broad reason is more prosaic. It is quite simply that the need for modernization was not immediately obvious. It became so, and policy slowly adapted in its pursuit (as we will see in detail in Chapter 4). But the economic indicators in general gave quite contradictory signals to politicians and their economic advisers through the 1950s and 1960s. They certainly indicated that the UK economy was growing less well over the period as a whole than were its major competitors; and indeed was falling steadily behind them year by year. But they also signalled that the UK economy was still achieving rates of growth — and sustained growth over a long period — of a level without precedent in its own history. The post-war economy grew faster and in a more sustained way than had the UK economy in the past. It was simply surrounded — as it did so — by economies which were — until the late 1980s at least — growing faster still.

The two sides of this UK economic performance — sustained growth, but with growth faster elsewhere — are evident in Table 2.1, which offers a 30 year view of the UK's economic performance and international standing.

Table 2.1 Thirty year economic record of the UK, 1950–80, and some international comparisons

Item	UK 30 year record (percentage change[1])			
	1950–60	1960–70	1970–80	1950–80
GDP at factor cost	30.3	33.8	18.6	106.7
Output of manufacturing industry	35.9	33.5	−3.1	75.8
GDP per head of population	25.4	26.6	17.5	86.6
Consumers' expenditure	27.0	26.7	23.6	100.0
Consumers' expenditure per head of population	22.3	19.9	22.6	79.7
Gross fixed capital formation	69.5	63.5	6.7	195.5
Gross stock of fixed assets:				
Total (end of year)	31.1	45.9	35.7	159.6
In manufacturing (end of year)	51.5	44.7	28.6	181.9
International trade and payments:				
Exports of goods and services	29.8	64.7	54.4	230.3
Imports of goods and services	51.0	51.2	42.6	225.7
Balance of payments on current account (average for period) (£m)	64.6	88.4	−204.4	−17.1
Official reserves ($m) (end 1950 to end 1960 etc.)	−69	−404	24,649	24,176
Sterling exchange rate (average for period) (US $ per £)	2.802	2.680	2.188	2.557

| Item | Period | International comparisons[1] | | | | | |
		UK	USA	W. Germany	France	Italy	Japan
Output and expenditure:							
GDP	1960–70	31.5	46.0	58.3	71.9	71.3	187.5
	1970–80	20.2	32.1	32.1	43.8	47.8	67.5
Manufacturing output	1960–70	32.3	61.6	79.2	82.2	101.2	283.1
	1970–80	−0.3	37.0	23.0	35.0	38.0	56.0
GDP per head of population	1960–70	24.4	29.4	38.7	54.6	58.2	159.2
	1970–80	19.1	18.3	30.2	36.1	39.2	48.2
Consumers' expenditure per head of population	1960–70	18.6	32.2	42.3	51.9	76.1	120.3
	1970–80	24.4	21.8	33.6	44.6	31.1	46.5
Gross fixed capital formation per head of population	1960–70	54.3	30.8	39.4	90.7	49.8	282.6
	1970–80	0.1	6.3	20.6	24.9	15.4	35.3
Trade and payments:							
Exports of goods and services	1960–70	59.7	79.1	112.0	129.2	187.9	304.6
	1970–80	47.8	92.4	91.5	104.8	75.0	239.5
Imports of goods and services	1960–70	47.9	111.3	141.8	163.1	190.6	288.9
	1970–80	38.1	59.5	99.2	114.4	71.2	111.0
Share in value exports of manufacturers of top 11 industrial economies	percentage in 1960	16.5	21.6	19.3	9.6	5.1	6.9
	in 1970	10.8	18.5	19.8	8.7	7.2	11.7
	in 1980	10.3	16.9	19.8	10.0	7.8	14.9

[1] Except where indicated the figures show the percentage rise over the decade.
Source: Reddaway (1983, pp.222–3).

From Table 2.1 we can see that — between 1950 and 1980 — GDP more than doubled (it rose 106.7 per cent on the 1950 level), total consumer expenditure doubled, exports more than doubled, and consumption per head rose by nearly 80 per cent. But we can also see that — in the last 20 years of the period — the UK growth figures on GDP (and on manufacturing output as part of that GDP) compared unfavourably with those of the United States, West Germany, France, Italy and especially Japan; and that the UK share in the value of manufactured exports from the leading eleven industrial nations fell steadily.

There can be no doubt that the post-war economy performed well — when set against its own history. Between the wars, industrial production slumped and unemployment soared; and though standards of living did improve for those in work in the 1930s (not least because prices fell, to increase their real wages) that improvement was extremely modest, and general life styles (certainly when compared to those attainable by comparable groups in the US) remained low. Immediately after the war, though there was full employment, shortages of even basic foodstuffs remained acute. Rationing actually intensified in the mid 1940s. But thereafter, until 1974, the UK economy experienced its longest sustained period of unbroken economic growth. It also experienced full employment, and a steady (and eventually marked) increase in the standard of living (if that standard is to be measured in terms of the consumption of food, manufactured goods and services). By the mid 1970s a generation had come into existence who had known 25 years of secure employment, who expected their standard of living steadily to improve, and who took for granted state provision of what — by comparison with the past — were generous degrees of access to education, health care and pensions. Income inequality remained entrenched. People did not share equally in rising prosperity. Significant sections of the population remained poor in relative terms, as we shall see, but by the mid 1970s the general standard of living was light years better than the life styles which had been virtually universal only a generation before.

Economic life in the UK after 1974 took a different shape. After 1974 regular and sustained economic growth could no longer be taken for granted. The 1980s did in fact see remarkable rates of economic growth, but only after very heavy recession and in quite new economic circumstances. The economic growth of the 1980s followed what, between 1979 and 1981, was without question the most severe recession ever experienced by the UK manufacturing sector. In the brief period between June 1979 and January 1981 19.6 per cent of manufacturing output was lost: and though 'the subsequent recovery in manufacturing activity — halting at first but then gradually gaining in momentum — has taken manufacturing to ... an all time high ... even so by [the fourth quarter of 1988] manufacturing output was only 6.8 per cent higher than the level it was when Mrs Thatcher first came to office (in May 1979)' (Wells, 1989, p.25). By then large scale unemployment had returned to replace the labour scarcity of the 1950s and 1960s. Inflation had quickened to double figures. International competition had intensified; and the balance of payments had developed a volatility largely absent in the previous 25 years. Some of this more recent volatility is evident in Figure 2.1. There you can see that after 1973 movements in growth, unemployment, inflation and the balance of payments became far more marked than they had been in the previous two decades.

We can see the weakening of the UK's position as an economic power by tracing the fate of the UK as a player in world trade. The share of world trade captured by the manufacturing sector of the UK economy fell from 25.9 per cent in 1950 to 7.6 per cent in 1984. In the same period foreign manufacturers increased their share of the UK domestic market: from 6 per cent in 1955 to 25 per cent by 1979 — to the point in 1983 when, for the first time since the Industrial Revolution, the UK became a net importer of manufactured goods. The twin movement — of foreign-made goods in, and of fewer UK manufactured goods selling abroad — is captured in Table 2.2.

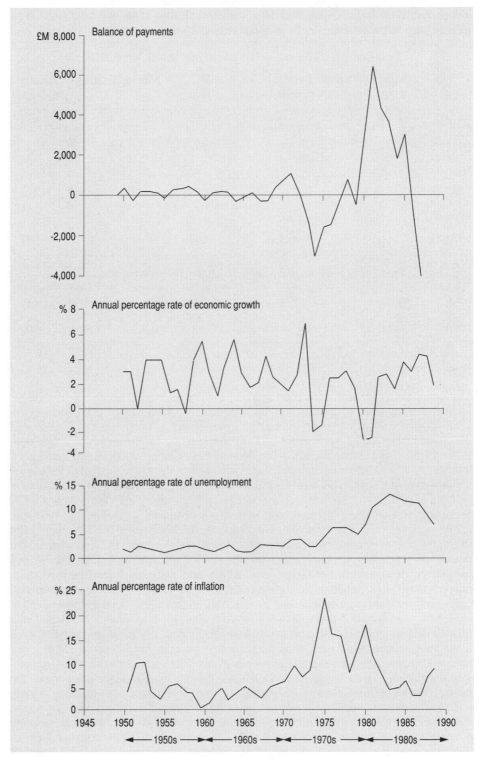

Figure 2.1 *Post-war economic performance: growth, inflation, unemployment and the balance of payments, 1950–90*

Table 2.2 UK balance of trade on selected items, 1946–86, and British percentage of world trade in manufactured goods, 1950–84

Balance of trade on selected items (as % of GDP)					
	Manufactures	Primary products		Manufactures	Primary products
1946–50	+8.6	−11.4	1976–80	+3.2	−4.6
1951–5	+8.8	−12.4	1981–2	+1.6	−0.4
1956–60	+8.0	−9.1	1983	−0.5	+0.3
1961–5	+6.4	−7.1	1984	−1.1	−0.3
1966–70	+4.9	−5.7	1985	−0.7	−0.3
1971–5	+3.5	−6.2	1986	−1.3	−0.9

Percentage of world trade in manufactured goods							
1950	25.9	1959	17.7	1969	11.2	1979	9.1
1954	20.5	1964	14.2	1974	8.8	1984	7.6

Source: Harris (1988, p.17) and House of Lords Select Committee on Overseas Trade (1985, vol.1, p.23).

The long boom in the UK economy to 1973 was based on the generalized application of Fordist productive techniques to a new set of core industries. This involved considerable industrial restructuring: with the decline of old industries, the redeployment of labour, and a shift in the geographical location of UK manufacturing industry. That the economy would be restructured in this way was not immediately apparent after the war. The dislocation of foreign competitors, and the desperate shortage of foreign currency, gave a last lease of life to the leading industries of the now departed years of UK economic dominance: to coal, cotton and shipbuilding. As late as 1956 the number of miners, for example, was still at the 1947 level (of 700,000), kept there by an 'overwhelming demand for coal in this period' and the initial post-war slowness of coal mechanization (Barrett Brown, 1972, p.5). But thereafter these industries went into rapid and sustained decline (in scale, employment and profits); and only later revived to a degree on the basis of extensive investment in entirely new technologies. The textile industry, for example, contracted from 200,000 employees in 1961 to only 59,000 in 1980. Pits closed at the rate of one a week through the 1960s, as exhausted coal faces were abandoned and miners moved from coal field to coal field. Contraction began again in the 1980s, particularly after the defeat of the miners' strike of 1984–5, leaving a much smaller industry, increasingly dependent for its output on a few 'super pits' using fully-mechanized coal cutting equipment. These contractions in their turn then altered the 'weight' of these industries in the occupational structure of the post-war UK, with associated consequences — as we will see in later chapters — for the composition of the class structure, the character of the labour movement, and the relative prosperity of different regions.

That was the *downside* of the restructuring of the post-war economy: the collapse of old industries. But there was an *upside* too.

The post-war years saw the emergence of new capital-intensive industrial systems, producing high quality, high volume consumer goods. The term 'Fordism' is particularly appropriate for this because of the centrality of vehicle construction to the new pattern of growth and generalized affluence. Semi-automated production systems in vehicle construction, and in other light engineering industries, combined with continuous flow production in the chemical industry, in oil and pharmaceuticals, to generate sizable and sustainable increases in the productivity of labour. Parallel changes occurred in agriculture too: where the application of the products of the vehicle and agro-chemical industries generated an equivalent leap in output and productivity.

Changes of this magnitude then had a ripple effect out onto the structure of the economy as a whole, and onto the occupational distribution it sustained. The contribution to GNP of the new industries grew steadily through the 1950s and 1960s. Cars in particular became the main export earner of the UK economy. The weight of the new industries in the UK's industrial profile by 1968 is shown in Table 2.3.

Table 2.3 Percentage share of manufacturing employment and net output, selected industries in 1968

Industry	Employment		Net output	
	000s	% share of all manufacturing	£ million	% share of all manufacturing
Chemicals	407.6	5.2	1,334.2	8.7
Mechanical engineering	977.2	12.5	1,963.0	12.8
Instrument engineering	171.2	2.2	299.3	2.0
Electrical engineering	753.7	9.6	1,375.3	9.0
Vehicles	788.4	10.1	1,578.7	10.3
(of which, motor vehicles)	457.0	5.8	945.6	6.2
Textiles	666.2	8.5	1,058.3	7.0
Clothing and footwear	445.1	5.7	484.2	3.2

Source: Allen and Massey (1988, p.157).

The state too came to take up more and more of the gross national product. For Fordism in the UK, as elsewhere in the advanced capitalist world, was associated with the growing involvement of the state in the management of the economy, in the provision of industrial infrastructure, and in the servicing and training of the labour force. State employment grew steadily through the 1950s and 1960s. State aid to industry expanded in commensurate fashion; and the share of GNP passing through the hands of the state increased year by year. The growth of state spending — particularly on welfare services and of state employment — is well captured in Table 2.4. At its peak in 1975, 'total state expenditure as a percentage of GNP at factor cost

The Ford production line at Dagenham

was 57.9%' (Coates, 1984, p.219) and 7.2 million people were directly employed by the state, its agencies and its nationalized industries.

Table 2.4   Scale of state spending and employment, 1921–75

| | State expenditure as % of GNP | | | | | | |
	1921	1931	1937	1951	1961	1971	1975
Total state expenditure	29.4	28.8	25.9	44.9	42.1	50.3	57.9
Resource spending	16.2	14.2	16.0	25.1	22.5	26.8	29.6
Transfer spending	13.2	14.6	10.0	19.8	19.6	23.5	28.3

| | Number of state employees (000s) | | | | | |
	1923	1931	1951	1961	1971	1975
Central government	160	110	1,136	1,302	1,561	1,910
Local government	227	292	1,415	1,782	2,651	2,993
Nationalized industries	—	—	2,789	2,196	2,001	2,003
Armed forces	250	189	827	474	368	336
Total	637	591	6,167	5,754	6,581	7,242

Source: Coates (1984, p.220).

So if we stop the picture in 1973 — on the eve of the first oil crisis — the UK economy looks like a splendid example of the new Fordism: new industries, a new and generalized prosperity and an active Keynesian welfare state. And so it was: but it was also an economy of considerable frailty. Large UK-based companies in the early 1970s were in growing difficulties. Profit rates were low and falling. Industrial militancy was high and rising. Inflation and unemployment lay around the corner. The intensification of international competition had already begun; and whole industries would soon be swept away (motor bikes, textiles, boot and shoe manufacture, and the hold of the UK car industry in both domestic and foreign markets). For the UK growth of the 1950s and 1960s was based on what — in retrospect — was only a flawed version of Fordism. The UK was strong on the welfare state side of the whole Fordist package, but weak — as we said earlier — on the industrial investment and economic modernization vital to sustain high levels of economic competitiveness and welfare spending. As Bob Jessop has rightly observed: in the post-war UK

> although mass production industries, their suppliers and their distributors grew at the expense of traditional staple industries in the 1950s, they did not fully secure the fruits of the Fordist revolution. British-owned industry based at home rarely got the same returns from the new techniques of mass production as its overseas competitors or, indeed, as foreign-owned multinationals did inside Britain. Among the factors which contributed to this productivity gap were the slow rate of growth in Britain, the impact of Britain's distinctive form of union organisation, and the inadequate managerial skills of British entrepreneurs. Among the consequences of this productivity gap, given the government's commitment to maintaining full employment levels of demand and to an expanding social wage, was the increasing satisfaction of mass consumption demand through imported goods rather than domestic output.
>
> (Jessop, 1988, p.8)

What the UK experienced — if we follow the line of Jessop's argument — was a 'flawed Fordism'. 'British mass producers, unlike their American counterparts ... never fully embraced Fordism, but ... rather persisted with a hybrid type of mass/batch production better suited to Britain's more diverse product markets' (C. Smith, 1990, p.217). Even in the growth years of the 1950s and 1960s, the UK economy only experienced 'a limited expansion of mass production, relatively poor productivity growth, union strength producing wage increases from the 1960s onwards not justified by productivity growth, a precocious commitment to social welfare and jobs for all, growing import penetration from the 1960s to satisfy the mass consumer market and, from the mid 1970s, to meet demand for capital goods' (Jessop, 1988, p.8). The economy could appear to do well only while the period of immediate post-war reconstruction created a seller's market, only until foreign competitors could effectively reorganize themselves after wartime defeat, and only for so long as the generalized application of Fordist modes of organizing production was generating growth across the capitalist bloc as a whole. But as competition intensified and the conditions for Fordist growth weakened, it was economies like the UK's — uncompetitive across a whole range of even Fordist industries — which experienced the biggest

Car imports into Britain in the 1980s: Volvos being unloaded at Immingham

deficits on their balance of payments, and the biggest need rapidly to re-structure industrial investment, work organization and levels of employment.

The crisis of the Fordist economy in the UK was thus particularly acute, and its restructuring to a new level of competitive strength dominated policy in the 1980s. The 'new industries' of the 1950s were themselves extensively reorganized in that decade. New computerized production systems were introduced, tight managerial control of the labour process was reasserted, and employment levels were cut. That was the fate of the car industry from 1975, of steel from 1980–1, and in a different way, of coal too after 1985. 'Between 1979 and 1987 manufacturing employment fell from 7.4 million to 5.4 million — a reduction of 2 million or 27% of the 1979 manufacturing labour force' (Wells, 1989, p.25). By 1990 employment in manufacturing industry had fallen to less than 5 million: and with that smaller manufacturing sector, new industries rose to prominence as employers of labour, earners of foreign currency and contributors to GNP. The UK became an oil exporting country in the 1980s. Its financial services sector made an increasingly vital contribution to the balance of payments, and employment in service industries grew rapidly as employment in both 'old' from 'new' manufacturing stagnated. 'Employment in services rose between 1979 and 1987 from 14.7 million to 16.7 million — an increase of 2 million (or about the same as the decline in manufacturing employment), representing a rise of 13.6% relative to the 1979 service labour force.' (Wells, 1989, p.26.) The state too 'retreated' from economic life in the 1980s. It sold off sizeable parts of the public sector — particularly its manufacturing bits. It curtailed its aid to private industry; and it pruned (and increasingly subjected to market/commercial forces) the staff that it employed in its welfare and administrative bureaucracies.

Overall, the crisis of Fordism which beset the UK economy after 1973 was tackled in the 1980s by exposing greater and greater percentages of economic life to the full thrust of *market* forces, at the cost of dismantling a significant proportion of the collective bargaining and political *networks* built up around UK industry in the years of Fordist-inspired growth. The building of those networks, and their later dismantling, will occupy us in Section 3.1.2 of this chapter and in the second part of Chapter 4. But what we need to establish first is the character of the economy — and the modes of its operation — which have emerged from two decades of easy post-war growth and two of stagnation and restructuring. It is to this task that we now turn.

SUMMARY

- The indicators of economic performance for the post-war UK economy tell two stories: of sustained growth and prosperity superior to anything achieved previously in the UK; and of a steady diminution in the strength of the manufacturing sector of the UK economy relative to the manufacturing sectors of its major competitors.

- UK economic growth in the 1950s and 1960s was based on the application and dissemination of Fordist modes of organizing production, and brought with it fundamental changes in the industrial structure and in the role of the state.

- Events after 1973 demonstrated the limited and flawed nature of the Fordist restructuring of the post-war UK economy, and precipitated major recession and industrial change in the 1980s.

2 THE CONTEMPORARY ECONOMY

All this has left an economy with a particular structure, geography, pattern of ownership and place in the international system.

2.1 THE STRUCTURE OF THE CONTEMPORARY ECONOMY

The dwindling competitiveness of UK-based manufacturing industry has had a direct impact on the structure of employment in the economy as a whole. The pattern of change here is clear enough. There has been a shift of workers out of agriculture and industry and into service employment, both privately and publicly provided. The timing of these shifts in employment has not been uniform however. Agricultural employment has steadily diminished. 1.8 million people worked the land in 1947. That figure was down to 1 million by 1987. Service employment had reached 10 million by 1960, and 14 million by 1987. It is manufacturing employment that has risen and fallen in a less uniform way.

> In the immediate post-war years, under the impetus of reconstruction and a government-sponsored export drive, employment in these industries increased rapidly. Then in the 1950s the pace of expansion slackened. Employment continued to rise in manufacturing and construction, though at a slower pace than before: while coal mining began to shed labour as pits were closed because of competition from oil. For a time the new jobs created in manufacturing and construction more than offset those lost in mining, with the result that industrial employment as a whole carried on rising through the 1960s. However this expansion came to a halt in 1966 ... Since that time industrial employment of all kinds — mining, manufacturing and construction alike — has fallen dramatically. From an all-time peak of 11.5 million in 1966, the total number of people employed in industry had fallen to less than 7 million by 1984.

> (Rowthorn, 1986, p.2)

On the surface of things then, the UK economy recently has experienced a degree of de-industrialization — in that the weight of the manufacturing sector (both in its contribution to GNP and to employment) has fallen. What the figures show is that '1973–4 appears to mark an important turning point in the fortunes of UK industry, because, since then, the trend in UK manufacturing output has been more or less flat'. Even now indeed 'manufacturing output is ... only slightly ahead of its previous peak annual and quarterly levels (recorded in 1973 and in 1974 respectively)' (Wells, 1989, p.32). However it is probably better to think of recent changes as ones of restructuring rather than de-industrializing. The leading manufacturing sectors of the 1960s (metals, mechanical engineering, textiles, shipping and motors) have now 'disappeared from the top flight' and others (tobacco, brewing, food manufacture) 'have slipped well down'. What has replaced them 'are major new forces in new sectors: in electrical engineering ... in health and household goods, and in retail and distribution' (Spence, 1985, pp.126–7). Under the impact of intensifying international competition, capital in the UK in the 1980s regrouped around a new set of key industries and around the provision of services. The growth figures for employment in the service sector are given in Table 2.5.

This pattern of post-war economic restructuring has also left an economy with a particular geography. It was always true of course that there was a spatial dimension to economic development, and that the combined and uneven trajectory of capitalism has left a world unevenly developed in spatial terms. There are, in fact, many economic geographies still overlapping and visible in the contemporary UK. There is the nineteenth century geography of the Belfast–Liverpool–Glasgow triangle: the concentration of heavy industry in the northern economy. There is also the nineteenth century concentration of commercial, financial and political institutions in London and the South East. Indeed that North–South polarity remains the starkest one, with the decline of the North firmly rooted in the decline of the heavy

Table 2.5   Employment change in the service industries for the UK, 1959–81

	Employment (000s)		Change (000s)	Percentage change
	1959	**1981**	**1959–81**	
Public passenger transport (roads and railways)	705	393	−312	−44.3
Goods transport and storage (road haulage, warehousing, wholesale distribution)	1,030	1,269	+239	+23.2
Sea and air transport	317	218	−99	−31.3
Private motoring services (garages)	339	482	+143	+42.2
Retail distribution	1,844	1,846	+2	+0.1
Post and telecommunications	334	430	+96	+28.7
Financial services (insurance, banking, finance)	458	779	+321	+70.0
Other business services (property, advertising, business services, unallocated central offices, law, accountancy, research and development, other business related professions)	464	1,070	+606	+130.7
Leisure and recreation services (including broadcasting and gambling)	238	334	+96	+40.2
Hotels and catering	665	928	+263	+39.6
Other personal services (hairdressing, laundries, dry cleaning, shoe repairers, private domestic services)	268	157	−111	−41.3
Public administration (central and local government)	1,255	1,400	+145	+11.6
Health and education	1,616	3,124	+1,508	+99.3
Welfare services (social services, voluntary organizations, religious organizations)	259	675	+416	+160.6
All service industries	9,797	13,105	+3,308	+33.8
Share of total employment (percentage)	44.79	61.48		

Source: Allen (1988a, p.99).

industry it monopolized. The North, once prosperous if grimy, is now more desolate, if cleaner: a site for new industry attracted by its cheap and amenable labour, and a site also for the new leisure industries of 'museum Britain'.

Prosperity in the 1950s and 1960s shifted south and inland, to a new spatial block bordered by Manchester, Sheffield, Birmingham and Coventry. 'In 1959 the geography of British manufacturing employment was dominated by the big cities and by the central regions of the West Midlands and the South East' (Massey, 1986, p.36). Much of this has now also gone. 'Between 1962 and 1982 London lost 60 per cent of its manufacturing jobs' (ibid., p.38) and the big Northern and West Midlands conurbations lost 43 per cent of theirs. Manufacturing in London, in Sheffield, in the West Midlands and in the North West was devastated by the draconian restructuring of the 1979–81 recession. Indeed there was a clear 'North–South' differentiation to that particular recession. 'The fall in manufacturing employment in the "north" amounted to a staggering 1.386 million (34.3%) between 1979 and 1986, as against a reduction of 726,000 (23.2%) in the "south". The greater part of this collapse occurred during the deep recession of the early 1980s.' (Martin, 1989, pp.84–5.) Moreover in the 1980s at least, the geographical spread of service employment did not compensate for the loss of manufacturing employment. In the 1970s the story had been different.

> During the 1970s ... the growth in service employment was evenly spread between the 'north' and 'south': between 1971–9 the northern region as a whole gained 859,000 new jobs in services (an increase of 16.5%), not far short of the rise of 1.02 million (16.6%) in the 'south' ... However during the 1980s both the nature and pattern of job creation in the service sector have been rather different ... Between 1979 and 1986 service employment in the four southern regions rose by 1.16 million or 16.1% ... By comparison, the numbers employed in services in the 'north' increased by only 493,000 or 7.4% ... and in the North-West and in Wales service employment actually fell.
>
> (Martin, 1989, p.87)

There is a heavy concentration of prosperity now in the South and the South East — along the M4 corridor and into London. This is what Doreen Massey has called 'a sunbelt' (Massey, 1986, p.32) — 'the favoured location for executive, administrative and research and development functions in the new industries, centring on electronics, advanced engineering, and pharmaceutical and health products' (Spence, 1985, p.128). 'Of the million or so new jobs created since 1983, the great bulk, some 849,000, have been located in the four southern regions' (Martin, 1989, p.88). 'Even within the South itself, the boom has been very uneven, a boom of some places and people rather than others' (ibid., p.94). Inner London depression contrasts with City affluence, the recession of the car towns with the prosperity of the new 'sunrise corridors' along the M4 and the M11.

All this may not last. In the sunbelt 'full or nearly full employment, skill shortages and high housing costs have created serious labour recruitment problems for employers, both in the sunrise and associated industries themselves, and in consumer and public services' (Martin, 1989, p.94). Certainly the costs of so heavy a regional concentration of prosperity (on infrastruc-

Table 2.6   Regional divergence in employment growth

Percentage change in number of employees in employment

	1971–9	1979–83	1983–8	1979–88
South East	1.6	−5.2	6.9	1.3
East Anglia	15.6	−0.1	21.2	18.8
South West	20.6	−5.2	5.5	0.1
East Midlands	14.1	−7.6	9.3	0.3
'South'	6.5	−5.4	8.0	2.0
(absolute change)	691,000	−617,000	849,000	232,000
West Midlands	1.1	−11.2	5.7	−6.5
Yorkshire–Humberside	0.2	−11.9	2.6	−9.5
North West	−1.5	−13.9	−1.6	−15.4
Northern	1.5	−14.3	4.5	−11.5
Wales	7.4	−14.0	−1.6	−15.4
Scotland	4.9	−9.6	−0.5	−10.2
Northern Ireland	1.3	−7.2	0.0	−7.2
'North'	2.8	−12.5	2.0	−10.8
(absolute change)	323,000	−1,476,000	202,000	−1,274,000
UK	4.6	−9.0	5.0	−4.5
(absolute change)	1,014,000	−2,093,000	1,051,000	−1,042,000

Source: Martin (1989, p.88).

ture, housing and so on) are already driving some sections of finance and administration out of London and away from the main motorways, and this redevelopment has become a possibility because of the new technologies of communication. 'Old industrial towns around London, such as Luton, Reading and Slough, have benefited from this trend, as have a number of new towns such as Bracknell and Milton Keynes, and so too have major provincial cities further afield such as Bristol, Ipswich and Cambridge.' (Allen, 1988a, p.128.) For similar reasons there is also a particularly middle class prosperity emerging too in the northern suburban complexes around Newcastle, Leeds and Manchester. The economic geography of the nineteenth century was one of industrial dynamism in northern river valleys. That of the 1950s and 1960s was one of Midlands revival. The economic geography of the 1990s is more complex. It combines a definite North–South divide with an increasingly potent division of urban squalor and suburban affluence.

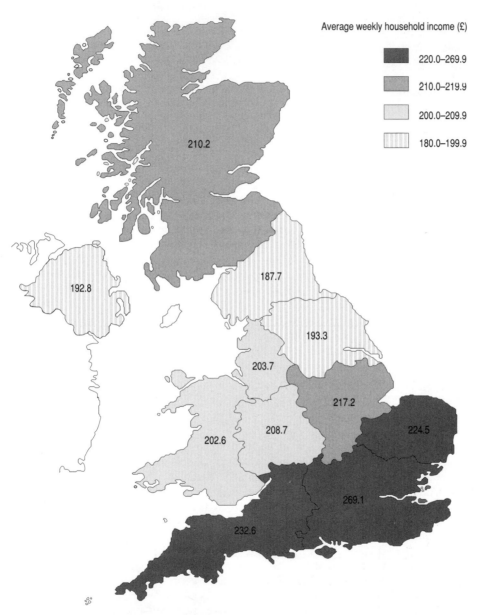

Figure 2.2 *Average weekly household income (£), 1985–6*
Source: Hudson and Williams (1989, p.174).

SUMMARY

- The structure of the UK economy has changed since 1945: with a decline in agricultural employment, the rise and fall of manufacturing, and the recent expansion of service employment. This is less a process of de-industrialization than of restructuring around a new set of key industries (including oil, high-tech electronic, financial services, retailing and distribution).

- The contemporary UK economy has a particular geography built around the sedimentation of various previous ones: the Northern monopoly of Victorian heavy industry, the concentration of trade and administration in the South East, and the rise and fall of Midlands prosperity in the post-war period. New spatial differentiations — between urban and suburban areas, and between sunbelts and rustbelts, have added an extra dimension to that geography in the last 20 years.

2.2 OWNERSHIP AND CONTROL IN THE CONTEMPORARY ECONOMY

The commanding heights of the UK economy remain firmly in private hands, and economic activity remains dominated by the pursuit of profit. The contemporary UK economy, in keeping with the UK economy throughout the entire post-war period, remains overwhelmingly capitalist in ownership and control. This has had a number of important consequences for the way the economy is run.

It means that what goes on inside companies is very largely their affair. It splits the economy into a private world of production (of whose precise details little is publicly known — and where commercial and industrial secrecy is the order of the day) and a more public world in which what is privately produced is then consumed and evaluated. But though privately experienced, the imperatives released into production by the dominance of private ownership are still general to all producers. Companies that are privately owned in reality enjoy little private freedom. The need to make profits builds into the private organization of production an imperative to organize life *hierarchically* — the better to allow central control of costs (especially labour costs) in a situation in which the survival of the production unit (and therefore of the employment it generates for those who work in it) in the end depends on survival in the competitive struggle of the *market* place. Employment and profit in the private sector are never guaranteed or planned. They have to be won, perpetually struggled for, and are always precarious: and that instability has profound consequences (as we will see later) for the way production processes are organized and managed in the closed world behind the factory gate and the office door.

The provision of primary products, manufactured goods and a whole series of services by private initiative in return for private profit, is of course as old as capitalism itself. What is new is the way in which competition between capitalists has created a particular structure of ownership. The contemporary UK is now dominated by remarkable variations in size between corporate structures, remarkable that is when set against the far more uniformly sized companies of the Victorian period. In those years, the vast majority of companies were small. They had a single owner rather than a corporate board, and they employed relatively few people. It remains the case that the vast majority of companies are still of this kind. The 1980s in particular saw a flowering of small business enterprise: and successive governments, Left as well as Right, have encouraged such a flowering. But in the contemporary economy such firms, though numerous, are no longer dominant. Instead, in each productive sector, the vast bulk of output comes from just a handful of firms. Indeed the UK economy is now one of the most monopolized of all the advanced capitalist economies; and that degree of monopolization has grown over time, fuelled at least in part by great merger booms in the 1920s and 1970s. 'Between 1950 and 1970 the top 100 manufacturing firms increased their share of total net output from just over 20 per cent to just over 40 per cent: and that degree of economic concentration has stabilised around 40 per cent since then.' (Allen, 1988b, p.193.) In 1986, to take just one example, over $1\frac{1}{4}$ million workers — some 5 per cent of the total workforce — had jobs with the 40 largest manufacturing firms in the UK.

The single most striking feature of the scale of activity of these large firms is that most of them are world players in their own right. Some — the trading companies — have always been: Unilever (trading in oils), Shell UK (trading in oil itself). But others which began with local markets as their sole/main focus of operation now operate in a multitude of markets. This is true of ICI, GEC and many others. Many UK firms have now bought their way into the production systems of major competitor economies, particularly the American. UK-based companies now occupy high positions in the league table of world companies. In 1985 46 per cent of the top 500 Western European industrial and commercial companies were UK based, and 'the leading 50 British manufacturing companies [that year produced] 44 per cent of their output from overseas subsidiaries' (Spence, 1985, p.123).

Indeed 'in many ways, the British manufacturing industry is now split in two. On the one hand there is the highly international and dynamic sector. On the other there is a small domestic industry turning over quietly when it can and not wishing to be disturbed' (Massey, 1986, p.46). 'The UK is a globalized economy locked by traditions and institutions into the world system. It is one that combines poor quality local performance with the possession of more multinational companies than any other country apart from the USA' (Gamble, 1981, p.113) and possibly West Germany. And indeed the local manufacturing base is in part so poor precisely because the orientation of its key institutions is so heavily external and global. The physical base of UK industry remains so under-developed, in part at least, because British capital is so massively invested abroad (Massey, 1986, p.47).

Many big UK manufacturing concerns are now foreign owned, to the extent that 'one in seven workers in manufacturing is [now] employed by a foreign-owned firm' (Auerbach, 1989, p.263). Though the 'UK economy has historically always been a highly open economy' (Harris, 1988, p.9) until recently the vast majority of UK-based firms — and certainly the most important ones — were locally owned and run. But things have changed now, and are changing still. In the past, if foreign firms did establish subsidiaries here, they were largely American (Singer, Ford and so on ...) and invariably found themselves surrounded by strong locally-based competitors. But all this has altered. Japanese, West German, French, Italian and Swedish companies are now based in the UK, attracted by factors of language, labour skills and low wage bills. Japanese inward investment in motor vehicle construction in the 1980s has been particularly significant, raising to 55 per cent the level of car production in the UK which is foreign owned. Japanese car firms have been attracted partly by the UK's presence inside the tariff walls of the European Community. They have also been attracted by the fact that 'UK labour costs (gross hourly wages, benefits and social costs) are, along with those in Spain, the lowest in Western Europe by a significant margin, and British car workers labour (including overtime) the greatest number of hours per year' (Auerbach, 1989, p.272). This inward investment by foreign-based multinational companies means that UK firms are often locked into complex trading and producing relationships with foreign-based concerns. This is particularly so in the new growth industries and in banking: with the result that much of the UK's overseas trade and capital movements are in truth movements of money and goods *within* multinational corporations, rather than movements *between* independent producers in the UK and abroad.

It is also worth noting the global orientation as well as the global organization of particularly the financial institutions within the UK economy. In the nineteenth century the UK was *the* great exporter of capital — on the eve of World War I 'foreign investment by British capital was running at twice the rate of domestic investment'; and though that changed temporarily between the wars, in the post-war period the global reach and concerns of UK-based banks and finance houses have reappeared. 'In the early 1970s UK capital exports were running at £0.6 billion per annum, and by the end of the decade it had reached £2 billion per annum. Following the abolition of exchange controls in 1979 the floodgates were open: and in 1979 over £6$\frac{1}{2}$ billion was invested abroad, followed by £8 billion in 1980 and £10.7 billion in 1981.' (Spence, 1985, p.124.) Indeed in 1988 'Britain was the world leader in foreign acquisitions, with an absolute level (£26 billion) four times as high as that of its nearest rivals. It also possessed the highest ratio in the world (34%) of foreign acquisitions to gross domestic fixed capital formation, other large countries having ratios such as 6% (France), 1.3% (the US and Japan) and 1.1% (West Germany).' (Auerbach, 1989, p.263.) Of course investment also flowed into the UK as well in the same period, but by no means on the same scale. Consistently through the 1980s, the UK was a net *exporter* of capital, as the figures in Table 2.7 show.

It is this overseas orientation of the UK private sector, just as much as the presence within it of foreign-owned firms, that makes industrial restructuring in the UK so difficult to organize from the political centre. Though we are entering the 1990s still in possession of a national economy with a national currency, industrial and financial firms of a certain size now operate and survive only in transnational markets of a regional or even global kind. They operate as European units, or as world players, or as UK offshoots of Asian, European or American concerns: and in doing so raise very serious questions indeed about who — if anyone — can run the economy, if by run we mean control the activities of its key units from some national centre.

Table 2.7 Private transfers overseas (£ million), 1978–88

	UK investment overseas		Overseas investment in the UK		Balance of capital flows	
	direct	portfolio	direct	portfolio	direct	portfolio
1978	3,520	1,037	1,962	−139	−1,558	1,212
1979	5,889	887	3,030	1,549	−2,859	662
1980	4,886	3,230	4,335	1,499	−531	−1,731
1981	6,005	4,300	2,932	323	−3,073	−3,977
1982	4,091	7,563	3,027	225	−1,064	−7,338
1983	5,417	7,193	3,386	1,888	−2,031	−5,305
1984	6,003	9,866	−181	1,419	−6,184	−8,447
1985	8,653	19,440	4,213	7,121	−4,440	−12,319
1986	11,525	25,243	4,176	8,447	−7,349	−16,796
1987	15,372	6,463	5,953	10,805	−9,419	4,342
1988[1]	6,918	6,600	2,969	981	−3,949	−5,619

[1] First six months.

Source: Toporowski (1989, p.252).

Economic management by national governments is still an important influence on the behaviour of even large and transnational corporations; but these days the activities of such corporations are fixed much less by government policy than by the competitive conditions they find prevailing in the international market place in which they must survive.

For it is clear that national governments do now experience difficulties in establishing and maintaining detailed and effective control over the activities of multinational companies, and that very few of them try. The reasons are presumably fairly obvious. At the most superficial they are administrative. It is just impossible for the state bureaucracy to monitor and intervene in the day to day running of complex, hierarchically organized and highly secretive large corporations. It is also political: in that if they try, it is always open to large corporations to move their basis of operation elsewhere, to more politically sympathetic (i.e. less interventionist) political regimes. And it is also economic: in that governments can, at most, influence levels of demand and costs in their local economy, whilst the companies are global players. If rates of interest are too high in the UK, they will borrow elsewhere. If the UK government wants them to export more to say, Germany, they will do so only if that does not disturb their overall global corporate plan, including any plans they might have for their production unit in Germany itself. And of course it is also technical: in that, in certain sectors at least, national units no longer produce whole commodities. Ford build their engine blocks in country X, their carburettors in country Y and so on. National governments often find that what they have is only part of a production system which is integrated world-wide; and when that occurs, they are no more equipped to control outcomes than Dagenham local council would have been when facing the Ford Motor Co. in the 1950s.

Nonetheless economic activity does need to be co-ordinated, and though movements in world *markets* are the key co-ordinator at the international level, neither big companies nor democratically-elected governments are happy to leave all their futures to the anarchic interplay of supply and demand. Instead market forces are softened as co-ordinators by all sorts of *networking* arrangements. The political institutions of the EC are a site for negotiations between multinational companies and alliances of European states: for tariff terms, investment aid, capital movements, labour codes and environmental constraints. National states play a key role in economic co-ordination too. Departments of industry still keep close relations with key local subsidiaries, and through them with the multinationals' headquarters; and departments of defence (with the power of the purse string to deploy) have particularly close relations with large engineering and electrical suppliers. And in the field of slightly smaller companies, the banks play critical co-ordinating roles. Behind the façade of corporate independence, we can see blocs of companies sharing common points of co-ordination organized through the banking networks which finance them.

Regional networks, national corporatist relationships and banking co-ordination remain critical mechanisms for organizing the increasingly international interplay of large economic actors — softening but not removing the ultimate co-ordination of market competition itself. But what characterizes those mechanisms of co-ordination is the limited access they allow for consciously planned democratically-inspired co-ordination at national governmental level. The national economic system that politicians ran so successfully in the Fordist years has spawned international linkages which increasingly shift its running up to the supra-national level, out of the domain of governments and public sectors, into the quiet and private world of the large corporation and the bank. The problem this leaves for national politics will be one of our final concerns in Chapter 4.

SUMMARY

- The private ownership of the means of production continues to give a particular feel to the UK economy: prioritizing the role of profits, leaving the internal affairs of even large companies intensely private and secret, facilitating the growth of monopolies, and giving a particular and limited role to the state.

- The overseas orientation of the UK economy has been increasingly marked of late: with the arrival of foreign-owned multinational companies, the continuing involvement of large UK financial institutions in the financing of foreign trade and production, and the growing involvement of large UK-based manufacturing companies in the organization of production overseas.

3 PRODUCTION AND CONSUMPTION IN THE UK ECONOMY

This growing overseas involvement of key parts of the UK economy has made it much more difficult to 'run' production and consumption from Whitehall. It was never easy, but it is now significantly more difficult to shape the behaviour of economic actors simply by adopting one set of macro-economic policies rather than another. That is why, when we look at those policies in detail in Chapter 4, the story we will examine then will largely be one of policy failures and policy constraints. But not all those constraints are global ones. The restructuring of the UK economy has had important local consequences too: shaping the internal as well as the external distribution of power and affecting both the personnel involved, and the character of the policies being pursued, in the running of the contemporary UK. In what remains of this chapter, and in the entirety of the next, we need to map those local consequences and constraints in a systematic way. We will do so here by concentrating on the immediate effects of economic change on the way production is organized and consumption fuelled. Then in Chapter 3 we will shift the focus of our enquiry to more general social consequences — and move away from our concern here with the economic.

3.1 PRODUCTION

Economic development in the post-war UK has altered both the categories and content of the jobs people have been called upon to perform. The transformation of agricultural production, for example, continued the decline of agricultural employment and qualitatively altered the range of tasks that fell to agricultural labour. Farm-hands now mind machinery, and use industrially-made raw materials (chemicals, fertilizers, building materials) of a kind familiar to more factory-based labour. In the factories themselves (those of the post-war growth industries of cars and light engineering) machine-minding and conveyor belt work became commonplace; and the supervisory and clerical tasks vital to the lubrication of continuous flow production proliferated. It was white collar rather than manual labour which grew in importance and volume as the Fordist regime of accumulation consolidated itself: designers and draughtsmen creating the new products, managers and supervisors over-seeing the new production lines, and clerical and sales staff handling the greater output. Alongside them, we find greater numbers of workers too in retailing and transport; and a proliferation of state employees of a non-manual kind: teachers, social workers, nurses, doctors and civil servants. When people went out to work in the post-war economy, many went — as earlier generations had done — to perform manual work in factories and mines. But still more now went to manage the workers, to train and heal them, and to move the paper on which the distribution of the growing abundance of goods increasingly depended. The result, by 1981, was a distribution of the occupied labour force as shown in Table 2.8.

Table 2.8   Distribution of the employed labour force, 1911–81

Occupation	Number of persons in major occupational groups (000s)							
	1911	1921	1931	1951	1961	1966	1971	1981
Employers and proprietors	1,232	1,318	1,407	1,117	1,139	832	—	—
Non-manual workers	3,433	4,094	4,841	6,948	8,478	9,461	11,072	13,278
(a) managers	631	704	770	1,245	1,268	1,514	2,460	3,489
(b) higher professionals	184	196	240	435	718	829	945	1,218
(c) lower professionals and technicians	560	679	728	1,059	1,418	1,604	1,938	2,681
(d) forepersons and inspectors	237	279	323	590	682	736	754	1,042
(e) clerical and related employees	832	1,256	1,404	2,341	2,994	3,262	347	3,687
(f) sales employees	989	980	1,376	1,278	1,398	1,516	1,428	1,161
Manual workers	13,685	13,920	14,776	14,450	14,022	14,393	13,949	12,128
Total occupied population	18,350	19,332	21,024	22,515	23,639	24,686	25,021	25,406

Source: Halsey (1988, p.163).

3.1.1   CHANGES IN THE LABOUR PROCESS

Global figures of this kind, though a vital first guide to patterns of change, obscure as much as they illuminate. They cannot by themselves capture the qualitative transformations in the labour process characteristic of the post-war period. From the many such transformations that we could discuss here, it is worth mentioning four.

1   One is the changing pattern of skill and status in the labour force as a whole. Some occupations have retained both their skill content and their social standing throughout the post-war period. Others have not. The traditional professions (doctors, lawyers, accountants) and senior managers have retained all their pre-existing social prestige and the salary levels commensurate with it. The lesser professions (teaching particularly, though nursing too) have seen their working conditions, public standing and levels of remuneration erode as their numbers have increased; and indeed the 1980s witnessed industrial action by both these groups — action which would have been inconceivable a generation before. Craft skills have been undermined in the 1980s too: this time by the virtual destruction of apprenticeships; and office work has been entirely routinized and proletarianized over the post-war period as a whole. So the lower professions, white collar work and skilled craft labour no longer have the social standing or income cushion they enjoyed in 1945, even though the skill level of office work in particular (as IT spreads through the administrative system) continues to rise. Indeed the skills required to cope with the new computer-based technology are changing again, but because they are general, they are not providing a base for the emergence of any new aristocracy of labour.

Office work in the 1980s: the hidden face of the Open University

2   The failure of office work to generate a new labour aristocracy of highly paid high-status administrative workers is in part a product of a second major shift in the character of the contemporary labour process — namely the gendering of office work. One of the most striking features of clerical work in the post-war period — and of teaching too, especially at primary level — is the emergence of a sharply divided labour hierarchy: with a bottom layer of almost exclusively female labour, topped by tiny supervisory strata disproportionately male in composition. The entry of married women into the paid labour force in increasing numbers in recent decades has enabled a minority of women to rise to senior executive positions — and thereby to create the impression of greater gender equality. But in truth employment patterns in the contemporary UK remain gendered in important ways. Most women who go out to work work with other women. There is a remarkable degree of gender segregation in paid employment. Those women who work with men have a far greater chance of being supervised by them than they do of finding themselves in supervisory positions over men; and the gendering of a particular occupation/job category is invariably an opportunity for the employer to reduce the status and wages of those working there. It is not that women fail to capture top jobs. It is rather that jobs captured by women fail to remain top.

3   It is worth noting too that different categories of work have grown in importance in recent years. Most jobs on offer remain full-time ones, but part-time work is now becoming increasingly common, particularly 'in the service industries, in health and education, retailing, hotels and catering, and in a wide variety of miscellaneous services' (Allen, 1988b, p.207). 'The number of part-time workers rose by 4.7 million between 1951 and 1987, to constitute by then 23 per cent of the total labour force' (ibid., p.206). 'In the 1970s alone, over one million part-time jobs were created in the service

Table 2.9 **Occupations listed according to the degree to which they are dominated by one sex[1]**

Predominantly female occupations	Predominantly male occupations and groupings of occupations
90% or over	*90% or over*
Hand and machine sewers and embroiderers	Miners and quarrymen
Nurses	Furnace, forge, foundries, etc.
Maids, valets, etc.	Electrical and electronic (excluding assemblers)
Canteen assistants	Engineering trades (excluding inspectors)
Typists, shorthand writers, secretaries	Woodworkers
	Butchers and meat cutters
75–90%	Construction workers
Shop salesmen and assistants	Painters and decorators
Charwomen, cleaners and sweepers	Drivers of stationary engines, cranes, etc.
Kitchen hands	Building and contracting labourers
Office machine operators	Drivers: road-passenger service and goods vehicles
Hairdressers, manicurists and beauticians	Postmen and mail sorters
Telephone operators	Commercial travellers, etc.
	Police
60–75%	Administrators and managers
Clerks and cashiers	Engineers
Waiters and waitresses	Technical and related workers
Primary and secondary schoolteachers	Armed forces
Packers, labellers and related workers	Groundsmen and gardeners
Cooks	
Bartenders	

[1] The titles of occupations used in this table are taken from the Official Census; those with the suffix '-men' may include employees of both sexes.
Source: Webb (1989, p.146).

industries. In 1984 almost 90 per cent of the 4.9 million part-time workers in Britain were in the service sector, and the overwhelming majority of those jobs were occupied by women' (Allen, 1988a, p.106).

Self-employment has also increased — to about 10 per cent of the labour force; and maybe as many as 8 per cent of the total work force are best described as temporary labour. This is not entirely a new phenomenon. Temporary labour has long been a feature of the way work is organized in many service sectors of the UK economy. But the scale of this peripheral labour does seem to be increasing slightly, if not in manufacturing then at least in the service industries: in the private sector, in hotels and catering, and miscellaneous services; and in the public sector, in education, health and public administration. There seems no doubt that the occupational structure of the UK in the 1990s will increasingly become a *dual* one as manufacturing

Figure 2.3 *The flexible firm*
Source: Atkinson (1984, p.29).

employment diminishes and service employment grows: one divided into
core workers and a periphery of less unionized, less well-paid and less
secure employees. A much cited diagram to capture this is that of Atkinson's 'flexible firm' holding on to its core workers while sub-contracting out
to other workers to give maximum flexibility to respond to changes in
demand and costs. The diagram (Figure 2.3) may be an ideal-typical one,
but it does alert us to the cleavages in position and experience of different
groups of workers in the contemporary UK economy.

4   The intensity of work has also changed over time, for reasons that we
will discuss in more detail in a moment. The pace of work has always
differed between classes in a capitalist economy, as has the degree of super-
vision/autonomy to which workers are exposed. In general it has always
been the case that the pace of work, and the degree of supervision to which
it is subject, has been greater the lower you go down the occupational
hierarchy — and that still remains so. But there have been changes. The
introduction of Fordism subordinated more and more manual workers to
work rhythms fixed by the speed of the line, such that the intensity of work
depended on who controlled the line itself. As we will see next, the pace of
work in assembly-line production has quickened significantly in the 1970s
and 1980s, after the easier and slower working pace of the two decades
before. The impulse behind that change has largely been the growth of
market competition: and it is clear that a quickening of competitive pressure
in the 1970s and 1980s intensified the burden of work, and the degree of
insecurity, for management too. As the managerial hierarchy extended with
the growth of company size, and as the need for greater labour productivity
on the shop floor manifested itself in tighter managerial control of the entire
work process, lower and even middle management came to experience their

work as to a degree proletarianized. The squeezing of middle management has therefore been a marked feature of the labour process in the 1980s. So too has been an intensification of work in the public sector — introduced there largely by increasing the volume of throughput to be handled by a no longer growing labour force: by increasing class sizes, by introducing tighter costing systems into universities, by increasing the turnover of patients, and so on. What the big tables of figures on occupational structure hide is the degree to which — within any one category of job — people are working harder in the late 1980s than they were two decades ago.

SUMMARY

- The occupational distribution in the UK has altered significantly since the war: with the rise of white collar work, the spread of the managerial function, and the expansion of public sector employment. White collar and public sector employment both experienced cut-backs after 1979.

- Key changes in the labour process include: a particular pattern of skilling and de-skilling; the persistent gendering of jobs; the growth of part-time and temporary work; and a generalized intensification of the work process in the 1980s.

3.1.2 CHANGES IN POWER

Behind these structural changes in the distribution of paid labour lie significant changes in the balance of power inside UK industry. The post-war years have seen a prolonged and largely invisible struggle to determine who actually runs the economy. We need as clear a picture as we can of the contours and parameters of that particular struggle.

In the years to 1940 there was no doubt who ran the UK economy. It was run by those who owned what was produced, rather than by those who actually did the producing. The rights of property to 'manage' had been enshrined in English common law since medieval times; and any restrictions on the terms on which labour could be employed had been swept away in the first flush of liberal political economy after 1800. Managers managed before 1940 subject only to two very limited sets of constraints. There was a degree of state regulation — a number of Factory Acts and so on — which set limits on the length of the working day and prescribed certain minimum standards for the organization of work itself. And there were pockets — and they were pockets, nothing more — of trade union power, islands of job control established by skilled workers organized in craft unions. These controls were plentiful in the 1890s: indeed craft unions unilaterally set rates for the job in building, engineering and parts of the textile industry until employers forced collective bargaining on them in a prolonged 'employers offensive' in the years to 1900. But even these craft controls were minute when set in the context of generalized lack of job control by the bulk of unskilled and unorganized manual labour; and certainly by the 1930s even craft controls had gone in the main — swept away by the wartime dilution of skilled labour between 1914 and 1918, and by the mass unemployment of the inter-war years.

Wartime and post-war full employment changed all that. It made labour scarce — particularly skilled labour — and it gave management an incentive to hang on to the labour it had, at virtually any price. And in any case the new production systems of the Fordist era altered the balance of costs within the production system, so that at least certain groups of workers found themselves in a quite novel bargaining position. There was no queue of labour waiting outside the factory gate to take the jobs of the recalcitrant. Instead, inside the factory, expensive capital equipment could easily be immobilized, at great expense to the employer, by the industrial action of just a few workers: an expense which employers could easily avoid by meeting demands for higher wages and better working conditions, secure in the knowledge that any extra costs could be passed on — in the easy market conditions of the 1950s and 1960s — in the form of higher prices at the factory gate.

Not all workers found themselves so placed in the 1950s. Workers in agriculture, retailing and banking did not. Nor did the expanding numbers of white collar workers feel their industrial power grow, either in private industry or in the expanding bureaucracies of the state. But increasingly manual workers in the growth centres of the private economy did: in cars and light engineering most of all. There, organized work groups emerged in the 1950s, willing and able to exploit local shortages of labour to improve on the rates of pay and conditions of employment negotiated on their behalf at national level by full-time trade union officials and representatives of the employers. Local bargaining through local shop stewards became the order of the day. A gap opened between nationally-negotiated wage rates and actual take-home pay, as earnings were bolstered by company bonuses and systematic overtime. Unofficial stoppages became a feature of industrial relations in coal mining, cars, electrical engineering and in shipbuilding, as local groups of workers downed tools to win these extra earnings, and to consolidate a degree of control over aspects of their work situation (over the pace and organization of work, over levels of manning and the availability of overtime, and even over questions of discipline and dismissal).

The degree of job control achieved by such work groups at the heart of UK manufacturing industry in the 1950s and 1960s was never very great. It was always a control won (and constantly having to be re-won) in negotiations with local management. It varied with the degree of organization and militancy achieved by particular groups of workers, and never returned to the unilateral control of wage rates enjoyed by certain groups of nineteenth century craft workers. But it was significant nonetheless. It represented a class shift in who was running a key part of the economy, and as such it attracted widespread publicity and condemnation in the media of the early 1960s. It was attacked there as 'the English disease', as a mixture of restrictive practices, wage drift and unofficial militancy that was supposedly contributing massively to the dwindling fortunes of UK-based manufacturing industry.

As we have seen, such shifts in class power did not — in the main — occur in the public sector. Miners apart — where a combination of working practices and long-established traditions of militancy did keep proletarian challenges to management alive and effective — most wages and conditions in the public sector in the 1950s and 1960s were settled (as they are settled still) by national negotiations between trade union officials and senior management. Wage drift was not a problem there. Nor were unofficial strikes. But productivity was. The productivity of public sector employees was both difficult to measure (large parts of the public sector provided services whose quality would not easily quantify) and where it could be measured, was invariably low. Broadly speaking, in the 1950s and 1960s the public sector traded job security for modest wage increases; and lacking any competitive pressures to hold down its unit costs, let its labour:output ratios rise. The public sector side of the Fordist accumulation regime was large-scale public bureaucracies, laxly managed, with easy working routines, high levels of job security and relatively low pay.

As the Fordist crisis deepened, however, all this began to change. It was the growing awareness amongst senior state personnel of the generalized crisis of productivity in the state sector, and of the need to set an example on wages to the private, that led governments in the 1960s and 1970s to run a series of wage policies on its own employees, and in the 1980s to introduce commercially-based performance indicators and large-scale redundancies into the public sector. The result in both cases (both of the earlier wage policies and the later retrenchments in spending) was major industrial unrest across the public sector. Indeed (as we will see in more detail in Chapter 4) this pattern of public sector resistance inspired Labour governments in the 1970s to negotiate a trade-off with the unions between higher social provision and lower public sector unit costs. It also inspired the later Conservative government to go for a more aggressive confrontation: facing out its own unions in a series of long strikes in the first half of the 1980s (of which the year-long miners' strike was the most protracted), altering legal codes to cripple effective trade union resistance, and keeping unemployment at what — for the post-war period — were record heights.

What the Conservative policies of the 1980s did — in ways which Labour governments in the 1970s had not — was to push class power back from labour to capital. The Conservative governments led by Margaret Thatcher created the conditions in which, once more, management could manage unchallenged. They led their own employers' offensive, and created the conditions for an employers' offensive by others. Indeed that was already underway in the 1970s. The tougher market conditions of the period after 1973 had already led many private companies to centralize wage bargaining away from the shop floor, even before the Conservatives came to power. Once there, Conservative legislative changes, government example, high unemployment and tough competitive conditions combined to encourage a more generalized assault on established working practices.

The full details of changes in labour practices under the Conservatives remain to be determined. But already we know certain things about industrial relations in the 1980s. We know that as early as 1984 over 80 per cent of manufacturing plants surveyed had introduced changes in working practices in the previous two years — changes which 'often involved a higher intensity of labour effort and the introduction of more flexible forms of working which in the majority of cases also meant the relaxation of well-established demarcation lines' (Rubery, 1986, p.96). We know, that is, that throughout the 1980s larger and larger groups of workers were signing collective agreements that involved significant changes in working practices (and by

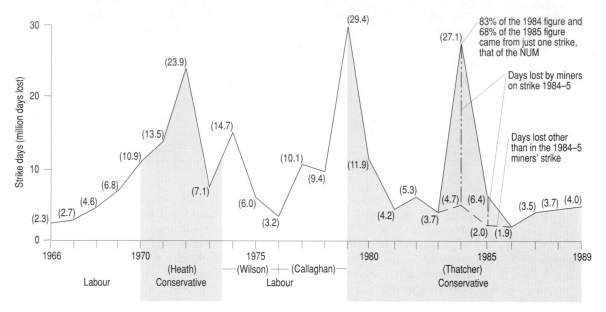

Figure 2.4 *Strike days, 1966–89*
Source: Department of Employment, Employment Gazette.

implication an intensification in the rate and effectiveness of work). We know that wages in the UK in the 1980s were amongst the lowest in Europe. We know that a percentage of industrial production was shifted to green field sites without trade unionism; and that new manufacturing plant was opened by foreign (especially Japanese) capital in regions where the labour movement had already been defeated and demoralized by long-term unemployment. And we know that these changes combined in the 1980s to generate a steady increase in the productivity of labour across the manufacturing sector of a now slimmed down but more competitive industrial base, and to produce a steady (and by international standards in the 1980s) impressive rate of economic growth.

Only the 1990s will make clear what is as yet uncertain — namely the depth and quality of the restructuring of the UK economy in the 1980s. But what we do not know is the likely longevity of this economic improvement. There are signs however as the decade opens that the restructuring has not been as complete as Conservative ministers like to claim.

One sign is the scale of the UK deficit on the balance of payments in 1989 and 1990, which suggests that serious imbalances remain in the structure of the economy as a whole. The UK still seems to have de-industrialized to too great a degree — with too slimmed down a manufacturing sector to meet local demand for manufactured goods. Between 1973 and 1988 domestic demand for such goods rose by 30 per cent but local output did not. On the contrary, and as we saw earlier, 'domestic output of manufactures ... can be said to be broadly stationary comparing 1973 and 1988 — with large troughs in output registered between each of these local peaks' (Wells, 1989, p.41). The shortfall in manufactured goods — and the resulting importation of them in increasing volume — was covered in the late 1970s and early 1980s

Table 2.10 Comparative economic performance, 1979–86

	UK	W.Germany	France	Italy	USA	Japan
Increase in GDP (%)						
1979–86	+10.3	+10.6	+10.0	+12.1	+16.0	+29.0
1979–81	−3.6	+1.5	+1.5	+4.0	+1.6	+8.0
1981–6	+14.8	+9.0	+8.5	+7.8	+13.8	+19.6
Increase in industrial production (%)						
1979–86	+2.8	+7.0	0	+5.0	+13.0	+26.0
1979–81	−9.4	−1.0	−1.0	+3.0	0	+5.0
1981–6	+13.4	+8.0	+1.0	+2.0	+13.0	+21.0
Unemployment as a percentage of the labour force						
1979	5.0	3.3	5.9	7.6	5.8	2.1
1981	9.8	4.4	7.3	8.3	7.5	2.2
1986	13.4	8.5	10.4	11.0	7.0	2.8
Inflation (% per annum)						
1979	13.4	4.1	10.8	14.8	11.3	3.6
1986	3.4	−0.3	2.6	5.8	2.0	0.4

Source: Maynard (1988, p.95).

by the export of primary produce (particularly North Sea oil); but of late, only by borrowing heavily abroad. The balance of payments *surpluses* of 1981–2 (of 3.8 and 2.6 per cent of GDP) had by 1988 given way to a *deficit* equivalent to 3.8 per cent of GDP (ibid., p.41). In spite of a decade of Thatcherism, the UK still seems locked in a tension between finance and industry, between short-term palliatives and long-term requirements for industrial investment — with high rates of interest necessary to protect the pound, and to hold money in London to cover the payments deficit, eating away at the industrial investment vital to correct that deficit in the longer term.

Moreover, wage levels continued to grow faster than output in Thatcherite Britain in the 1980s — indicating both considerable residual industrial strength by labour and the persistence of shortages of skilled workers in key parts of the economy as it revived. Productivity too continued to lag behind earnings, in spite of a decade of restructuring. Indeed the 'productivity miracle' of the 1980s looks less solidly-based than the figures first suggest. Much of it seems to be based either on a once and for all scrapping of redundant capacity, or on an associated intensification of the work process by a labour force fearful of unemployment. As Table 2.11 shows, UK industry seemed incapable by the end of the decade of sustaining the rapid increase in labour productivity achieved in the mid 1980s; and a detailed examination of the latest figures available to us suggests that 'the boom of the 1980s failed to eliminate the productivity gap between Britain and its industrial competitors'. In 1989 'output per hour among French manufacturing employees was 22 per cent above Britain's', while the gap between UK productivity levels and those of West Germany and the Netherlands, Japan and America, was 'even bigger' (D. Smith, 1990, p.4).

Table 2.11 Manufacturing productivity (% year on year)

		1986	1987	1988	1989	1990[1]
Output	official	1.2	5.2	7.3	4.3	2.0
	adjusted	1.7	5.4	7.8	4.5	2.6
Labour input	official	−2.6	−1.1	1.3	−0.1	−0.9
	adjusted	−2.9	−0.2	1.9	−1.3	−1.8
Productivity	official	3.4	6.2	5.5	3.7	2.5
	adjusted	4.7	5.6	5.8	5.7	4.1

[1] Second quarter.
Source: D. Smith (1990, p.4).

The scrapping of redundant capacity and the intensification of the work process in the UK in the 1980s seem only to have produced what Peter Nolan has called 'a series of step by step increases in measured productivity' rather than any 'fundamental and sweeping transformation of production relations' (Nolan, 1989, p.114). Little of the productivity gain seems to rest on the generalized application of qualitatively new productive processes. Investment levels in manufacturing plant and equipment remain too low for that. Indeed

> leaving aside the special case of oil and gas extraction ... real manufacturing investment in 1987 was nearly one-tenth lower than in 1979 ... Investment by banking, finance and insurance, by contrast, more than doubled ... with investment in business services close behind. All the growth in investment occurred in services, with falling investment in agriculture and industry.
>
> (Glyn, 1989, p.72)

Moreover, any move that we do see towards a new production base seems threatened by serious skill shortages and a decade of inadequate industrial retraining. All that we know so far about social and technological change in the 1980s in industries as disparate as textiles, motor components and foundries shows

> a complex picture of piecemeal and uneven adaption to new design, production and marketing systems. Above all else they show how firms in the 1980s, often hedged in by cash shortages and fierce market pressures, have sought incrementally, and not always successfully, to apply new microelectronic systems and a range of not so much new as different labour management techniques. The process of change has been partial and slow.
>
> (Nolan, 1989, p.117)

So a big question mark still hangs over production in the contemporary UK. Big supply side problems remain to threaten the viability of the UK industrial recovery in the 1990s. The UK still lacks 'a *sufficient* volume of manufacturing capacity capable of producing the sorts of products people require in both domestic and overseas markets' (Wells, 1989, p.58). Industrial weaknesses still dominate the agenda of those who would run the economy, and of those who would use any economic strength for social reconstruction. It is therefore hardly surprising that fierce political debate persists as how best to run the UK economy most effectively in the 1990s. It is a debate which we will examine in more detail in Chapter 4.

SUMMARY

- UK industry saw a shift in class power towards organized work groups and their stewards in key sections of manufacturing industry in the full employment conditions of the 1950s and 1960s.

- Public sector workers (miners apart) largely missed out on this: and attempts to restrict their wages from the 1960s stimulated waves of public sector strikes — in the late 1960s and early 1970s, and again in the late 1970s and early 1980s.

- In the 1980s, Conservative governments made strenuous efforts to push back working class industrial power, to restructure industry and to generate increased productivity and competitiveness. It is not yet clear however how successful these attempts have been.

3.2 CONSUMPTION

So power has shifted within industry in the 1980s, from workers to management; and within the economy generally power has shifted a little from producers to consumers. Since individuals play both sets of roles (they are both producers and consumers) what they have lost on one they have gained on the other. Certainly this has been the Thatcherite trade-off canvassed at them for a decade now. Work hard and consume more: and define yourself not as a producer (a member of a social class, a trade union or a professional body) but as a consumer (of goods, services, housing, law and order and national glory).

What Fordism did was to augment the purchasing power of consumers without significantly increasing their market power. The emergence of some kind of post-Fordist regime of accumulation has added to the power consumers can exercise over producers, by giving them the money with which to choose, and the competition from which to select, a growing range of ever more sophisticated consumer goods and services. The key allocative devices linking producers and consumers in the Fordist period were managed ones. Big hierarchically-organized firms provided goods in greater quantities than ever before to customers with no previous experience of affluence; and operated in markets largely of their own design and choosing. They did so in an economic climate managed by governments keen to make purchasing and selling easy, and able to effect those easy conditions by nationally-based macro-economic policies.

In the different economic conditions prevailing in the late 1980s and 1990s much of this has gone. Governments neither can nor will play that role any longer. Consumer confidence and purchasing power has grown, as a generation used to affluence has emerged — to demand more and better things. Competition has intensified, and firms have been compelled to compete with each other in the quality and particularity of their products as much as in the quantity and cheapness of their provision. Of course, much of the product differentiation characteristic of the modern consumer goods sector is clearly trivial and false (a new facia panel on a basically unchanged washing machine, three coloured buttons on a basically unchanged stereo system, etc.). But the new technology of computerization has made it possible both to stimulate, and then to meet, increasingly nuanced demands for higher quality and more personalized products. Producers now have had to reach out — and capture — markets in which product competition is intense: and in the process the unmanaged market has reasserted itself as a key co-ordinating institution in contemporary economic activity.

3.2.1 CONSUMPTION IN THE POST-WAR PERIOD

There are a number of important things to note about the changing pattern and experience of consumption in the post-war period.

1 The first is the steady and general transformation in the quality of everyday life brought forward by successful Fordist regimes of accumulation. Some of that provision is public and universal. The post-war years have seen transformations in the quality and availability of health care and education. It is commonplace these days to complain about the detail and decay of welfare provision, and its costs. But there is no escaping the fact that standards of welfare care are years ahead now of those available in the 1930s, and that this represents a real increase in the effective rights of citizenship. These rights may be receding at the margin now. My generation — born as the war ended — may prove to have been the privileged one, the generation of Fordism at its height. Certainly the fiscal crisis of the state, with its steady if incremental privatization of welfare provision, looks set to create a two-tier welfare system. Even in the 1950s and 1960s access to welfare provision was skewed by class, gender and ethnicity: and was always supplemented by a parallel system of private provision of higher quality care, available only to the rich. That private sector is now flourishing as never before; but it remains the case that the bulk of the universal welfare state is still in place, and is still providing a range of services and facilities to its consumers of a quality beyond the imagination of reformers in the inter-war period.

But the bulk of what is consumed is privately chosen, bought and used. The volume and quality of wage goods consumed has also reached a level beyond the imagination of the inter-war generation; in things such as housing, food, clothing, domestic appliances, transport, communications and leisure activities. The range of options available to consumers has been transformed. The quality of what is on offer is far higher than ever before;

and the social range of those participating in high-volume high-quality consumption is unprecedented. What only the rich had/could reasonably aspire to in 1945 (their own houses, holidays, cars, telephones, good clothes and a generous diet) the skilled working class have today. The vast majority of us now consume — and take for granted as a norm — things unanticipated in 1945: our private leisure pursuits (colour televisions, videos, stereo systems), our holidays, our domestic appliances. In the process other things have gone — domestic servants for the middle class, cinema for the workers (though cinema attendance is beginning to rise again). But overall, standards of living have risen, and have done so in waves: improvements in basic food and clothing (in the 1950s), the spread of basic consumer durables (in the 1960s), the beginning of the leisure boom (in the 1970s) and the increasingly sophisticated domestic consumption and leisure experience of the 1980s. The post-war years have moved many of us from rationing to Ratners, and from Blackpool to Benidorm.

2   The second thing to say is that not everyone has been able to participate fully in this consumer bonanza. Poverty remains a large-scale feature of the consumption patterns of the post-war UK. As the affluence of the majority has grown, the consumption patterns of a sizeable minority have lagged steadily (and in the 1980s increasingly) behind. What we are talking about here is not absolute poverty in the main (though there is that again — with young people sleeping rough on the London streets — and the emergence there nightly of a cardboard city of the homeless). The welfare safety net is in place, and in general it is still up-graded in line with inflation. But the net has holes, and as with any holes, things fall through. Indeed, a number of the holes in the welfare net were widened in the 1980s to encourage the

Cardboard city: sleeping rough in London in the 1980s

young and unemployed to take low paid jobs, and to push the cost of main-taining certain unproductive groups (youth, the disabled, and the old) increasingly back onto families and the private sector — and thus increas-ingly onto the unpaid labour of women.

However, most modern poverty is relative poverty. It is poverty relative to the consumption standards of the majority. And poverty in this sense is now massive. In 1985, between 17 and 29 per cent of the population still lived at or just above Supplementary Benefit level. By the mid 1980s, there were anywhere between 6 and 12 million poor people in the UK, of whom as many as 2.6 million faced intense poverty (Hudson and Williams, 1989, p.23). The distribution of this poverty is not even in the society as a whole. It is skewed regionally, as we might expect, given the uneven development of the economy from which so much of it derives. The North is poorer than the South, the peripheral regions more than the centre, the cities more than the countryside and the suburbs. There is a gender dimension to poverty. Women share a larger burden of poverty than do men. The distribution of poverty is also skewed by ethnicity, by age and by class. Low pay and unemployment are key elements of contemporary poverty. And the bases of poverty cumulatively combine: to be female, black, unskilled and living in some 'northern' city is to increase your chances of exposure to poverty way above the norm.

So private affluence has its underside — in the creation of a new class of peripheral labour and state welfare clients locked in poverty amid affluence — a class moreover which is increasingly vulnerable to any post-Fordism restructuring of the economy and to the privatization of much welfare provision. It is this class which continues to bear the brunt of the private affluence and public squalor characteristic of UK society in the 1990s.

3 What makes you poor in the UK is your place in the inequalities of class, gender, ethnicity, region and age. What stigmatizes you as poor is your inability to obtain particular kinds of credit. The financing and organization of consumption is a third key feature of the way contemporary life has been moulded by the exigencies of first a Fordist and now, perhaps, some kind of emerging post-Fordist regime of accumulation. In accumula-tion regimes of low consumption of the pre-war type, there was no need to diversify the kinds and types of money. Cash in hand, and the weekly pay packet, were enough for the working class — with the post office or sock beneath the bed for any vestigial saving, and the pawn shop (and the slate at the local corner store) as the last resort when money ran out. A monthly cheque, and a modest network of branch banks in which to cash them, was all that the middle class required to establish its status and to lubricate its consumption. But when consumption went up a gear in the years of Fordist-based economic growth, the circuit of finance necessary to fuel the process had to gear up as well. The development of credit now began to relate, 'not just to the managing of poverty, but to the growth of affluence' (Ford, 1988, p.73). The 1950s saw an expansion in the already well-established provision of hire purchase arrangements by retailers, and the spread of mail order shopping. The 1960s and 1970s saw the spread of cheque books and bank accounts down into the skilled working class; and the expansion of the scale of trading by finance houses (to facilitate the purchase of cars, large items of domestic expenditure and houses). The 1980s saw a total revolution in both the availability, scale and distribution of credit. Money went plastic; and

The new plastic face of money

saving became a real possibility for large sections of the employed population. Credit and saving institutions (from banks to building societies) grew to absorb those savings, and to re-process them as credit. My Halifax account pays less than 10 per cent. My Halifax credit card charges me about 30 per cent. I borrow my own money back, pay 20 per cent for the privilege, and watch the Halifax grow! As Janet Ford put it:

> In the mid 1960s bank credit cards were unknown. Today approximately 22 million have been issued by Access and Barclaycard. There are thought to be over 6 million retail store cards in circulation ... In early 1987 total personal credit granted but still outstanding was in excess of £30,000 million. In addition approximately 7 million households have credit for house purchase ... In 1986 the outstanding credit for house purchase totalled £153,666 million ... considering only consumer credit, in 1986 the average family owed £1,500 and spent 6% of its income servicing the agreements.

> (Ford, 1988, p.3)

SUMMARY

- There has been a large and sustained increase in living standards for the majority of the population since the war — living standards generated both by the public provision of welfare services and the private provision of consumer goods.

- Poverty remained a feature of post-war UK life. Not all sections of the community participated in the rising affluence.

- Rising affluence has been accompanied by a transformation in the availability of credit and in the scale of personal debt.

3.2.2 THE CONSUMER REVOLUTION AND ITS LIMITS

Selling is now big business. Behind the credit boom lies a complete revolution in retailing, banking and leisure. Long established traditions of retailing were one of the casualties of affluence in the 1970s and 1980s. Until then a plethora of small and corner shops — in the food area selling unpacked goods and providing home deliveries — increasingly gave way to supermarkets and hypermarkets. Retailing became as monopolized as every other sector of the UK economy. High Streets transformed themselves into a standardized array of the same 10–20 retail companies, now household names: Marks & Spencer, Burtons and British Home Stores in clothes, Boots the chemists, WH Smiths for newspapers, Dixons and Currys for electrical goods, Habitat and MFI for furniture, Laura Ashley or Liberty's for materials, Mothercare for baby provisions, Woolworths, Debenhams and the John Lewis partnership for general goods. Older household names either went (John Collier) or survived in revamped form by going slightly up market (Woolworths). And as the details on the back of your storecards show, even this limited range of names on the High Street obscured the even greater degree of concentration of ownership that lay behind them. BHS, Mothercare and Habitat are all linked together on my storecard, and so on.

People also began to shop even for groceries by car: first in urban-based supermarkets, then in out of town sites surrounded by other shopping outlets (especially DIY stores and fast food chains). Whole hypermarkets and shopping malls sprang up in the 1980s, combining shops with restaurants, play areas and multi-view cinema complexes. For by then family shopping expeditions had become the UK's second most popular leisure activity after watching television. Spending had become the thing people liked to do to relax. Consumption had become an end in itself, available to all who had money to spend, access to credit, and private transport to reach the shops and to carry the goods home. The poor did not participate, but everyone else did.

This consumer revolution absorbed much of the private time, energy and aspirations of vast swathes of the UK middle class and skilled manual working class throughout the 1980s. Affluence spawned whole new social categories — yuppies, lager louts — and completely altered patterns of private relaxation. For people consumed services as well as goods — particularly leisure services — and whole industries flourished on that servicing alone. The increase in domestic expenditure on manufactures actually matched that on services in the 1980s — with spending high particularly on cars, electronic goods, electrical appliances and clothes — all areas in which 'the UK lacks an adequate volume of internationally competitive capacity' (Wells, 1989, p.43). Hence the worsening in the UK balance of trade. The sale of alcohol reached new heights, and lost its male, macho, pub location and image. People drank in the 1980s, and drank everywhere: at home, in the new leisure-oriented pubs, and in restaurants. They drank (as indeed they ate) a wider and more foreign-based range of products: wines as well as spirits, lagers as well as beers. They holidayed abroad too in increasing numbers, as the foreign package holiday replaced the seaside jaunt of the 1950s for more and more people.

The other index of this consumer revolution which is worth noting too is the scale of house ownership and the rising price of housing. Over the 45 years since 1945 the UK has moved from a society that rented its accommodation (from councils and private landlords) to one that owned its own housing and rented only when it could not afford to buy. There are regional variations in all this of course (Scotland in particular) and the usual variations of class and age apply. The lower down the social ladder you go, and the younger you are, the more common renting becomes (particularly from councils by the poor, and from private landlords by the young). But otherwise house ownership has increasingly become the norm: made possible by the greater availability of funds for house purchase from building societies, and made necessary by the curtailment of publicly-funded housing provision under Conservative governments after 1979.

Growing affluence, the availability of credit, shortfalls in the rate of growth of the housing stock, and the continued regional imbalance in economic growth, all combined to fuel a dramatic inflation in house prices in the 1980s. This began in the South East, and then spread; to eat away at the capacity of the consuming middle classes to sustain their flight of high consumption into the 1990s. The housing price boom of the 1980s left a serious crisis of housing consumption in place as the 1990s opened: one borne disproportionately by the young and by those on low incomes. They could not afford to get into the housing market as owners; and if they did, high interest rates threatened the ability of many of them to repay their mortgages. The number of people with mortgage arrears of over six months doubled in 1989–90, to bring the total to nearly 100,000 families, and to increase the number of home repossessions by building societies to record levels — 14,390 in the first six months of 1990, as compared to 13,740 in the *whole* of 1989 (*The Times*, 13 August 1990, p.2 and 14 August 1990, p.7). And even for those able to keep up with the rising cost of housing, the burden of repayments ate away at their ability to participate in the helter-skelter of consumption on which the manufacturing and retail sectors had come so heavily to depend.

Inflation is indeed the point at which the crisis of consumption and the problems of production continue to come together in the contemporary UK. Inflation was not a major problem in the Fordist years. Then the rates of productivity grew with sufficient speed and the flow of labour was sufficiently generous, to keep wage levels in line with production. But as we saw earlier, inflation quickened everywhere in the late 1960s and early 1970s, as the world trade cycle reappeared (increasing commodity prices, especially that of oil), as labour supplies dried up (increasing wages) and as the rate of growth of productivity slowed (as the full dissemination of Fordist production systems was achieved). The inflationary end of the Fordist boom, as we saw, was experienced as a crisis of stagflation and as a crisis of government spending. High government spending no longer helped to lubricate private capital accumulation. It just kept labour in short supply, added a tax burden to the already squeezed profits of the private sector, and made its own contribution to inflationary pressures.

Table 2.12 Inflationary over-heating of the 'South' in the 1980s

	Percentage increase, 1983–8, in	
	average house prices	average hourly earnings
South East	156.7	52.5
Greater London	169.8	55.0
Rest of the South East	138.6	48.9
East Anglia	148.3	43.1
South West	115.5	42.7
East Midlands	92.0	40.7
'South'	145.9	47.3
West Midlands	90.4	40.4
Yorkshire–Humberside	57.6	38.1
North West	57.7	39.3
Northern	43.1	36.6
Wales	58.1	36.0
Scotland	29.8	38.8
'North'	56.7	37.6
Great Britain	104.8	43.9

Source: Martin (1989, p.93).

These pressures were then eased by attempts at some sort of post-Fordist restructuring of the economy — one that again increased productivity, increased unemployment and cut government spending. But that restructuring only eased the problem of inflation. It did not take it away in the UK. Productivity remained too low to permit high wage rises, and wages stayed high through the self-confidence and entrenched organizations of core workers. The supply side problems of the UK economy persisted throughout the 1980s — and because they did, we are entering the 1990s with a gap between demand and supply that is keeping inflation and the balance of payments at the forefront of domestic politics. We are entering the 1990s, that is, with the same economic agenda with which each of the last three decades has also begun.

SUMMARY

- The dramatic rise in living standards in the 1980s was accompanied by a revolution in credit provision and in retailing. Consumption is now the UK's second most popular form of relaxation (after watching television).

- Problems loom in the 1990s: with domestically-generated supplies of manufactured goods insufficient to meet local demand, with rising house prices eating away at spending levels, and with inflation quickening again.

CHAPTER 3:   THE SOCIETY

So far we have built a picture of a society in flux, but one largely peopled by economic producers and consumers. If you look back over the arguments of the last two chapters, you will find that we have already noted the existence of many important processes of social change: but so far those processes of social change have entered our story only because they have been directly linked to economic developments inside the UK since 1945. We have seen, for example, that the number of people working or mining the land, or spending much of their working time engaged in heavy manual labour, has fallen dramatically in the post-war period. We have noted too that more people now than before work alongside machines (as minders/supervisors), have managerial posts, work as state administrators, occupy white collar jobs or provide services of a wide variety of kinds. We have already observed that more married women go out to paid work in the 1990s than was the case in the late 1940s; and that a small but significant percentage of the workforce are now members of ethnic minorities. The Irish and Jewish communities of inter-war Britain have recently been joined by West Indian and South Asian ethnic minorities as well. And we have emphasized that, to a degree within these ethnic communities, and far more within the wider society which surrounds them, the consumption of wage goods (and the general experience of steadily rising living standards) has been a key feature of the experience of more and more people in the UK since 1945. Poverty persists, but for the 75–80 per cent of the UK population who have escaped it, the 1980s in particular have been years of unprecedented prosperity.

So we are beginning to put together a certain view of how UK society has been organized, and has changed, in the post-war period. But our concerns so far have not focused on the society as such. We have concentrated on economic issues, even though societies are far more than just sites for economic activity. It is time now to leave this preoccupation with 'the economic' behind. Though there are occasions on which it makes sense to think of the UK as simply being an economy, more normally it helps to think of the United Kingdom and its people as constituting a whole 'civil society'. For in the UK, as in all other societies, people play social roles other than those of producers and consumers. They are parents, lovers, friends, church goers, members of clubs, watchers of sports and so on; and as such rely on institutions and networks (families, social groupings, private organizations) which also have to be run. If therefore we are to fill out the 'big picture' of how the UK has been run since 1945, we need to look at civil society as well as at the economy which sustains it. That is our task in this chapter.

In the space available to us, we cannot hope to do more than touch briefly on some of the key aspects of social life in the post-war UK. The principles of selection here will be taken, as they are elsewhere in this book, from the set of concerns which underpin the project as a whole. We are concerned throughout with 'the running of the country': preoccupied less with the character of the society than with the ways in which its various parts are organized, co-ordinated and led. Since our focus is on the 'running' of the contemporary UK, we can use this chapter both to examine those who do the running, and the principles of social organization available to them as they do so. That is why questions of social structure and dominant social values will occupy us here as we trace patterns of continuity and change in post-war UK society.

1 THE RUNNERS

No society has yet been devised which did not, over a long period, develop its own internal patterns of social stratification. Certainly UK society has been, and remains, riddled with strongly entrenched social divisions. Access to both the material and psychic goods available in the society (to its distribution of power and status as well as to its consumer goods and work routines) is not enjoyed in equal measure by all sections of the community. Most obviously perhaps, degrees of access to such things vary over time and between generations. In the UK the set of life chances open to the generation born in 1945 has been greater than that open earlier to the generation born in the 1920s. What the inter-war generation faced, after all, was unemployment, fascism and war: and they had to survive without the televisions, foreign holidays and private motor cars apparently so essential to contemporary middle class life. It is not of course that history here is necessarily best understood as a story of unbroken material progress. It may well be that the children of the 1940s baby boom were the fortunate ones. In many ways their options are still proving to be more bountiful than those facing their children born in the 1960s, now emerging as young adults into a world subject to higher inflation, unemployment and house prices than their parents faced a generation before. Time alone will show how the life chances of each generation compare to those on either side of it; but what we know already is that, *within* generations, access to the riches of society varies on other lines.

It varies between ethnic groups, being easier for European-born groups and their offspring than it is for families with roots in colonial Asia, Africa and the Caribbean. Access to social prestige and power also varies between genders. Men rather than women find wider routes before them to power, status and high incomes. And access varies by social class. It is just so much easier to come to wealth and power in this society if you pick your parents with care. As we will see, it is the children of aristocratic, professional and higher managerial parents who have the greatest likelihood of rising to the top in UK society, and the children of manual workers for whom the chances are least. There is a degree of short-scale social mobility. There are even examples of exceptional individuals who leave their working class background far behind. But those examples confirm the character of the class system in the contemporary UK rather than imply its absence. For leaving their social origins behind is what proletarian children have to do if they wish to be successful in this society: and indeed the more they do that, the more they will know how successful they have been.

To enjoy the greatest material rewards this society has to offer — and certainly to be in the best position to exercise power within it — it helps to be a white middle-aged male from a middle/upper class social background.

UK society is to a remarkable degree run by a limited number of individuals of just this type. Not everyone with those personal and social characteristics has power in the contemporary UK, but very few people have power who do not occupy a central place in this narrow social band.

1.1 SOURCES OF PRIVILEGE AND POWER

There is nothing inevitable or pre-ordained about the existence of such a monopoly of power by so small and distinctive a group. Such concentrations of power are themselves the product of long and complex histories; and their persistence into the 1990s is a testimony to the amount of human effort that has gone, and that continues to go, into their protection and reproduction. We lack the space to examine either the history or the reproduction of social privilege in any detail (that detail can be found in Scott, 1991; Bottomore and Brym, 1989; and Thompson, 1979). But what we can do is emphasize the importance of past patterns of class rule to the way the contemporary UK is run, and point to the legacy of those past patterns in many features of contemporary UK life.

The legacies of past patterns of class rule are everywhere about us in the contemporary UK: in the institution of the monarchy, in the persistence of

The Queen at Ascot, June 1989

titles and country estates, in the rituals of church and state — even in the way we learn our history as a story of kings and cavaliers. This should not surprise us, for 'the British upper class of today is the outcome of a long process of historical development in which successive upper classes have fused, split and allied themselves in a variety of ways' (Scott, 1985, p.30). The seventeenth century civil wars may have been personally traumatic for Charles I, but they did not involve any root and branch destruction of the old feudal order. Instead after 1660, the English aristocracy and landed gentry transmuted themselves into a highly successful agrarian capitalist class, and in alliance with first merchant capitalists, and later with industrialists, ran the eighteenth and nineteenth century UK state and society in ways which facilitated the accumulation of private capital and the persistence of social privilege. The particular agrarian anchorages of English landed wealth did not survive the general agrarian depression of the last quarter of the nineteenth century; but the symbols, forms and attitudes of agrarian wealth did. Landed wealth moved into finance, into trade and to a lesser degree into industry, at the very moment at which successful industrial capitalists were buying themselves into land, into titles and into banking. The result was that by 1945 the UK was run — not by aristocrats or a rising industrial middle class — but by a fusion of these two classes into one — into a class whose wealth depended on successful capital accumulation, but a wealth no longer dependent either on land or on UK-based industrial development alone.

In the post-war years, as we have seen, responsibility for the generation of national wealth has come to rest in the hands of fewer and fewer companies. Accordingly power over economic resources has come to lie almost exclusively with the senior figures inside those companies. These figures are rarely the owners: most of the companies they head are publicly quoted ones, owned by shareholders and run on a day to day basis by boards of directors/professional managers. The old capitalist class of individual owner-managers has gone from the world of large companies (though it remains, of course, still very much the norm in the world of small business). Legacies of it are still evident at top corporate level, in the presence there of a few family firms, with family retention of controlling blocs of shares and direct family representation on the governing boards. This is particularly the case in retailing, food and drink, hotels and leisure, and merchant banking (Scott, 1991, p.79). But normally these days large industrial and financial firms are run by professional managers; and this has often been enough to sustain claims that there has been a 'managerial revolution' which has transformed capitalism and its ruling class into some post-capitalist meritocratic ruling order (see Burnham, 1945, *passim*).

Merit does have much to do with progress to the top of managerial structures in today's highly competitive industrial system. But so too does capital ownership and birth. The fragmentation of share ownership can be vastly overdrawn; and the dispersal of industrial power associated with it certainly can. In the 1980s share ownership in the UK increased dramatically, as the Conservative government privatized large state enterprises in schemes which actively encouraged the small saver to buy industrial shares and to play the Stock Market. As a result, nearly one in five of the UK adult population held shares by 1988. But paradoxically this very dispersal weakened popular control of the new popular capitalism, by diluting still

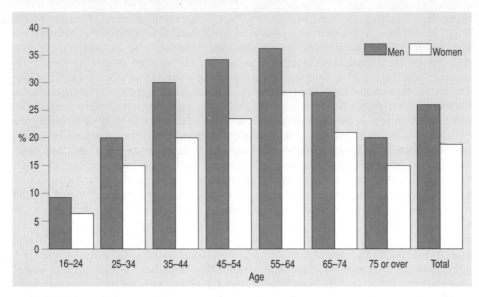

Figure 3.1 *Share ownership in the UK by age and sex in 1988*
Source: The Times *(5 November 1990, p.5).*

further shareholders' challenges to two features of contemporary share ownership which together enable a small group of men to keep a controlling hold on much of UK economic life.

The first is that significant blocs of industrial shares were, and still are, held by financial institutions — by merchant and commercial banks, by pension funds, and by insurance companies. Nearly a half of the top 200 industrial companies in the UK can now be said to be formally controlled by institutions of this kind (Scott, 1991, p.78). The men who run these financial institutions are well placed to exercise industrial leadership and co-ordination. The directors they appoint to the boards of companies which they partly own play a key role in co-ordinating economic activity between firms, and in holding together blocs of companies in loose finance-led coalitions. The second is that senior managers themselves receive large salaries and shares — as their prize for industrial success — and are thereby in a much stronger position than individual shareholders to mould economic activity to their plans and preferences. For these reasons, the spread of popular capitalism has not changed the distribution of power very much. It still remains the case that certain key players dominate industrial decision-making through the positions they occupy at the command posts of the largest industrial and financial concerns.

It is also clear that these people are both prepared and able to transmit their power and privileges to their children — and particularly to their sons. The most reliable way of being rich and powerful in the contemporary UK is still to be born rich, to be born to the powerful. Inheritance remains a potent source of wealth. It is true, of course, that wealth has been redistributed to a degree this century, but in the main that redistribution has 'not been between the rich and the poor but between successive generations of the same family and between husbands and wives' (Urry, 1985, p.60). That is, it has largely been a distribution between the rich, as Table 3.1 makes clear.

Table 3.1 Share of total personal wealth (%), England and Wales, 1923–72

| | Percentage of total population | | | |
	top 1%	next 4%	next 5%	next 5%
1923	60.9	21.1	7.1	5.1
1972	31.7	24.3	14.4	14.5

Source: Urry (1985, p.60).

Privileged education also remains a critical channel into senior posts — particularly in merchant banking but also in much of industry. The social profile of leading industrialists and financiers continues to show a higher than average presence there of individuals of aristocratic descent and of former public schoolboys. Even the state bureaucracy — open as it is as a career to talent — shows a heavy presence at its senior levels of Oxbridge products and ex-public schoolboys. As late as 1970, 69 per cent of top civil servants had an Oxbridge background, and 62 per cent had been to one of the major public schools (Scott, 1985, p.48). Indeed the hold of Oxbridge on the loyalties of senior civil servants is actually growing stronger. The latest research shows that — for permanent secretaries at least — 66.7 per cent came from Oxford or Cambridge between 1945 and 1964, a figure which rose to 75 per cent for the 1965–86 group (the figure for 1900–19 was 62.7 per cent) (Theakston and Fry, 1989, p.132).

Ruling circles in the contemporary UK society are not closed to talent from below; but they are exclusive in their membership and cohesive in their attitudes and values. Indeed the test of membership of senior positions has been one that new members have normally been only too willing to meet: to socialize themselves into existing attitudes and practices, and to transmit both those values and their privileges to their offspring. The public school and, to a lesser degree, Oxbridge have acted, and continue to act, as the crucial mechanisms for the production of those values and for the transmission of that privilege. The result has been the consolidation of a self-confident, coherent and remarkably self-conscious Establishment, a whole network of privileged and interconnected people consolidated around a set of important institutions and productive of a climate of values, opinions and preoccupations. There may be social mobility of a limited kind, but that does not alter the fact that the Establishment is alive and well in the UK, and still firmly in control of access to the command posts of the society. What we still face in the UK is what we have faced consistently from 1945: the monopoly of privilege by the privileged within the monopolies.

Table 3.2   The educational background of élite groups

(a) The public school background

	Total	Percentage from public schools
14 year olds in England and Wales (1967)	642,977	2.6
Conservative MPs (1970)	330	64.4
Conservative cabinet (1970)	18	77.7
Royal Navy (Rear-Admirals and above, 1970)	76	88.9
Army (Major-Generals and above, 1970)	117	86.1
RAF (Air Vice-Marshals and above, 1971)	85	62.5
Ambassadors (1971)	80	82.5
High Court and Appeal Court judges (1971)	91	80.2
Church of England bishops (1971)	133	67.4
Directors of 40 major industrial firms (1971)	261	67.8
Directors of clearing banks (1971)	99	79.9
Directors of merchant banks (1971)	106	77.4
Directors of major insurance companies (1971)	118	83.1
Governors and directors of the Bank of England (1971)	18	55.5

(b) Grammar school education in eight élite groups (%)

	1939	1950	1960	1970–1
Civil service (under-secretary and above)	6.6	25.5	25.8	31.4
Ambassadors	0.0	11.8	9.5	12.0
High Court and Appeal Court judges	5.0	6.1	10.3	9.5
Royal Navy (Rear-Admirals and above)	19.0	6.3	5.0	12.9
Army (Major-Generals and above)	4.6	10.2	4.2	8.3
RAF (Air Vice-Marshals and above)	0.0	5.5	8.6	23.5
Church of England (assistant bishops and above)	4.5	11.5	15.1	17.9
Directors of clearing banks	3.9	5.8	10.1	9.0

Source: Noble (1975, p.314).

SUMMARY

- Life chances are unevenly divided in society: between generations, and within generations, between ethnic groups, genders and classes. The contemporary UK is run in the main by middle-aged white males.

- Existing patterns of class rule are the product of centuries-long accommodations between aristocratic privilege and industrial/ financial wealth. Dominant groups in the UK owe their power to their ownership of capital and their control of key economic institutions.

- Social privilege is transmitted between generations mainly by the inheritance of wealth and participation in privileged forms of education.

1.2   THE EXISTENCE OF A 'PROPERTIED CLASS'

So those who run the economy and state are largely the children of those who ran it before, or those newcomers who were educated with them. Together these people make up a key element of a slightly wider 'propertied class', the core of which is made up of the owners and controllers of the big industrial and financial concerns.

John Scott has categorized these core individuals as a mixture of entrepreneurial, internal and finance capitalists: that is, as a mixture of those who control firms by virtue of being members of the founding family, those who have risen up the internal managerial ladder, and those who link finance and industry by holding directorships in both sectors. As we said earlier, entrepreneurial capitalists still control a number of the UK's top 250 companies. (27 out of 250, on Scott's latest figures; Scott, 1991, p.78.) The other 200 or so companies are run by professional managers without specific family connections, and many are linked by an 'inner circle' of co-ordinating directors. The size of this inner circle depends very much on how many of the large enterprises fall within our purview. However if we take the top 200 large companies in the UK in 1988, Scott reckons that they were linked by no more than 290 people — 285 men and 5 women — two-thirds of whom sat on the board of at least one bank or insurance company, and half of whom were actually bank/insurance executives (ibid., pp.78–9).

Table 3.3   The top 27 finance capitalists, 1976

	No. of directorships in top 250 companies		No. of directorships in top 250 companies
Sir David H. Barran	5	Daniel Meinertzhagen	4
John A.F. Binny	4	Baron Netherthorpe (Turner family)	5
Sir George S. Bishop	4	Sir David L. Nicolson	5
Viscount Caldecote	4	Sir Anthony Part	4
E. Philip Chappell	4	Sir John Partridge	5
Sir Robert A. Clark	5	Lord Pritchard	4
Earl of Cromer (Baring family)	4	Baron Remnant	4
Ian J. Fraser	5	Baron Robens	5
Sir Reay Geddes	4	Sir Eric Roll	4
Baron Greenhill	6	Sir Francis E.P. Sandilands	6
Barrie Heath	4	Philip Shelbourne	5
John F.C. Hull	4	Harry Smith	4
Earl of Inchcape (Mackay family)	5	Sir Gerald B. Thorley	4
Sir Peter A. Matthews	4	Total	121

Source: Scott (1985, p.43).

The 290 are John Scott's 'finance capitalists'. Table 3.3 lists the 27 most important of them from a slightly earlier study of 1976. This is how Scott described their character and role then.

> The third group within the core of the upper class, the finance capitalists, is also the smallest group. It consists of those who are recruited from among the internal and entrepreneurial capitalists to the boards of directors of enterprises other than those in which they began their careers. Many of them may be recruited from politics, the civil service and other areas outside the world of business. Such people therefore hold directorships in two or more enterprises in various sectors of the economy and they play a key role in co-ordinating the operations of the business system as a whole. They are the co-ordinating controllers of monopoly capital. [The table] lists 27 finance capitalists who sat on four or more boards amongst the top 250 companies of 1976. All but seven of these men had some kind of title — hereditary peerages, life peerages and knighthoods. They can be considered as the 'elder statesmen' of the business system. Through their directorships the finance capitalists link many of the large companies ... tie together the diverse capitalist interests and provide a basis for some degree of co-ordination.
>
> (Scott, 1985, pp.43–4)

Numbers like 290 or 27 should not mislead us here. It is actually very difficult to get a precise figure on these 'core members' of the propertied class — on those who actually run the top industrial and financial concerns — those whose personal wealth derives from their ownership and control of 'giant business enterprises, large landed estates and massive share portfolios' (Scott, 1991, p.65). John Scott believes that altogether 'the core of the capitalist business class comprise about 0.1% of the adult population, about 43,500 people' who collectively owned '7% of total wealth in 1986' (Scott, 1991, p.82). His list of the UK's wealthiest families is reproduced in Table 3.4.

Table 3.4   Britain's rich, 1990

	Family	Estimated wealth (£ million)	Main source of wealth
1	The Royal family	6,700	land and urban property
2	Grosvenor (Duke of Westminster)	4,200	land and urban property
3	Rausing	2,040	food packaging
4	Sainsbury	1,777	food retailing
5	Weston	1,674	food production and retailing
6	Moores	1,670	football pools and retailing
7	Vestey	1,420	food production
8	Getty	1,350	oil
9	Maxwell	1,100	publishing
10	Feeney	1,020	retailing
11	Hinduja	1,000	trading
12	Livanos	930	shipping
13	Goldsmith	750	retailing and finance
14	Swire	692	shipping and aviation
15	Ronson	548	urban property and petrol distribution
16	Barclay[1]	500	hotels and urban property
17	Branson	488	music and aviation
18	Cadogan (Earl Cadogan)	450	land and urban property
19	Jerwood	400	trading
20	Portman (Viscount Portman)	400	land and urban property
21	Thompson	400	food processing and property

[1] Not the family associated with Barclays Bank.

Source: Scott (1991, p.83).

These 'core members' of the propertied class are then surrounded by maybe 100,000 other souls, people linked into the propertied class by kinship, education, social bonds and a shared culture, whilst not themselves being directly involved in industry and finance as such. Here we find perhaps 1–2 per cent of the population, differentially dependent on finance, industry, rents or the professions, but commonly dependent for their privileges on the maintenance and success of the monopolies, and on the preservation of highly unequal rights and rewards between top management and the rest. These people constitute a class of the socially privileged, a class whose privileges derive from the possession within them and their families of large amounts of private capital and private property (see Coates, 1989b, pp.34–5). They are 'the great and the good', the people who head the key social institutions (the church, the law, the military, and the media) and who sit on the advisory committees of the state.

This 1–2 per cent of the UK population play a disproportionate part in the running of the non-economic aspects of contemporary UK society. Once again, public school education can be used as a reliable guide to the membership of this group, and to their disproportionate occupation of key social and state positions. In spite of the professionalization of the armed services, the established church, the legal profession and the state bureaucracy in the twentieth century, public school representation at senior levels in each remains high (as Table 3.2 showed). Whatever else is going on in the contemporary UK, the demise of the public school, and the diminution of its importance as a route to privilege and power, are not amongst them.

The potency of public school and traditional university education as a route to public as well as private power is evident too in the figures on cabinet composition this century. As late as 1983 over three quarters of cabinet ministers had an Oxbridge education, and 'two thirds of the cabinet members that year had attended *both* a public school and one of the two traditional universities' (Scott, 1991, p.132). Indeed one public school in particular — Eton — managed to provide one in three of all UK cabinet ministers between 1950 and 1970. Things may be changing a little now. None of the last three Conservative Prime Ministers have had a conventional upper class education: and the percentage of Conservative MPs — as distinct from cabinet ministers — without a public school background has recently reached the giddy heights of 25 per cent (*The Times*, 27 November 1990, p.4). There does seem to be a tendency abroad in recent Conservative cabinets to eschew 'establishment figures'; both by falling out with other sections of the Establishment (particularly the Church of England) and by appointing cabinets that are full of state-educated and minor public school figures (see Paxman, 1990, for details). But these are only shifts of emphasis within two continuing truths: the importance of public school and Oxbridge education to social advancement in the contemporary UK; and the importance to the smooth running of the government and the country of connections made between senior figures in their youth — at school, at home and at university.

We need to be clear here on what key mechanisms of co-ordination are at work at the top of UK society, and what are not. It would be wrong to create the impression that the key political, financial, economic and social institutions in the contemporary UK are entirely run and dominated — as arguably they were between the wars — by a closed upper circle. They are not. In the contemporary UK, the 'establishment' understood in that way —

as an 'all pervasive social and political force dominating all parts of the state apparatus ... and drawn from the highly restricted social background of the upper circle ... continues to exist, but in only an attenuated form of its old self' (Scott, 1991, pp.125, 138). The networks binding the privileged together are looser now than once there were. The linkages between the state apparatus and private economic power are no longer as heavily based on family and social connections as they were before 1945. But these exclusive social networks, though looser, still remain — and still retain their importance as sources of power and privilege. Public school attendance and membership of Oxbridge colleges still facilitates access to privilege and power in ways that attendance at state schools and other universities does not. After a century of social reform it still remains the case that — at the most senior positions within the society — the interaction of the large *hierarchical* structures which run the UK is lubricated by a *network* of individuals linked to varying degrees by personal connections, common social circles and shared values. The UK may be run hierarchically, but those who do the running are linked together in complex and important social networks of a non-hierarchical kind.

These ruling networks are not entirely closed however. Rather, ruling circles in the UK are open in at least three ways.

1   Part of the ruling structure has been democratized to a degree; and that which has — that nearest to the state — is in consequence the least immersed in any upper-class or aristocratic embrace. The labour and trade union movement has been the vehicle which this century has broken down some of the walls of privilege: not removing the walls as such, just pushing some of their people through gaps in the brickwork, there invariably to be socialized into the mores of the still dominant social order. Working class men (as trade unionists) sit on the board of the Bank of England, the board of the BBC, and on other advisory committees of the state; and are joined there by a smattering of middle class women and the token black face. But this process of democratization, though important, has not gone very far even in the civil service, as our figures earlier show, and attempts to extend it in recent years have met serious opposition. This last systematic attempt to extend democratic control occurred in the 1970s, when the Labour Party tried very modestly to put worker representatives on the board of industrial firms (tried, that is, to extend the democratization process beyond the confines of the state by introducing a modest degree of industrial democracy). This was totally blocked by a CBI-led campaign of unprecedented intensity (for details, see Coates, 1980, pp.131–42). Democracy, apparently, was good enough for trade unions, but not for industry and finance.

2   Ruling groups in the contemporary UK are not closed in two other ways as well. There is now a significant foreign element in the ruling circles of industry and finance. This has always been true to a degree. The Ford Motor Co. is a classic example of the big foreign firm co-habiting with local industry: and local industry has often turned outside to recruit foreign entrepreneurial skill (a Michael Edwardes, or an Ian MacGregor). But in the 1980s the scale of all this changed, as the foreign presence in industry and finance grew.

3   And, of course, the whole system of economic and social control is open to a limited amount of long-range social mobility — that movement from factory floor to boardroom so beloved of the 'rags to riches' thesis on leader-

ship recruitment. There are examples currently with us — Lord King at British Airways is one; John Major at No. 10 is another. But there are not many. Merchant banking still seems the most closed sector to this kind of leadership recruitment, retailing possibly the least. But as we have seen, these newcomers represent no challenge to the structure of privilege. On the contrary, they assimilate well, and help to give greater longevity and dynamism to the system of privilege they enter. Indeed their presence among the ranks of the great helps in a democratic culture to legitimate the existence of rank itself, and maintains the vital fiction that merit, not birth, is the key to success in the contemporary UK.

In fact the arena of merit lies slightly lower down the social ladder. Just beneath the élite strata there have been very big changes indeed. Here 'a career open to talent' is very much the order of the day. The post-war elongation of lines of industrial command, the fragmentation of managerial tasks, and the need for tighter labour supervision, all combined to open managerial careers to a new service class. These middle managers were recruited in the 1950s and 1960s from working class and lower middle class homes — from boys who went to grammar school and on to university. In fact two new middle classes have been created in the UK in the post-war years, both meritocratic in recruitment and organization. One is a commercial and industrial middle class — employed by private capital — imbued with market values and paid high managerial salaries. The other is a state employed middle class — working in the expanded education, health and welfare bureaucracies of the post-war state. This middle class tends to be less market-oriented, less well-paid, and more left-wing in its politics.

In both cases, the expansion of middle class tasks stimulated social mobility for at least a generation. In the years after the war there were too many spaces to fill, and too many new spaces at that, for all of them to fall to the children of the existing middle class. These spaces were in any case too functional/technical in their tasks to be occupied by the uneducated and the untrained. So into them poured the brightest children of the lower orders. Yet that movement was in large measure a one generational phenomenon. For this new middle class was not only prolific in skill. It was also prolific in children. The lot recruited into new middle class posts in the years of the Fordist boom bred the next generation of managers and schoolteachers in their spare time. The contemporary universe has fewer middle class spaces to fill, and the first generation are in any case still largely in post. When they have gone, the odds are that the posts they vacate will be filled by their own.

So the greater social mobility of the immediate post-war period may not persist: and in any case social mobility in the UK throughout the post-war years has been largely short-scale mobility by white males. Though the expansion of middle management roles in both state bureaucracies and private companies has increased the *absolute* amount of social mobility visible since 1945, the *relative* chances of men from different social classes reaching very senior positions in society has remained virtually unchanged. The Nuffield Mobility Study — the most recent and comprehensive study of post-war social mobility available to us — split the male population into seven classes. It then found that those born into the bottom two classes remained more than three times less likely, and those born in the middle three classes more than twice as unlikely, to end up in the top two classes as those who were born to parents already there. Overall therefore, 'in most institutions the evidence suggests that there has been a broadening of the social base of entrants to lower positions of leadership, but little change at the top' (Salaman and Thompson, 1978, p.283). At the top, now as before, a propertied class remains firmly in control.

The representation of ethnic minorities in the senior echelons of the society is also very limited. There is some; particularly through the Jewish community's concentration on work in the law and in medicine. But the Asian and Caribbean migrations of the post-war years have not turned the UK into a melting pot society. Asian immigrants have generated their own business class. Afro-Caribbean intellectuals and entertainers have occasionally slipped into public prominence. But the power structure in the UK is in every other respect still overwhelmingly white in its composition, attitudes and self-definitions.

It is also overwhelmingly male. Gender patterning has only altered at the margin. Monarchy periodically generates a leading woman — first out of the litter. Politics did so for the first time in 1979 with Margaret Thatcher's long tenure as Prime Minister. But few women have yet come to

Table 3.5   Women in senior positions

(a) Women as a proportion of total staff in various civil service grades

	1979		1982	
	women as % of total	total staff	women as % of total	total staff
Permanent secretary	0	41	0	40
Deputy secretary	2	158	3	143
Under secretary	4	615	5	554
Executive directing (middle)	4	52	2	97
Executive directing (lower)	0	18	3	152
Assistant secretary	5	1,155	4	4,000
Senior principal	3	710	8	4,200
Principal	8	4,456	7	13,900
Senior executive officer	8	8,060	6	22,900
Higher executive	16	22,382	12	50,900
Executive officer	37	47,395	27	132,100
Clerical officer	65	89,436	61	185,900
Clerical assistant	79	75,329	81	119,800

(b) Numbers of women and men holding parliamentary office, 1950–87

	Cabinet ministers		Ministers not in cabinet		Under secretaries		Parliamentary secretaries	
	women	men	women	men	women	men	women	men
1950	0	17	1	15	1	7	0	17
1960	0	19	0	20	0	11	1	16
1968	1	23	2	31	2	15	1	19

	Cabinet ministers		Ministers not in cabinet		women	men
1970	1	17	1	20	0	30
1974	2	19	1	26	2	30
1975	2	21	1	27	3	35
1979	1	21	2	27	1	36
1987	0	22	3	26	4	31

(c) UK university academic staff (full time), by sex, 1984–5

All departments	Women	Men	Women (%)	Men (%)
Professors	101	4,049	2	98
Readers and senior lecturers	614	8,300	7	93
Lecturers and assistant lecturers	4,657	22,022	18	82
Others	1,521	2,928	34	6
All	6,893	37,299	16	84

Source: Reid and Strata (1989).

senior positions in industry and finance. There are no women in charge of merchant banks or big multinationals. Women are beginning to come to positions of prominence in the trade unions. There is some social mobility for women in teaching, in culture and the arts, and just a little in the older professions. But women are still struggling for entry to some of the established institutions of male power — from the Anglican priesthood to the Stock Exchange. The UK is still run by men: and the presence of women in senior positions still has the feel of the token and the exception.

Men of power: John Major's cabinet, April 1991

That is why it is still possible to say that the UK is run — in the main — by a tiny strata of middle-aged men — by a generation born in the 1930s and 1940s — a generation whose attitudes were forged in the years of Fordist prosperity, and who have risen to power in the more difficult conditions of the late 1970s and 1980s. They have taken over from the generation that fought the Second World War, and they will soon give way to a generation forged in the years of Thatcherism. There is generational change here, but no fundamental transformation yet of the social origins and characteristics of those who lead us within each generation.

SUMMARY

- UK society is dominated by a propertied class whose members run most major social institutions.

- This class is open to a degree to entry from outside: by democratically-sponsored figures, elements of foreign ruling groups and the meritocratic. The bulk of social mobility by merit, however, occurs just below the ruling group, into a service class of professional managers and administrators.

- Movement into that strata is largely the preserve of the white male section of the population.

2 'THE RUN'

There is a long standing debate in the social sciences about the relationship between 'structure' and 'agency': between those who see social realities as given sets of relationships into which individuals are inserted (and which they then create/'bear' by the way they see themselves and treat others) and those who give greater weight in social explanation to the role of individual actors, to people making their own history by the autonomy of their own decisions. The powerful often see themselves in this second way: as free agents creating the social order over which they preside. But in reality the powerful invariably enjoy their power because of the positions they occupy in hierarchically-organized social institutions; and those institutions remain to award power to their successors when one generation of the powerful gives way to the next.

If it is that way for the powerful, so it is also for the rest of us. We occupy particular social positions — and experience those positions as our own individuality. We act freely, within the constraint of our resources, only to find that we are shaped in our individuality by the positions we occupy, and by the social forces released upon us. We learn how to behave and think: both from those who have occupied our positions before us, and from those — more powerful in our own generation — who would have us act in particular ways. Neither the traditions of the past, nor the pressures of the present, push us into a dull uniformity; but they do heavily prescribe the parameters within which we are free to shape our lives afresh: and we in our turn, by what we do, by what we say and think, and by what we expect of others, help to reproduce a stable social order which will then mould the generation to come. We are both made, make ourselves, and make others.

This has important consequences for the running of the contemporary UK. The existence of principles of social organization which are universally accepted throughout society as valid (if not always as desirable) both creates the capacity of the society to be run, and sets limits on the direction in which it can be taken. Perhaps the general point is made best by an example. In most families in the UK, it is women who take predominant responsibility for looking after children, and it is men who do not. There is a powerful principle of gender structuring the social division of labour, a principle which is sustained by, and sustains in its turn, a whole cluster of sexist attitudes and practices. The existence of that principle is not the direct product of any one powerful individual/institution — nor indeed is it the product of all powerful individuals/institutions, though many of them help by their attitudes and practices to keep the principle alive. But because that principle exists, it is possible to run the society in a particular way. It is easy, for example, for employers to pay women less when they enter office jobs/factory work, because the women have dual responsibilities (as mothers and workers) which erode their bargaining power as paid employees. But it would not be as easy for employers to promote only women to senior managerial positions. It could be done, of course, but only in the face of powerful resistance and only by the recasting of a whole range of other forms of social provision (most noticeably those for looking after children). It is easier to promote men, and it is men who get promoted — not because men are better than women, but because certain principles of social organization govern how the society is organized, and how therefore it can most easily be run.

Three such principles seem to me to be of particular importance in the shaping of the contemporary UK, and of the way it is run:

1 that material rewards are tied to positions of economic command;

2 that ethnic backgrounds vary in social importance; and

3 that social roles are allocated on the basis of gender.

Class, ethnicity and gender structure contemporary UK society: and because they do, UK society is run in a particular and highly unequal way. It is time now to explore each of these in turn.

2.1 CLASS

The relationship between power, position and income is not just a feature of the top of the social hierarchy. It applies all the way down. Written into the whole way that labour is rewarded in this society are clear sets of social priorities. Only certain forms of work are rewarded materially at all — child care and family sustenance is not, commodity production is. And in the sphere of paid labour, mental work is rewarded more highly than manual labour, and the managerial function more than the labouring one. Labour in plentiful supply is rewarded less than labour which is scarce, and within management, though not in manual work, age normally brings higher rewards. We generally take it for granted that professional skills will be more rewarded than craft skills, that those who supervise will earn more than those they supervise, and that senior management will receive a level of monetary and non-monetary rewards that are systematically denied to those they manage. The whole structure is justified by arguments about incentives, the weight of responsibility and the need (once the structure is in place) to pay the going rate: but in truth the system of wage payments is inherited, is inherently unfair, and can be traced back to the inequalities of power between capital and labour at the start of the process of industrialization.

So one obvious thing to say about UK society in the 1990s is that it is still stratified by *class*, and by being stratified in that way is open to being run by those who occupy superior class positions. The 'agency' and 'structure' dimensions of this are both crucial to our argument here. For individual *social actors*, whether you own capital or not — and if you do not whether you sell your labour power, in what job, for how much — has a critical bearing on your life chances, your existing style of life, and your degree of personal power and control. It is not the only determinant of those things, as we will see in a moment, but it is a crucial one. For the *social structure* as a whole, because of the prior existence of such social inequality, key distinct and definite loci of power are created. It is possible to locate who is likely to exercise social power independently of knowing anything about the actual individuals involved.

The shape of the social structure in a society such as the UK is primarily fixed by the character and development of the economy on which it depends. Changes in industrial structure, work organization and production techniques filter out into broader changes of a class kind. In the post-war UK, we have already seen a number of these linked economic and social changes.

- We have seen a steadily rising productivity in industry after industry since 1945, the production there of ever greater quantities of goods and services. This has meant that — at every level of the class structure — access to goods and services has grown (even when access to status and power has remained largely unchanged). The life-style of a manual worker in the 1980s is likely to be richer in many ways than was that of a senior managerial figure one/two generations ago; and the differences in life-styles between classes has now diminished in significant ways. There is a similarity in dress, in leisure pursuits, and in family concerns between social classes that was largely lacking prior to 1945. There has been a convergence between classes in the quality of housing, consumer durables and services on which they all draw. Significant differences in consumption remain, and the degree of social interaction between classes is still low. In the main, manual workers still socialize with manual workers, professionals with professionals and so on. So the walls of class remain, but it is no longer as possible as it was in 1945 to spot the social position of individuals by their accent, clothing or attitudes. The society *looks* more egalitarian, and thinks of itself as more universally middle class, than it did in 1945. Class differences remain — in income, work experience and access to power and status — but class differences are no longer as visible as once they were.

- Though class divisions are no longer as obvious as they were for the majority of the UK population, the terms on which people enter the labour markets of a capitalist economy continue to be a prime determinant of their effective access to social resources. As we first observed in Chapter 2, income inequality remains an important feature of contemporary UK life, and has changed little — in relative terms — over the post-war period. In 1954 the top 10 per cent of income earners in the UK took 25.3 per cent of total income after tax, and 25 years later still took 23.4 per cent. Over the same period the bottom 30 per cent of income earners took only 11.6 per cent of total income in 1954 and 12.1 per cent in 1979. The bottom group (three times as large as the top group) took only half as much income as top people did, consistently, year after year (see Coates, 1984, p.125); and this pattern of inequality persisted well into the 1980s, as Table 3.6 makes clear.

Table 3.6   The distribution of incomes (percentages), 1976–84

	Quintile groups of households				
	bottom fifth	next fifth	middle fifth	next fifth	top fifth
Original income					
1976	0.8	9.4	18.8	26.6	44.4
1981	0.6	8.1	18.0	26.9	46.4
1982	0.4	7.1	18.2	27.2	47.1
1983	0.3	6.7	17.7	27.2	48.0
Disposable income					
1976	7.0	12.6	18.2	24.1	38.1
1981	6.7	12.1	17.7	24.1	39.4
1982	6.8	11.8	17.6	24.2	39.6
1983	6.9	11.9	17.6	24.0	39.6
Final income					
1976	7.4	12.7	18.0	24.0	37.9
1981	7.1	12.4	17.9	24.0	38.6
1982	6.9	12.0	17.6	24.1	39.4
1983	6.9	12.2	17.6	24.0	39.3
1984	7.1	12.1	17.5	24.0	39.0

Source: Central Statistical Office, *Social Trends* (1986).

Indeed Table 3.6 hints at another feature of income inequality which has been striking in recent years, and which we also mentioned in passing in Chapter 2, namely the way in which poverty intensified in the 1980s. The CPAG has recently estimated that more than 10 million people were living in poverty (defined as at or just over Supplementary Benefit level) in the UK in 1987; and that between 1975 and 1985 poverty in the UK rose more rapidly than in any other EEC country (*The Independent*, 1 November 1990). In fact, 'the gap between the pay of high and low paid employees is now wider than at any time since records began in 1886', as the government's own earnings survey shows. Over the last ten years (from 1980) 'the best paid group has enjoyed a real pay rise sixteen times as large as the worst paid group' (*The Independent on Sunday*, 30 September 1990, p.1).

In the next chapter we will look at the government policies which generated such poverty. What we need to remember now, however, is that these inequalities are the product of more than variations in state activity. Governments can make income inequality grow or diminish, but they cannot by themselves call that inequality into existence in the

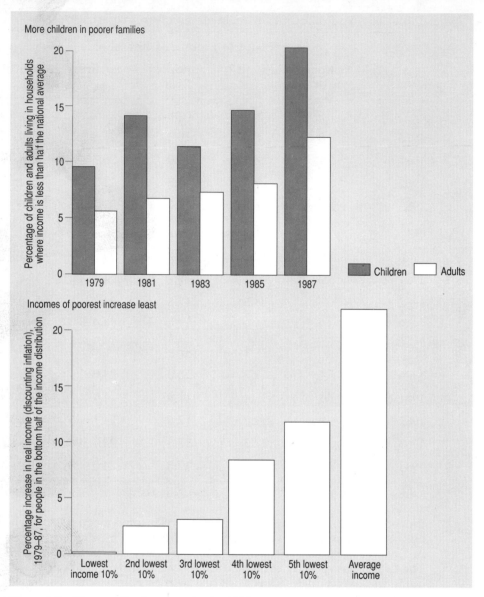

Figure **3.2** *The growth of poverty in the 1980s*
Source: The Independent on Sunday *(29 July 1990).*

first place. Powerful structural forces at work in society do that for them.

The poor — those at the bottom of the income distribution — remain fixed there by their class position. That is, the poor in the post-war UK continue to be those who receive low incomes for paid work, suffer involuntary unemployment from paid work, or are shut out of paid work altogether (by age, disability or domestic responsibilities). There is an important gender and ethnic dimension to this, to which we will come. But gender and ethnicity apart, the factor determining who are the people who actually experience low pay, unemployment and disability is one of *class*. It was — and it remains — individual members of the manual working class who have by far the greatest exposure to low pay and unemployment, and who are left in old age dependent on an inadequate state pension. Class and poverty go together in the UK: and in this respect at least, little has changed since 1945.

- We have seen a systematic change in the balance of manual and non-manual work in the modern labour process, and the associated growth of white collar employment. White collar work was traditionally lower middle class in status in the UK. It attracted, prior to 1945, higher wages, better conditions and greater job security than did manual work. Residues of that privileged past remain. White collar workers still tend to be paid monthly rather than weekly (as manual work still largely is), they tend to start at a later hour, have greater flexibility of hours of work, and face a salary structure which brings higher earnings the longer you are in the job. But these are residues. They are differences which are patchy and in decline. In the main, routine white collar work has now been effectively proletarianized, as the numbers of white collar workers have grown. White collar work in general no longer has a clear differential on wages and conditions when compared to manual work; and white collar workers are now as exposed as other sections of the working class to short time, speed-up and redundancy.

- We have already commented upon the growth of large firms since 1945, and the appearance of a new strata of professional managers — a new 'service class'. These men in particular have earned higher salaries, received better working conditions and non-monetary 'perks', and attracted to themselves higher status than have other white collar workers: and they have used that income and status to buy themselves a particular style of life. It is a way of living which is largely suburban in location, and is built around the spending of large and regular sums on conspicuous consumption. For this group, more than for any other, personal success has been judged by the quality of the house, the age and size of the car, the length and exoticness of the holiday, and so on. At the senior echelons of this new service class, income has been used too to buy privilege: private health care, private leisure facilities and even private education for their children. To 'go private' continues to carry status in the contemporary UK; and where an earlier middle class went private without fuss or pretentiousness, this new middle class tends to consume private privileges as publicly as possible.

- We have also seen a growth in state employment, which has created yet another major new middle class category in the post-war UK — the public sector welfare employee. The range of incomes, jobs and status allocated to its employees by the state in the post-war years has mirrored that found in private sector employment. There are public sector manual workers, cleaners and domestic helps. There are public sector routine white collar workers: in the civil service, in educational administration and in the health service. There are public sector semi-professionals: teachers, probation officers and social workers. And a strata of the public sector is similar to the service class and traditional professionals of the private world: senior managers in health authorities, university vice-chancellors, consultants and general practitioners. The arrival of the state as a major employer in the UK in the post-war years has added to the ranks of those who see themselves as middle class, but it has not fundamentally recast the social relations of production in a more egalitarian way. Hierarchies are, if anything, stronger in the public sector than in the private: and if the ownership of capital is not the ultimate determinant of power there, seniority in bureaucratic structures certainly is.

For even in the public sector, and definitely in the private, it has remained the case down the years in the post-war UK that in a basic sense, capital rules, and that the rules of capital apply. Those who own control those who do not. Those who hire and fire control those who are hired and fired. Those who make and sell control those who buy and consume. Class inequality of this kind does not bring absolute power, of course; and power relationships shift over time. We have already seen this, in our earlier discussion of shop floor power in the 1960s, and of consumerism in the 1980s. Consumers collectively set limits to what can be sold. Workers collectively can limit the terms on which they are hired. Those without capital can democratically regulate the use of private wealth, and determine the terms on which it is retained. What the class system does is to fix the gradient on which the interplay of producers and consumers, managers and workers, owners and non-owners is played out. The owners, managers and producers stand at the top of the hill, rolling their set of interests down the slope, running easily with the gradient; whilst the consumers, workers and non-owners push up — against the slope, working all the time against the gradient just to stand still.

The existence of unequal social relationships of a class kind then enables the society to be run on a day to day basis in ways which give a particular inflection to each of the three modes of decision-making with which we are concerned here. Most obviously it gives a central role to the *hierarchical* allocation of tasks and rewards. Individuals sell their labour power to hierarchically-structured institutions with lines of managerial command and with salary structures which parallel the hierarchy itself. The higher you are, the more you earn. To be employed by such a structure brings money in the first place, and to rise within it brings more. This then enables *market* methods of allocation to work in ways which reproduce class inequalities. People can be left 'free' to buy — because the limit to what they can buy is already predetermined by their income, and their aspirations to buy more can be harnessed to the preservation of class inequality — disciplining them to corporate loyalty and legitimating the whole system as meritocratic. But the different life-styles which the inequalities of work and consumption then sustain divide individuals into different social *networks* — hermetically sealing the rich from the poor — lowering the gaze of resentment and aspiration to the edge of the immediate peer group, and consolidating linkages of a social and attitudinal kind which keep the groups in their place. If things were otherwise — if income equality was the norm, and if productive capital was socially-owned — the running of the society would have to be different. Markets might still work and networks exist, but not in ways that pulled social groups apart: and the role of hierarchical allocation would have to be very differently organized.* But in the contemporary UK, class

---

* See Breitenbach *et al.* (1990) for an exploration of how much inequality is endemic to industrial society, how much contingent on a capitalist way of organizing that society. This particular study presents socialism as a different package of market, hierarchy and network.

inequalities are strong: and daily life is run through a fusion of hierarchical direction, unequal market participation, and powerful social networking.

SUMMARY

- Class positions in UK society are fixed by the social relationships surrounding the production process. Individuals live within given sets of such relationships, which carry their own rules/principles of social allocation.

- There have been major changes in the post-war class structure, created by changes in the underlying economy. There has been a general rise in affluence and an associated decline in the visibility of class divisions. There has been a general expansion of jobs carrying middle class status. Public sector employment has grown; and poverty has persisted.

- Class patterns have changed to a degree, but the importance and impact of class itself has not. Class divisions continue to affect the way hierarchies, markets and networks allocate social resources.

2.2   ETHNICITY AND GENDER

It would be quite wrong to see class as the only structuring variable at play in the organization of contemporary society. Many other principles of social organization run through contemporary UK life as well — offering ways of running the show, but also setting real limits on how it can be run. Resources are allocated by physical ability: this is not a society that is particularly generous to the disabled and to the sick. Resources are also allocated by age: within any one class band, control of resources is denied until 18/21, and tapers off after 60/65. Resources are also allocated by ethnicity and gender.

Indeed, one of the striking features of contemporary society is the gap between its public rhetoric and its private realities. Much of the public discourse now is about equality, freedom, liberty and choice. This is a society run within a liberal, secular and democratic culture, as we will discuss in more detail later. It is certainly not a society, as once it was, in which it is easy to legitimate inequalities which cannot be tied back to the distribution of individual abilities, or to justify inequalities which push individuals down into immense deprivation. With the exception of the monarchy, the justification of social rank by virtue of birth has no general credibility now; nor has the justification of social inequality by virtue of ethnic differences or gender. The 'natural superiority of the white' or of 'the male' which — as late as 1945 — was the normal discourse of politicians and private citizens alike in the UK, is no longer publicly acceptable. Indeed legislation now exists to render it illegal to discriminate on the grounds of gender and ethnicity, or to incite racial/sexual violence. But racial and sexual violence still exists, ethnic and gender discrimination is rife, and privately residues of earlier belief-

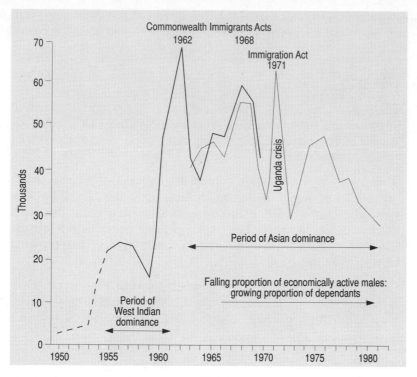

Figure 3.3   *Immigration to the UK, 1950–82*
Source: Hudson and Williams (1989, p.125).

systems abound. It is this gap between public rhetoric and private reality — and the economic and social functions that gap fulfils — that continue to reinforce ethnic and gender discrimination in the contemporary UK.

We can see this very clearly in the social position and life chances of various ethnic minorities in the contemporary UK.

- Migration into the UK by ethnic minority groups from the Caribbean and South Asia was a feature of UK life in the 1950s and 1960s. They were not the only immigrants — steady flows came too from the Old Commonwealth, Ireland and continental Europe — but in a racist society, it was their coming which attracted most comment and most opposition. With their arrival the balance of 'foreigners' resident in Britain altered from its 1951 position (of 1.6 million people living in Britain who were born outside the UK, of whom only 0.2 million were born in the New Commonwealth) to the 1971 census report of 3.0 million (1.2 million of whom were from the New Commonwealth), and to the 1976 position of 1.6 million people of New Commonwealth origin (Coates, 1984, p.174).

- The job levels of Asian and West Indian workers continues to be — as they have been ever since immigration began — substantially lower than those of white equivalents. Immigrant workers are heavily concentrated in industries (textiles, building, car assembly, transport, catering and health care) in which low pay, shift work, unpleasant working conditions and unsocial working hours still prevail.

Asian night-shift worker, Bradford, ca 1981

- Outside the Afro-Asian and Hindu communities, few black workers are to be found higher than at the skilled manual level. Not only are black migrants predominantly manual workers but also more than two-fifths of them are in semi and unskilled jobs. Black workers in this society find themselves disproportionately exposed to 'small scale productive labour in sweat shop conditions' (particularly if they are women), long hours and menial tasks 'under the enervating conditions typical of low skill work in the catering trades and service sectors' (Hall *et al.*, 1978, pp.341–2) or to shift work in heavily capitalized routine assembly/textile industries.

Table 3.7   Socio-economic category by ethnic group (percentages), 1982

Job level	White	West Indian	Asian	Indian	Pakistani	Bangla-deshi	African Asian	Muslim	Hindu	Sikh
Professional, employer, management	19	5	13	11	10	10	22	11	20	4
Other non-manual	23	10	13	13	8	7	21	8	26	8
Skilled manual and foreman	42	48	33	34	39	13	31	33	20	48
Semi-skilled manual	13	26	34	36	35	57	22	39	28	33
Unskilled manual	3	9	6	5	8	12	3	8	3	6

Source: Abercrombie *et al.* (1988, p.255).

There is also very clear evidence of gender structuring. We can see this in the allocation of domestic tasks, the distribution of women in the paid labour force (jobs, pay, promotion) and in patterns of sexual violence.

• Women still carry overwhelming responsibility for the maintenance of the home, for domestic tasks and for the care of dependants. Even in the 1980s, on the latest figures available, men do very little housework and very few take responsibility for childcare. Indeed, of the almost 100,000 one-parent families in the UK, over 90 per cent are headed by women.

Table 3.8 Household division of labour in the UK, 1984

	Allocation of tasks between couples, percentage[1] undertaken by:		
	men	**women**	**shared equally**
Household tasks:			
Washing and ironing	1	88	9
Preparation of evening meal	5	77	16
Household cleaning	3	72	23
Household shopping	6	54	39
Evening dishes	18	37	41
Organization of household money and bills	32	38	28
Repairs of household equipment	83	6	8
Child-rearing:			
Looking after the children when they are sick	1	63	35
Teaching the children discipline	10	12	77

[1] 'Don't knows' and non-responses mean that some categories do not sum to 100%.
Source: Hudson and Williams (1989, p.113).

• Women carry a particularly heavy share of whatever degree of poverty is prevalent. They are more dependent than men on the earnings of others, on state benefits, or on low pay themselves. They live longer on average than do men — so are a majority of the elderly — and indeed of the disabled. In every category of the contemporary poor, there are more women than men; and the figures on the proportion of the poor who are female remain unchanged over the century as a whole, let alone since 1945.

Table 3.9   Women, income and poverty in the twentieth century

	1890s (%)	1980s (%)
Women as a proportion of the economically active population	31	39
Women's earnings as a proportion of total earnings	19	26
Women's share of direct income	15	25
Women's share of total income	45	44
Proportion of Pension/Supplementary Benefit recipients who are women	61[1]	60[2]

[1] 1908.
[2] 1983.

Source: Lewis and Piachaud (1987, pp.47–8).

- In the post-war years more and more women have gone out to work. Between 1881 and 1951 the percentage of women in the work-force aged 15 and over was relatively stable, ranging between 25 per cent and 27 per cent, with higher fluctuations during the two world wars. By 1971 that figure had reached 42.6 per cent, and by then 9.4 million women worked for wages. By 1976, 10 million women worked, 38 per cent of whom had dependent children. Women now constitute 40 per cent of the total labour force, and an overwhelming majority (59.4 per cent) of all married women have a job of some kind.

- But as we saw in Chapter 2, women in paid employment are heavily concentrated in just a few sectors. Over half are to be found 'in just three service sectors: in distributive trades, professional and secretarial work, and miscellaneous services (mainly hairdressing, catering, cleaning and laundry). Even among women employed in manufacturing industry, half work in just four sectors: food and drink, clothing and footwear, textiles and electrical engineering' (Coates, 1984, p.160). About 70 per cent of them work in segregated jobs — work, that is, almost exclusively only with other women — and they earn, on average, no more than two-thirds of the average earnings of male employees. In spite of equal pay legislation, women earn less: because more of them work part time than men, more have broken occupational careers (withdrawing for childbirth and childcare), more are locked in non-supervisory posts, and more are concentrated in industries with traditionally low levels of pay. And as we saw earlier, even in the professions, women fare badly. 'In the civil service, women hold only 10% of the 5000 Assistant Secretary and Principal posts, while in grades at the top of the higher civil service there are only 21 women as against 700 men. In the legal profession, despite steady increases in the recruitment of women, females represent only 12% of both barristers and solicitors' branches of the profession' though this is a 'staggering increase in the proportion thirty years ago, when ... only two or three per cent of practicing lawyers were women' (Cashmore, 1989, p.182).

Table 3.10   Average gross hourly earnings,[1] manual and non-manual employees, full time and part time, by sex, in the UK, 1986

	Manual occupations	Non-manual occupations	All (manual and non-manual) occupations
Earnings in pence per hour			
Women working part time	239	308	279
Women working full time	273	391	363
Men working full time	393	627	489
As % of male full-time hourly earnings			
Female part-time earnings	61	49	57
Female full-time earnings	70	62	74

[1] Earnings include any overtime pay.

Source: Webb (1989, p.138).

So what is going on here? What processes of resource allocation are at work? The main one — as we have defined them here — is *networking*: perhaps more accurately negative networking (or group closure as it is more commonly known in the literature). In each case, contemporary generations inherit sets of attitudes and policies, whole ideologies of racism and sexism. The roots of each are very recognizable. The roots of racism lie in the Empire, in the way in which colonial domination was justified in the nineteenth century. A culture was consolidated then in which the notion of distinct 'races' with distinct characteristics gained widespread currency: and an economic system was put in place which systematically under-developed colonies by extracting their surpluses to the 'mother country'. Colonial under-development spawned migration; and in conditions of labour scarcity in the UK in the 1950s and 1960s kept certain public services alive (in transport and health) and sustained under-capitalized industries (in textiles in particular) as cheap, unskilled, poorly organized and easily exploited colonial labour was locked into the bottom of the UK class structure. Once placed there, the routes up and out (through social mobility) for ethnic labour were then blocked. White workers co-operated to exclude black promotion and white house owners co-operated to head off ethnic expansion into suburbia — so that the general diffusion of ethnic minority populations into the society was aborted. The subtleties of UK racism (where it is perfectly in order to buy foreign food and cheap textiles, but not to live next door or to marry) allowed niches for ethnic business (in retailing and food production as well as in public sector employment) and permitted an ethnic middle class to emerge. But the general result was ghettoization, as a strong network of racial prejudice locked second and even third generation members of ethnic minorities into the very bottom of the indigenous class structure.

The roots of sexism as a culture, and of gender discrimination as a set of social practices, are older still — and remain the common currency of all class and ethnic groups in the contemporary UK. If class/ethnicity is the weave of UK society, sexism is its warp. To be a woman in this society is to experience a heavily prescribed and largely predetermined set of social roles and life chances. To be a working class woman is to know an even more prescribed set. To be a working class woman in an ethnic community is to be more prescribed still. And here the controlling force are men themselves — locked together in complex networks of assumptions, interests and force — and legitimated in their attitudes and practices by the ubiquitous nature of gender divisions in other societies, and in this one, since time immemorial.

The longevity of gender divisions gives them an apparent 'naturalness' which makes them all the harder to refute. But gender divisions, like ethnic ones, are social products, not natural ones; and recent changes in the technology of reproduction makes that particularly clear. Contraception and commercialized baby food have created the conditions in which men and women can rear their children equally and in the numbers they desire. That they do not do so equally, that the burden still falls predominantly on women, and this in spite of a generation of struggle for women's rights — is clear evidence that gender divisions are in the interests of men; and that men do exercise processes of group closure to keep women 'in their place'.

When powerful cultural systems operate in this way — as networks of relationships that shut out ethnic minorities from any normal distribution of their people through the class structure, and lock women into socially subordinate and heavily prescribed domestic roles — these networks reproduce themselves without any central direction and control. Indeed those who formally run this society have recently been prepared to design hierarchical structures to counter the worst excesses of gender and ethnic discrimination. This willingness is very recent, and a product of extensive agitation by counter-networks — of black activists and women's rights campaigners in alliance with progressive elements of the UK labour movement. Until then the State was quite happy to treat women and blacks as second class citizens — as servants and providers to a world predominantly defined as male. In fact, equal opportunities legislation, and the bureaucracies created to implement it, have made precious little inroads into the barriers created by strong networks of racial and sexual prejudice. They have made inroads. They have created routes along which a few male members of ethnic minorities, and a few women, have struggled to more privileged social positions: but these have been positions achieved only after far greater effort than their white male equivalents would have needed to deploy, and only at the cost of leaving other members of their ethnic minority, or other women, behind.

In the world of economics, markets and hierarchies may be the most powerful allocative devices available for the running of the contemporary UK. But in the sphere of the social, networks are extraordinarily strong; and it is their tenacity which gives UK society its conservative tone, and its resistance to change. UK society remains one networked by divisions of class, gender and ethnicity. It remains a society easy to run just as long as the running goes with the grain of these networks, and does not challenge them or disturb them in any fundamental way.

SUMMARY

- Access to social resources (including power) is unevenly divided in UK society by ethnicity and gender. The society ostensibly treats people equally, but in reality women, and even men in ethnic minority groups, face a heavily prescribed and limited set of life chances.

- This inequality manifests itself in the location of most ethnic minority males in the lower half of the UK class structure. It manifests itself too in the persistence of a division of tasks: with women carrying the bulk of domestic responsibilities, and being allowed only a limited and restricted participation in the world of paid work.

- State hierarchies have recently been created to offset the worst elements of this inequality: but their impact has been muted by strong networks of a sexist and racist kind.

3   THE RUNNING

There is thus a very real sense in which this society runs itself. Like all other societies, its social order is largely self-sustaining. There is change — and there are institutions geared to initiating change — but the continuities remain to contain the pace and direction of those who would run the society in a different direction or in a different way. Any form of social order is, at one and the same time, both apparently natural and visibly constructed. It is 'natural' in the sense of occurring automatically — out of the uncoordinated decisions of the multiplicity of its members — and it is natural too in the sense (and to the degree) that those decisions take a persistent and recognizable character, form a regular and unbroken pattern. It is contrived to the degree that the uncoordinated decisions of the multiplicity of its members clash, and have to be regulated; and it is contrived too to the degree that this regulation involves the privileging and toleration of some forms of activity and the suppression and denial of others. To the degree that the social order is 'natural', the society runs itself. To the degree that it is contrived, then the society has to be regulated and run.

The balance between the apparently natural and the visibly contrived is never constant over time, or constant between societies at any point in time. All societies experience periods of fundamental social change — when old ways have to be replaced by new — when problems of social order are general, and the maintenance of social order is difficult and time consuming. The transition from feudalism to capitalism, and the periodic crises of capitalist production, are periods of this kind. Wars and invasions are others. All societies tend to carry too — even in more settled times — particular groups, classes or regions to whom the dominant social order is less satisfactory than it is for others, and to whose appeals for change dominant institutions are resistant. Non-democratic societies tend to experience that pressure periodically from large sections of the population; democratic ones only from particular disadvantaged groups. In the nineteenth century, pre-democratic capitalist societies tended to face popular demands for franchise reform fused with early trade union struggles for recognition and social reform. Twentieth century democratic capitalist ones still experience periodic bouts of worker unrest, and invariably carry from their pre-capitalist past unresolved tensions of a non-class kind: tensions of religion, ethnicity or nation; but they at least contain political institutions geared to the articulation and management of social protest.

Seen in this light, the contemporary UK is more capable of running itself than of needing to be run. Its major periods of industrial change and democratic reform are now one/two centuries gone; and were achieved without violent revolutionary upheaval, without any sharp rupture with existing political and social forms. Nor did military defeat and foreign invasion taint the general legitimacy of the pre-capitalist and pre-democratic UK social order. Instead, UK history shows a general accommodation of monarchy and aristocracy first to capitalist wealth and later to democratic rule: so that contemporary UK political institutions manage to combine the legitimacy of age and tradition with that of formal democratic control. An absolutist monarchy became a constitutional one. An all-powerful aristocracy subsided into a largely redundant House of Lords. A Commons initially denied power against the King, and based on the narrowest of property franchises, gave way to a fully democratic and popularly elected legislative chamber. The prerogatives of monarchy became those of the prime minister — hidden only behind the fiction of what had once been a reality: that the prime minister was actually the monarch's minister, not the people's.

Those changes involved, of course, immense struggle. They were neither easy nor entirely peaceful to achieve. But after 1688 the process of economic, social and political change in the UK was never one marked by moments of violent upheaval. Rather it lent itself to re-interpretation as a story of conservative, incremental and reasonable change. What the UK experienced was a long and slow *liberal* revolution: one which established the liberal right to own property and the liberal right to vote as the twin pillars of what has come to be understood in the UK as the basis of freedom. The *content* of that revolution established in popular consciousness — indeed put there as common sense, as unquestionable truths — a whole nexus of liberal ideas and values (particularly that the *individual* is to be preferred to the collective, the *private* to the public and the *market* to the plan). The *slowness* and *manner* of that revolution shrouded those liberal values, and the social practices — of market capitalism — which they sustained, in a veneer of traditional legitimacy. They created the impression that the UK was both new and old, both revolutionary and conservative; and so pushed into popular attitudes a specification of 'normal and legitimate' behaviour which, on a daily basis, still helps to guarantee the stability of a capitalist social order.

So what is 'normal and legitimate' behaviour as far as UK popular culture is concerned? In the broadest sense what is normal is *capitalist social life*. What is legitimate is whatever is prescribed by *the rule of law*. What is desirable is whatever is specified as *'in the national interest'*. UK society runs itself —

quite automatically — as a liberal capitalist society. It regulates itself — quite automatically for most people most of the time — out of a respect for the integrity and basic fairness of governing institutions. And its people are bound together by a sense of themselves as a nation with a particular character, role and history. There is an extraordinarily powerful and dominant ruling culture in the contemporary UK — one which links people's sense of how it is proper for them to live in their private lives with their understanding of what/whom has the right to set limits on what privately and publicly they are free to do. Three of the key strands of that culture can be indicated as follows.

3.1 CAPITALIST SOCIAL LIFE

When bread shortages occurred in the 1770s, and local merchants put up the price of bread, local people rioted, insisting on a just price, and burning the odd baker's shop to see that price enforced. If bread was worth £x yesterday, it was worth just the same today: neither more nor less (see Thompson, 1961, pp.62–8). For in the early stages of industrial capitalism, there was a clash — not simply between social classes — but between different moralities, different moral economies. People had to learn about the laws of supply and demand, had to be persuaded that it was possible to 'earn a fair day's wage for a fair day's work', had to be persuaded that private profit

The end of 'a fair day's work'

was a socially desirable thing. Now two centuries later we have learnt those things so extraordinarily well that we have reached the point at which it seems literally inconceivable that an industrial society could be run on different lines. Indeed the ferocity of the Cold War against communism gathered its heat precisely here — from the fact that after 1917 an alternative specification to capitalism, an alternative model of industrial organization, was again available, and was being targeted at capitalism's subordinate classes. The 1990s failure of the communist experiment, and the headlong rush to consumer capitalism in Eastern Europe, has thus served to reinforce the lesson begun in the 1770s: that a proper organization of economic and social life has to be built on principles of private property, market exchange and the pursuit of profit.

Echoes of that earlier morality remain, of course, and have been reconstituted by moderate non-revolutionary cultural and political forces in each generation from the 1770s. For some, the source of this morality lies in pre-capitalist social values and institutions of a religious nature (Christianity in the main, but now also in Islam). For others, the source is a critique of the philosophy and practice of liberalism itself, by people who find its unbridled individualism morally repugnant, and its faith in unregulated competition unpersuasive. A managed humanized capitalism remains a major target of Centre-Left political parties in the UK: and a social life tempered by values of compassion, integrity and self-sacrifice remains a concern of more conservative political forces as well. But both impulses are reforming ones aimed at an otherwise widely accepted normal way of living; that people live in nuclear and individualized units, that their goals are largely private to that unit, that they go to work in order to come home to consume, and that as producers and consumers they compete with each other for affluence, status and power. The vast majority of people in the contemporary UK take as axiomatic, unquestionable and totally legitimate the rights of private property. And because they do — because they accept the power structure of a private economy as both inevitable and morally just — and live out their lives within its logics and requirements, then UK society reproduces itself on a daily basis, and without central direction, as a liberal capitalist one in which the 'dull logic of market forces' holds ultimate sway.

3.2 THE RULE OF LAW

Such a Hobbesian culture of atomistic and competitive individuals would, of course, produce anarchy rather than social order were it not tempered by sets of shared understandings about the limits of legitimate modes of behaviour in the pursuit of ends, and shared acceptance of the rights of particular institutions to specify those limits. In the UK, the daily consequence of so relatively tranquil a political past is visible in general public attitudes to parliament, to government and to law. The civic culture in the UK is a particularly passive one. It is very rare for significantly placed social groups to challenge the legitimacy of the existing state, or to question the neutrality and basic morality of the law. There are challenges: those that reflect a different and less tranquil history — in Northern Ireland — and those that reflect a response to a particularly partisan piece of legislation; the struggle against the Industrial Relations Act in 1971 was one such. But as we will discuss in more detail in the next chapter, generally UK society operates on a basic consensus on the nature of politics and the loci of legitimate power. People allow the society to be run by democratically elected politicians, operating through the passing and implementation of law.

It is worth emphasizing that popular attitudes to politics in the contemporary UK are best characterized by passive acceptance than by active participation; and that passivity is vital to the running of the system. This after all is a liberal culture — so politics is marginal. The private is the real, not the public. There is a general distaste for the political, and little interest in it. There is also widespread disenchantment with politicians. Politics is something others do, ostensibly in our interests but actually in theirs. But though politics and politicians have a low status, nonetheless throughout the post-war years in the UK there has been generalized acceptance of the norms of parliamentary democracy, a generalized agreement that laws have to be obeyed (even if made by parties for which you did not vote), that taxes have to be paid, and that state officials are, almost universally, beyond corruption, and beyond the partisan. That is why the 1989 riots against the poll tax were seen as so threatening: because they called into question a more generalized willingness of UK citizens to obey laws regardless of whether they happened to agree with them.

The law and its officials have a particular position and stature in UK political culture — outside Northern Ireland at least. Attitudes to the British police, for example, have been, and remain, different from attitudes to police forces in some other Western democracies: more benign, less cynical, more prepared to grant the police status and respect. Northern Ireland has been less easy to run precisely because the RUC has never managed to win among the Catholic community the status and support commonly given to police forces elsewhere in the UK. Citizens of the UK expect, and generally receive, honest and fair government and administration. Certainly there is little evidence of the corrupt civil servant, the back-hander, the paid-for political favour in post-war UK society. Senior civil servants do often retire into very comfortable jobs in industry and finance — but when they do, the morality of that move is invariably criticized by left-wing sections of the parliamentary élite. For in general in the post-war years, the society has been run — to a remarkable degree — without corruption, without overt favouritism, and by public officials who have been expected to show a high level of personal morality and restraint.

There has been and remains widespread acceptance too that only certain forms of political pressure and protest are legitimate: that it is illegitimate to resort to violence in the pursuit of political ends, that civil disobedience (if tolerated at all) has to stay within the bounds of peaceful protest, and that it is quite wrong to use economic power for political ends. This latter has been — and indeed still is — of particular importance to the way UK society is run and governed, and is a highly sophisticated and discriminating set of general beliefs. Certain forms of economic pressure on government are accepted as legitimate — indeed are thought of less as pressure than as facts of life. This would certainly be the case with movements of money and capital in/out of the City of London. But the equivalent use of industrial pressure by trade unions would be seen as illegitimate. In the post-war period individual strikes have often attracted popular support (when the government was the employer and the groups involved were popular for other reasons — nurses and other health workers, for example); but invariably that support has quickly dissipated if the strike moved away from immediate questions of wages/conditions into wider questions of public policy, or if the strike became in any way violent. Then the norms of parliamentary democracy are quickly reapplied in the public mind. In this way, public attitudes to trade unionism have — and continue — to set real limits to the way the UK is run, and to the groups or institutions by whom that running can legitimately be done.

3.3 'THE NATIONAL INTEREST'

British history — and the way it is retold — also reinforce a particular set of attitudes to the nation, and hence a willingness to be run by whoever manages to lay claim to the interests of the nation as a whole. In the main, the British learn their history as a story of progress, enlightenment and democracy. They learn about the eighteenth and nineteenth century Empire as a civilizing force, now transmuted into a Commonwealth of Nations which bridges the First World and the Third. They learn to think of the UK as a world power, with a leadership role at world level — different from other European nations of equivalent size (and certainly from any Asian/ African society) by virtue of geographical location, early industrialization, imperial past and particular culture. They learn of apparently specific national characteristics: of restraint, stoicism and integrity (the stiff upper lip). They learn, that is, to accept as quintessentially English a general cluster of self-definitions of the English upper class at a particular moment of imperial supremacy. Political self-definition in large parts of the UK is still, in the end, firmly rooted in the late Victorian era. It is white. It is imperial. It is xenophobic.

Time has not entirely frozen at 1890, however. The twentieth century has added new layers of self-definition — more popular and more democratic — to this imperial core. From the contrast between inter-war labour moderation in the UK and the 'excesses' of fascism and communism abroad, the British have learnt to praise their own capacity for political moderation, for problem-solving by rational discussion. From the courage and victory of war against fascism, the British have acquired an image of themselves as powerful though small — a Dunkirk spirit of inevitable if delayed superiority. And from the 1945–51 settlement, the British have come to see themselves as pioneers — in the pursuit of welfare provision, in the capacity to provide the best care for their own people. Pride in everything British has since then extended to pride in new British institutions — in the National Health Service as well as in the monarchy, and in universal education as well as in the Commonwealth of Nations.

3.4 CHANGE AND CHALLENGE IN THE DOMINANT CULTURE

We need to note four things about these clusters of belief, in addition to their specific content:

1 The first is that their existence both creates possibilities for how the UK can be run, and sets real limits on the direction in which it can be taken. Ideas, as well as institutions, help to mould the terrain on which resources are allocated in the contemporary UK.

2 The second is that the 'writ' of these ideas is not universal. Collectively they constitute a dominant political and social culture. But powerful counter-cultures, and the social forces to pursue them, exist too:

(a) Resistance to the inevitability of 'capitalist social life' has been, and remains, very vestigial, ephemeral and episodic in the contemporary UK. Dominant attitudes of support for capitalism extend out to encompass the Left as well as the Right. Challenges come only within its parameters, on the degree of management of capitalism (at party level) and against specific manifestations of capitalist excess (at the economic and social level). This is no longer a society in which any revolutionary socialist culture/force has any major presence. But it remains a society in which — the lower down the social hierarchy you go — the more you meet resignation and fatalism about capitalism and its imperatives, and the less you find enthusiastic identification with them (on this, see Mann, 1982; Beynon and Nichols, 1977; and Westergaard and Resler, 1975). Indeed, 'the evidence of the 1980s is that subordinate groups still

Clash between mourners and RUC officers at an IRA funeral, 1988

subscribe to a radical egalitarian and oppositional ideology' (Hill, 1989, p.6) — if not a full-blown anti-capitalist one. There is still plenty of evidence of popular unease with the distribution of wealth and privilege in the contemporary UK — plenty of evidence of what Hill calls 'cynicism about the democratic process' and radicalism on the way the UK is and ought to be run (ibid., p.7).

(b) In particular, there is considerable resistance to British nationalism. The imperial culture we have just described is almost exclusively an English one, and in reality a predominantly London-centred phenomenon. Antipathy to London is evident in the English regions, but is qualitatively greater in Wales, Scotland and Northern Ireland. Scottish nationalism in particular has at times in the post-war period been a political force setting limits on the degree to which the running of Scotland from London was seen as in any way legitimate. And in Northern Ireland the right of London to rule at all has been, and remains, under question, from a section of the Catholic community in what are still defined — by the IRA at least — as the six occupied counties.

(c) For groups do exist in the UK whose politics take them beyond the norms of parliamentary democracy. In so stable, conservative and ordered a society as the UK, we find the longest running civil war in Western Europe. We also find at times a highly militant and well-organized labour movement willing to use industrial power for political ends. A significant part of the UK's domestic political agenda in the 1980s was largely shaped by state determination to break the industrial and political power of organized trade unionism (as we will see in the next chapter); but no such resolution of the struggle in Northern Ireland loomed into view in that decade.

3   The strands of dominant culture which we have emphasized here have themselves been subject to change over time. The interpretation of each by the majority of the UK population does not take the same form now as it did in 1945. Attitudes to capitalism, to law and to nation have altered, to give each a new inflection. Years of full employment and rising living standards have added a hedonism (a preoccupation with consumption and leisure) missing from the more puritanical work-ethic and modest expectations of life under capitalism characteristic of the generation that fought the Second World War. That same sustained experience of affluence, peace and job security has eaten away too at traditional attitudes to authority and to social rank. UK society — while still law abiding in the main — is a less deferential and disciplined society than it was a generation ago (see Jowell *et al.*, 1984–90, for details). And though nationalism remains an extraordinarily powerful force in contemporary UK society, attitudes to foreigners have altered over time: as UK citizens have travelled abroad more, as television has linked culture to culture, and as the experience of wartime mobilization and peacetime national service is shared by smaller and ever ageing sections of the population. It is not as easy as it was to run the UK by relying on themes of national glory and obedience to traditional sources of authority. Contemporary UK culture is too hedonistic, individualistic, materialistic, secular and pragmatic for that. People these days are highly instrumental in their attitudes to work, authority and nation. They have to be mobilized on the basis of their own highly-privatized self-interest. No doubt in one sense

that was true in 1945 as well, but in the 1990s people have far higher expectations of life than they did then; and they expect to be rewarded accordingly.

4   Which brings us to the fourth and final element of that dominant culture which needs to be examined — namely the way in which its specifications are maintained. This apparently natural cluster of beliefs and practices is in fact a repeatedly reconstructed and enforced culture. There is enforcement and there is reconstruction. The enforcement is done — when challenged — by the coercive arm of the state: by the police and the army. (It is the army who hold the line in Northern Ireland, and the police who broke the 1984–5 miners' strike.) The reconstruction is done by institutions of ideological indoctrination and socialization: formerly (and to a degree still) by the old triad of family, church and school, but now increasingly by a new one of television, government and press. UK society runs itself, not simply because of the weight within it of particular sets of ideas, but because those ideas are consciously moulded by key institutions. And of those institutions, by far the most important is the State. That is why we need now to turn to look at the state itself, to see how (and to what degree) the post-war UK has been run by those at its political centre.

SUMMARY

- Societies like the UK in large measure run themselves, on lines fixed by the shared assumptions of the people who make them up. Dominant cultures hold the key to the way societies operate.

- Dominant ideas in the post-war UK have included: a particular view of the inevitability and legitimacy of capitalist modes of economic and social organization; the importance and integrity of law; and the particular power of the English nation.

- Those ideas, though dominant, have never been without challenge; and over time their particular inflection has shifted into a more libertarian form. Dominant ideas still need to be managed; and the state has a key role in that management.

CHAPTER 4:   THE STATE

Our argument throughout has been concerned with the location and use of power in the contemporary UK, and with the restraints imposed upon its use by the processes, institutions, social groups and ideas that structure the contemporary world. We have argued that fundamental economic and social processes generate unequal distributions of power, embodied in the differential capacities of individuals and social groups to achieve their own goals, and to shape the behaviour and goals of others. We have seen that the most fundamental of those processes has been that of the *market* — organized on capitalist lines — persistently obliging individuals and groups to survive and progress by repeatedly immersing themselves in never ending circuits of production and exchange. We have seen too the emergence, from those circuits, of key economic and social institutions — *hierarchically* organized in the main — whose leading personnel have acquired through their bureaucratic position levers of power over the lives and thoughts of those excluded from such positions of privilege. And we have seen too how the workings of both market forces and hierarchical structures have been moulded by the existence of powerful social and ideational *networks*: social networks largely of a class and gender kind, that have determined access to senior hierarchical positions; and networks of ideas, that have enabled both the powerful and the powerless to come to terms with the inequalities of market power and hierarchical position.

The relationship between networks, markets and hierarchies in the contemporary UK is a complex one. It is very difficult to trace the causal connections between the power which derives from the ownership of capital and that which comes from seniority in hierarchical structures, and it is still more difficult to see how exactly class inequality is linked to dominant patterns of ideas. There are simple models around, of course. One would say that there is no connection — there is just a plurality of social forces at play in contemporary society, and any one individual will have some involvement in a number of these — which collectively will shape his/her life situation and status. Another — quite different — would say the reverse; that there is a simple connection and organizing factor behind all this complexity: that of the ownership of capital. Those who own capital have power, control key social and economic institutions, dominate culture and the media, and effectively constrain the state. There is, in other words, a simple pluralist and a simple Marxist view of contemporary reality.

If I were asked to choose between the two, I would go for the Marxist before the pluralist; but I would prefer not to be asked to make a choice of that kind. For there is much mileage in pursuing a complex fusion of these two models, in building an ostensibly pluralist yet basically Marxist view of state power (on this, see Coates, 1984, pp.222–8). The Marxist position cannot be ignored. The outer constraints on the use of state power do lie, it seems to me, with those who own capital. Yet much of what goes on in contemporary UK society lies within those constraints, and is not easily reducible to them. Not all institutions serve capital, not all governmental decisions are capital-dominated, and dominant patterns of belief still leave space for a radical voice. The 'realities' of contemporary capitalist economic life set real limits on how the society can be run; but they do not thereby determine its precise line of march. About that there is, and will remain, fierce political argument. Indeed it is the quintessential role of the state to resolve that dispute, and to fix the general strategic goals for the society as a whole, within the limits imposed by the place of the UK in the dominant world order. How the state resolves that dispute will turn, in part, on the balance of social forces that immediately surround it, and on its own particular political predispositions. It will be resolved, that is, by reference to broader sets of political attitudes and expectations within the democratic electorate. Strategies have to be fought for, and won, since they involve the mobilization of an entire population — and it is the job of the state in a modern capitalist economy and society to do that mobilization.

It is time therefore to look at the state — and at its role in the running of the post-war UK: and to do so in ways which build upon the materials and arguments we have established in the chapters which have gone before. If you look back to Chapter 1 you will see that there we emphasized the crucial impact on UK life in the post-war period of two broad features of the international order — one political and military, the other economic. Those two parameters continue to provide a useful framework for a consideration of the way in which successive British governments have attempted to run the post-war UK. In the sphere of international politics and military relationships, UK policy has shifted down the years — but only with reluctance and without seriously dividing the major political parties. A bi-partisan and reluctant retreat from Empire has been followed by an equally reluctant and almost as bi-partisan a shift of focus from America to Europe. In the sphere of the economic, bi-partisanship was also the order of the day until the early 1970s. One particular economic project held general support. It no longer does. How the UK should be run economically is now among the most contentious of issues in contemporary UK politics. If we are to see how the UK is run by its state, we need to understand both the role of the UK on the world stage, and the way political power has been used to effect national economic change. We also need some sense of how those two organizing preoccupations of successive British governments — with their world role and with economic reform — interact.

1 THE SEARCH FOR A WORLD ROLE FOR THE POST-WAR UK

As we said in Chapter 1 the UK emerged from World War II with a considerable gap between its world role and the resources available to sustain that role. UK armed forces played a critical part in the defeat of fascism. The UK stood — with the two big superpowers — as one of the 'big three' in all the negotiations on the post-war settlement. In 1945 the Empire was intact. UK forces were distributed world-wide; and UK national pride was at its peak.

In that climate, policy-makers within the UK state settled into a particular set of assumptions about the post-war world role of the London government and its attendant military forces. The UK state was by that time in the hands of the Labour Party, but their ostensibly socialist credentials did not bring any major change in overall state perspectives. The UK was to remain a major military power. The Empire was to be retained as far as that was possible. The wartime alliance with the United States was to be maintained into the peace: and the UK was to join with the USA in resisting any further extension in the world role of the USSR as a military power, and of communism as an ideology. UK policy-makers looked out to the Atlantic, not into Europe, in 1945. The union of English-speaking peoples — the USA, the Dominions and the UK itself — were to be the bedrock of world peace: and the role of the United Kingdom on the world stage was to keep that world free from communism.

Armed with views of this kind, the Labour governments of the late 1940s made a number of key strategic decisions. They were instrumental in the setting up of NATO in 1949, as a military alliance to combat communism. (Later Conservative governments joined equivalent, if shorter-lived, regional military alliances in South East Asia and the Middle East.) The Attlee government decided — and decided secretly (even a majority of the cabinet were not informed) — to establish Britain as an independent nuclear power: and the first H-bomb was exploded by British forces in the South Pacific in 1952. The Attlee government conceded independence to India and Burma in 1946, but retained the rest of the Empire intact; and the government actually fell disputing the internal consequences (for the financing of the NHS) of their decision to back the American defence of South Korea against invasion by North Korea and by Chinese Communist forces in 1950–1. Though the Attlee government did pull UK troops out of Greece, and left that particular 'communist problem' to the Americans — and reluctantly withdrew troops from Palestine to allow the creation of the state of Israel — in every other respect the Attlee government attempted to maintain as extensive and independent a military and political role on the world stage as the UK had become accustomed to between 1939 and 1945.

The decades that followed then forced upon successive Conservative (and later also Labour) governments the realization that so extensive a role could no longer be sustained. The 1950s were particularly educative in this respect. A series of colonial wars (in Malaya, Kenya and Cyprus) forced upon British public opinion (and British colonial administrations) the recognition that imperial control was no longer acceptable to vast swathes of the Third World; and that the price of retaining the Empire — in terms of soldiers killed, atrocities perpetrated and dollars spent — was too high. By 1960 a Conservative Prime Minister was prepared to go to Pretoria, to welcome the 'winds of change' in Southern Africa; and to preside over an orderly retreat from Empire. That retreat was not without its hiccups, but after 1960 these came only when indigenous settler groups resisted the arrival of majority rule. Rhodesia declared UDI in 1965, under Ian Smith, to that end, and had to be pulled back into line by a bloody and prolonged civil war. The UK played no direct part in that victory. On the contrary, its 'sanctions' against the white Rhodesian rebels were blatantly porous and partisan. But at least in Rhodesia, black majority rule was eventually established, and Zimbabwe (as it became) was readmitted into the *Commonwealth of Nations* — a loose coalition of countries united only by a vestigial loyalty to London and a shared

British paratroops en route to Suez, 1956

legacy of UK colonial rule. South Africa left the Commonwealth in 1960 to avoid pressure to follow a similar black majority path, and remained an international pariah into the 1990s: and Nationalist unrest still continues in Northern Ireland, in the unresolved legacy of the UK's first attempt at decolonization under pressure in the twentieth century — the 1922 retreat of the UK from the rest of Ireland. But otherwise the UK did effect a largely peaceful retreat from Empire after 1950, shedding its colonial responsibilities if not yet the feelings of white supremacy which those colonial responsibilities engendered in the past. The Empire has now gone, but the 'mentality' of Empire has not.

If this retreat from Empire can be considered among the success stories of the UK's post-war adaption to new conditions and new constraints, its attempts to maintain an independent military role for itself ought not to be seen in quite that light. In 1956 UK armed forces invaded Suez — in a classic piece of gunboat diplomacy — only to be forced into a humiliating retreat, not by Egyptian resistance but by US financial pressure. The growing dependence on the United States — and the associated demotion of the UK to the status of junior partner within NATO — was then reinforced in 1960 by the UK's failure to develop its own independent missile-launching system (Blue Streak) and its decision instead to go cap-in-hand to Washington to buy Polaris. The Americans very reluctantly allowed that sale to take place, allowed the UK, that is, to retain an independent nuclear capacity within NATO: and indeed in the late 1980s allowed the UK to replace its ageing Polaris fleet of submarines with the American Trident. But by then it was clear that the UK was almost exclusively dependent on the United States for permission to use the weapons it had purchased. By then the UK still had the status of a nuclear power, but hardly the substance; and when the Russians wanted to talk about reducing nuclear stockpiles, they talked to the Americans alone.

This hankering of significant sections of British public and élite opinion for a return to older days of imperial glory still remains a potent internal political force, and helps to explain both the fact (and the popularity) of the Falklands campaign in 1982. Into the 1980s the UK continued to maintain a capacity for limited military action on a global scale, and indeed the Thatcher government was the first of America's NATO allies to send armed forces to the Gulf in 1990 in support of the American military initiative there. The word 'support' is the key one here. For as successive UK governments lost their economic and military capacity for independent world action, they clung tenaciously to the 'special relationship' with the USA which their predecessors had forged in the 'dark days' of the Second World War. They hung onto a world role designed in the 1940s: at a moment of immense Cold War tension. It was the Cold War which

> froze the European scene when Britain was only half-way down: still the victor and occupying power of 1945, still at the top table, one of the 'Big Three'. And it was this 'frozen tableau' which 'allowed us to nourish illusions' about the UK's own importance, and about a supposed 'special relationship' with the United States for far too long.
>
> (Garton Ash, 1990)

In the process, a popular mythology of untroubled wartime alliance between the two English-speaking democracies was used to sustain and justify close support for US foreign policy initiatives. Even though the 'special relationship' was more evident as a determinant of foreign policy in London than in Washington — from where Western Europe was increasingly seen as a whole, and largely German and French in leadership   UK governments claimed a special degree of influence over US policy-makers. Harold Wilson tried that role — as mediator — very unsuccessfully during the Vietnam War. Margaret Thatcher forged a more effective and certainly personally closer relationship with Ronald Reagan 20 years later. And that 'closeness' manifested itself in UK willingness to allow Cruise missiles into Britain in 1980, to allow US warplanes to fly from Britain to bomb Libya in 1987, and as we have just said, to send British forces quickly to the Gulf to support President Bush in 1990.

The underside of this pro-Americanism in UK foreign policy since 1945 has been a lack of enthusiasm in UK governing circles for closer UK involvement with the countries and supra-national institutions of Western Europe. Centuries of history, and the persistence of the Channel, continue to sustain in British popular culture the notion that Europe starts at Calais — that the off-shore position, naval power and imperial possessions of the UK set it apart from the rest of Western Europe. In the past they certainly did. Fighting across the Channel was more common than uniting above it. But in the post-war years, Western European economic (and to a limited degree, political) unity has been a growing force. The EEC was created without UK membership: and here, as in other areas of more obviously economic policy, that 'lost opportunity' in the 1950s shaped much of UK international economic policy thereafter.

'It is only now being fully appreciated how the Cold War gave [the United Kingdom] an international status beyond its real importance in the post-war world; and how its ending leaves Britain with a diminished international role' (*The Sunday Times*, 29 July 1990). The issue facing the UK in the 1990s is how best to protect and enhance its role inside a European Community under effective German leadership: but two decades ago the issue of Europe was understood here in quite a different way. The question then was not how to work *inside* Europe but rather whether to *participate* in the European Community at all; and the differing answers to that question split both the major political parties internally into pro- and anti-European lobbies. In the end, after an initial French veto on UK membership, the UK did join — in 1973 — and its membership was confirmed in a referendum in 1975. But anti-European feeling (and particularly unease about German economic and political power) remains intense; and governments continue to dispute internally the degree of involvement which the UK should undertake in an increasingly integrated and now much larger European Community. In the capitals of Europe, the UK is often seen as a 'reluctant European', and the impression is not a false one. UK governments are now having to learn how to gain a degree of international influence by participating in a club of European states, after more than two centuries of being used to having that influence as an independent world power. The institutions of the European Community are the focus for much of the resentment generated by this change, but they are hardly its cause. That cause lies deeper: in the loss of world power to which EC membership is now reluctantly seen as the only intelligible response.

The unease about European integration will dominate UK politics in the 1990s, but its existence also reminds us that there has been unease about UK foreign policy before. There was unease — in the late 1940s — among left-wing Labour MPs and their supporters — about the close connection being forged with the USA, about strident anti-communism and about NATO. These MPs sought a 'Keep Left' international policy of non-alignment; and though defeated then, were one of the strands feeding into the Campaign for Nuclear Disarmament which flourished in the UK between 1956 and 1963, and again in the 1980s. On each occasion, a strong undercurrent of left-wing opinion challenged the UK's place in, and acceptance of, Cold War definitions of the international order. These anti-nuclear groups were preoccupied with the creation by the UK of an independent, non-aligned foreign policy — one that was not set by governments elsewhere, but was democratically determined within the UK itself; and in their search for independence of that kind, they often found themselves in strange and uneasy agreement with groups on the far right of the political spectrum. Certainly when the question of EC membership surfaced, a broad coalition of left-wing forces resisted it on the grounds that it involved a loss of national sovereignty. For 20 years after 1960, official Labour Party policy opposed EC membership: and in the referendum of 1975, the bulk of the Labour Party rank and file campaigned against membership in alliance with right-wing political forces equally opposed to the loss of formal sovereignty involved.

What the Labour Party objected to about EC membership in the 1960s and 1970s was the UK's immersion in a European trade club built on liberal market principles. They saw in the terms of the Treaty of Rome a further barrier to their ability, when in office, to manage the economy in a social democratic (they would say, socialist) way. Conservative enthusiasm for Europe in those years was similarly fuelled by the EEC's existence as a trade club of this kind. But as the EC has come increasingly under German and French social democratic leadership (with even the German CDU keen to use state intervention in economic affairs), and as moves to European monetary and political union have quickened, Brussel's capacity to act as what Margaret Thatcher once called a 'backdoor route to socialism' has altered party attitudes inside the UK itself.

The Labour Party has now come to terms with Europe. Only a vestigial group of left-wing MPs maintain an anti-EC stance. But the unease on the Conservative Right about European integration remains far stronger. When the ultra-Thatcherite Nicholas Ridley spoke out against German power in 1990 (and lost his cabinet post in the process) he spoke for an important constituency of right-wing opinion. Indeed there is something of a paradox here. Left-wing opposition to Europe has been largely based on questions of *sovereignty*, that of the Right on the *loss of an independent world role*. The Left has now come to terms with European integration, as they realize that sovereignty can best be defended by being part of a larger and more effective economic and political unit. But as Margaret Thatcher's unexpected fall from power in 1990 made clear, the Right's hankering for national independence and imperial glory can find no such easy resolution: which is why the UK enters the 1990s with the Labour Party (the old opponent of EC membership) more committed to participation in Europe than the Conservative Party which took the United Kingdom in originally.

SUMMARY

- The UK began the post-war period as a major world power, and adopted military and colonial policies which fitted its perception of itself as such.

- Subsequent readjustments to the UK's diminished circumstances have included the retreat from Empire, the loss of effective control of the UK's independent nuclear deterrent, and the attempt to sustain a 'special relationship' with the United States.

- This 'Atlanticist' vision has left successive UK governments less than fully enthusiastic about involvement in the growing movement for Western European integration: and though that is where the UK's future seems inexorably to lie, it is a future which is more difficult for right-wing political forces to accept than it is for left-wing ones.

2 THE SEARCH FOR A PROSPEROUS ECONOMY

As we have already seen, not all the forces obliging the UK state to curtail its world role were global in origin. There were local sources of weakness as well. The global constraints were largely political (American pressure, movements of national independence, and so on) but economics was never far away. Certainly the rise of Europe as the new location for UK international activity in the 1990s was a rise predicted on the expansion and prosperity of particularly the West German economy. The balance of the political and the economic among the internal UK sources of weakness was, however, quite different. Internal political pressure to alter the UK's world role was almost always — as we have just seen — episodic, marginalized and ineffectual. But the economic forces obliging the UK to curtail its world role were overwhelming; and in their ubiquity produced a quite different pattern of political division within the UK itself.

On the shift from Atlanticism for Europeanism, the main line of political cleavage has always been *within* political parties. On the strategies for economic reconstruction it has largely been *between* parties. On the external role of the UK in the post-war years, national politics has been dominated by a broad consensus, challenged of late only by an anti-European minority in each of the two major political parties. On the question of economic management and reconstruction, there was a broad consensus between the parties until 1970 at least, but since then the sharpest of divides. For unlike the world of international relations, the world of economic management has seen not one dominant set of policy orientations but two — one social democratic, one neo-liberal — and if we are to grasp the options facing the contemporary state, we need to put those projects into play here.

2.1 SOCIAL DEMOCRACY

The broad political consensus on the management of the UK economy that was such a feature of UK national life between 1945 and the early 1970s has attracted many labels. It has been called 'Butskellism' — after the last Labour Chancellor of the Exchequer from the 1940s (Hugh Gaitskell) and his immediate Conservative successor (R.A. 'Rab' Butler) — to signify the broad party agreement that it involved. It has been labelled Keynesian (after the economist with whose writings government policy was most closely associated) or even corporatist (to signify its dependence on the voluntary co-operation of trade unions and organized business in the running of the economy). We shall label it 'social democracy' — partly to emphasize its centrality to the Labour Party's understanding of its post-war role, partly to differentiate it from the neo-liberal Conservatism with which in the end it would be replaced.

AND NOW—
WIN THE PEACE

VOTE LABOUR

Labour Party election poster, 1945

But no matter how labelled, the content of the package is clear enough. At its core were certain social and economic responsibilities accepted by the Coalition government in the last years of the war: responsibility for full employment, rising living standards, international competitiveness and generous welfare provision. Those guarantees were made possible by the wartime experience of government economic and social control, and by the availability — in the writings of John Maynard Keynes — of an economic theory which explained why and how governments could regulate private capitalism's institutions to achieve socially desirable ends. In the event, it did look immediately after the war that the economic conditions for the realization of wartime promises were no more congenial than those which followed 1918: but this time the Labour government was more determined and more fortunate. It was more determined: it nationalized a large series of unprofitable private industries, maintained for a while a whole series of wartime controls and rationing systems, and persevered in its creation of a National Health Service and broad social security net in spite of fierce opposition from Conservative quarters. It was also more fortunate, in that the United States was on hand with aid to lubricate the growth of world trade, and with new production technologies to generate rapidly rising labour productivity. The price of US help — as we have seen — was immersion in the whole Western anti-communist military, economic and ideological system. Keynesianism and the Cold War went together. But at least between them they produced a 25 year spell of unbroken UK prosperity.

The social democratic management of a rapidly growing capitalist economy in the 1950s and 1960s gave the state a particular and distinctive set of tasks. Direct administrative controls of investment, labour utilization and working methods were quickly abandoned, to be replaced by the indirect encouragement of economic growth and full employment by the management of Aggregate Demand. Governments altered the volume of their spending and borrowing, and used interest rate adjustments to affect levels of investment and consumer demand, to create the conditions in which firms could flourish and prosper, and in which jobs could be plentiful and secure. Since this was what, in the broadest sense, Keynes had advocated in the 1930s (and what his adherents insisted on in the 1950s) the policy package became known as Keynesianism; and Keynes himself was lionized posthumously as the mind which had found the key to the contradictions of capitalism.

The general set of responsibilities adopted by post-war governments then committed state action in other ways as well. A large public sector turned the economy from a wholly capitalist to a more mixed one; and government employment grew in the fields of education, health and social welfare. Governments came to be expected to give assistance on a large scale to industrial investment, and research and development, and to offset the regional imbalance in jobs and prosperity associated with undirected private capitalist investment. A generation of voters emerged used to full employment and to low but steadily rising living standards, a generation trained by the claims of politicians and the visible activity of governments to lay responsibility for their prosperity (and its continuance) on government itself. And in such a situation, governments were drawn into increasing involvement in the regulation of wider and wider areas of social life: funding massive housing programmes, establishing rent controls, liberalizing sexual relationships, and enforcing private competition. The cumulative consequence of this activity, of course, was that greater and greater percentages of the GNP passed through the hands of, or were directly generated by, the various agencies of the state. (The figures for that state spending in the period of social democracy were first reproduced in Table 2.4 in Chapter 2, to which you might now briefly refer.)

This particular pattern of spending and economic activity was not unique to the UK in the 1950s and 1960s. Governments in each of the major capitalist industrial powers played similar roles to varying degrees. For there was a close fit between greater government expenditure and the needs of key economic institutions in the post-war world order. Big companies needed a stable framework of exchange rates and steadily expanding internal markets if they were to realize the profits locked into the large volumes of goods they could produce in the new semi-automated production systems of the Fordist period. Strong self-confident trade unions were in a position to demand full employment and rising real wages; and the population as a whole had come to expect extensive welfare provision and growing affluence from the politicians they elected. Keynesianism in its widest sense — of big government — was a key element in the Fordist accumulation regime. That regime did not abandon markets as key allocators of economic resources. On the contrary, it required that markets grow in volume and scale. But market allocation was increasingly regulated and hedged about by political initiatives in the Fordist period. Large, hierarchically-organized, non-market driven state bureaucracies were established to educate, keep healthy and win the support of the labour force: and big government, full employment and buoyant home markets bred large companies and large unions free to a degree from direct market pressures. Their explicit agreement on wages and prices — a corporatist (or *networked*) managing of the Keynesian economy — was implicit in the shifting balance of power brought into market relationships by 25 years of state-supervised full employment and rising prosperity. It was a corporatist bias, moreover, which was to surface more visibly, in the UK at least, as the social democratic period neared its end.

Social democratic political management of the economy in the post-war UK moved through three phases: of establishment, ascendancy, and finally disintegration. In its period of ascendancy, in the 1950s, governments actually retreated from the degree of direct state intervention commonplace during the Second World War and the early post-war period. Rationing was steadily abolished. Incomes policies between 1948 and 1951 were not repeated. The nationalization of large industries stopped with the state purchase of the steel industry in 1950: and state direction of investment and labour was replaced, as we have said, by indirect controls of a fiscal and monetary kind. But by the mid 1950s, in the UK at least, two large limitations to that particular version of Keynesianism were already coming into view. The scale of government spending overseas, and the low levels of investment in manufacturing plant and equipment in the UK, were by then combining to produce balance of payments problems. There were in fact a whole series of balance of payments crises after 1955 (as we saw in Chapter 2, and as is visible there in Figure 2.1). Moreover, as we also saw in Chapter 2, full employment was eroding managerial power at the point of production, allowing inefficient labour practices to persist and wage-led inflation to emerge in the competitive heartland of British manufacturing industry. Dwindling competitiveness abroad, and wage drift at home, combined by 1961 to move the social democratic management of the UK economy into a more corporatist phase.

This extension of social democracy from Keynesianism to Keynesian-corporatism took a number of forms. Externally it was accompanied by an accelerated reduction in UK military commitments, and in 1967 by an actual devaluation of sterling. Internally the big policy change came with the re-introduction of incomes policies: as governments after 1961 attempted to square the circle of full employment and price stability by engineering voluntary wage restraint and increasing productivity from a by now fully-employed labour force. Sometimes the agreements were voluntary — as in 1964. At other times they were statutory (if the pressure on sterling was more intense) as in 1967. Occasionally wage norms were tied to productivity agreements (as in 1967) or supplemented by Industrial Relations legislation (as in 1969 with the Labour government, and after 1971 with Heath). And always they involved the government using its own wage settlements (in the public sector) as an example to the private. It was with such a public sector pay pause that the cycle of incomes policies between 1961 and 1979 began.

Table 4.1   Incomes policies, 1961–79

Conservative government: Macmillan	
July 1961	total public sector pay pause for 9 months
Mar. 1962	'guiding light' norm of $2–2\frac{1}{2}\%$
Labour government: Wilson	
Apr. 1965	norm of $3\frac{1}{2}\%$
July 1966	six month 'freeze' on all incomes
Jan. 1967	six month period of 'severe restraint' with a nil norm
July 1967	norm of $3\frac{1}{2}\%$
July 1968	norm of $4\frac{1}{2}\%$
Conservative government: Heath	
Nov. 1972	Stage 1: 90 day standstill on all wage and price rises
Mar. 1973	Stage 2: wage rises limited to '£1 plus 4% of total wage bill'
Nov. 1973	Stage 3: norm of 7%, with additional 'threshold payments' if inflation exceeded 7%
Labour government: Wilson/Callaghan	
July 1975	Stage 1: £6 maximum rise
July 1976	Stage 2: norm of $4\frac{1}{2}\%$
July 1977	Stage 3: norm of 10%
July 1978	Stage 4: norm of 5%

Throughout this eighteen year period, what governments did was to pull together national trade union officials and representatives of business, to negotiate a corporately agreed deal on prices, wages, productivity and investment. Governments used the NEDC for this purpose steadily through the 1960s, and the whole process peaked after 1970, when the Heath government used the CBI to police its price control policy, and the Labour government later signed a 'social contract' with the trade unions, exchanging wage restraint for full employment, price stability and union influence on a wide range of economic and social policies. At its most extensive in the first half of the 1970s, this corporatist phase* of the social democratic project involved massive government funding of industrial investment, research and development, and training — as government, unions and industry struggled to stave off the intensified pressures of foreign competition in manufactured goods that was evident not just in export markets but at home as well. It also involved a second wave of nationalization, extending the public sector

---

* The UK's experience of corporatism — often captured by the term 'tripartism' — was a very modest case of corporate political leadership. If the term 'corporatism' is new to you, you will find its meaning discussed fully in Section 3 of this chapter.

created between 1945 and 1951 by taking into public ownership a series of industries and firms which were in competitive difficulties (this time to have them run by a state holding company, the NEB).

Table 4.2 Public–private ownership changes in the UK, 1946–79

	To public ownership		To private ownership
1946–9	railways, road haulage, major airlines, coal, gas, electricity and steel industries, and Bank of England		
		1953	road haulage
		1953–63	steel industry
		1960	national airline monopoly ended
1967	steel industry re-nationalized		
1973	Rolls Royce nationalized	1971–3	Thomas Cook and Carlisle breweries privatized, and some national airline routes granted to a private airline
1975–8	British Leyland, British National Oil Corp., British Shipbuilders, British Aerospace, ICL and INMOS in computers, and holdings in 'high-tech' companies such as Ferranti, Amersham International, and Cable & Wireless.	1977	some British Petroleum shares privatized

Source: Anderson (1991, p.17).

The social democratic project for economic management disintegrated in the 1970s, as the social contract disintegrated, and as waves of international competition destroyed local industry after local industry. On the surface of things, that disintegration was local and particular, a product of uniquely UK characteristics: the defensive strength of the UK labour movement, and the weakness and failure of the UK state. Certainly trade union militancy, particularly in the public sector, was a key destroyer of incomes policies throughout the corporatist period — as 'winters of discontent' brought Labour governments to defeat in 1969–70 and again much more dramatically in 1978–9. Union leaders found it hard to deliver wage restraint year by year, because governments found it hard to persuade companies to hold their prices constant, and because unemployment steadily rose in spite of wage restraint.

Unemployment rose, of course, because the underlying economy remained internationally uncompetitive, and that in its turn was a measure of the failure of social democratic-inspired governments to modernize the manufacturing base of the UK economy in the 1950s and 1960s. No effective state planning and direction of resources for economic reconstruction took place in the 1950s. Instead, as we have seen, governments in that period retreated from such controls, and from such direct intervention: and when they woke up to the problem — in the 1960s — the corporatist structures they created allowed them only the space for loose indicative planning and the limited 'picking of winners' by government departments and economic development councils. The importance attached by unions, electorates and politicians to 'the welfare side of the post-war settlement meant that resources were side-tracked into redistribution rather than to modernisation' (Jessop, 1988, p.12). Politicians' loyalty to the UK's world role and sensitivity to the City blocked the modernization process in equal measure. The British state in its social democratic phase responded to growing economic difficulties in an *ad hoc*, temporary and crisis-driven manner, and did not develop either a coherent strategy, or a bloc of classes and institutions, capable of delivering a major restructuring of the UK's economic base.

But these inabilities were not just local phenomena, with UK roots alone. They were rather a local manifestation of deep-seated problems in the entire social democratic project for a managed capitalism. That management over 25 years had altered the balance of class forces in the UK, leaving the UK disproportionately exposed to strong trade unionism and to heavy government social expenditure. High government expenditure had everywhere shifted from being a facilitator of economic expansion to become a burden on corporate profits and investment, as the rate of productivity growth in industry had slowed, and as the low productivity of the state sector had turned into a source of inflation rather than employment. By the late 1970s the entire social democratic project was in disarray everywhere.

Across the entire capitalist system, high tax, high welfare spending, Keynesian-managed economies were subject to heavy competition — even in their internal markets — from foreign manufactured goods produced in economies with lower levels of taxation and welfare provision. In this climate, governments could no longer prevent unemployment by their own spending. Instead, with rates of growth of labour productivity slowing down, as the dissemination of Fordist production systems through the entire economy reached completion, taxes ate away at corporate profits and at the wages of well-protected employees, and added to inflation. By the late 1970s inflation and unemployment were rising together across the capitalist bloc as a whole; and social democratic governments could only wait for world economic growth miraculously to reappear, while containing their own industrial costs by long-term aid to investment and short-term statutory wage restraint. Invariably it was this wage restraint that broke political support for the whole edifice; and by 1979 in the UK (and 1980 in the USA) governments were in power that were no longer wedded to the social democratic consensus which an entire generation of politicians and voters in the UK had come to take for granted.

SUMMARY

- In the UK, the post-war settlement on economic policy attracted many labels; but was built on a particular set of government responsibilities (for full employment, economic growth, prosperity and price stability) and was underpinned by a particular economic theory derived from the writings of John Maynard Keynes.

- This gave the UK state an increasing number of roles and responsibilities, brought more and more of GNP through the hands of state agencies, and in general constituted the political dimension of the whole Fordist accumulation regime discussed in Chapter 1.

- Social democracy went through three phases, culminating in a tripartite way of running the economy — through incomes policy, indicative planning and industrial relations reform. Social democracy disintegrated in a series of 'winters of discontent' initiated by public sector wage militancy. These reflected an earlier failure to modernize the economic base.

2.2   NEO-LIBERALISM

The Conservative government led by Margaret Thatcher entered office in 1979 with a quite different explanation of economic decline, and a distinctive and proselytizing ideology of its own. Unemployment was no longer explained by deficiencies in demand but by inadequacies in the supply side of the UK economy. This was then tied to a particular imbalance of power between capital and labour (the excessive power of trade unionism). The roots of unemployment lay in inflation, not demand deficiency. The roots of inflation lay in excessive demand and inadequacies of supply. Inadequacies in growth, investment, research and development, training and competition were no longer to be remedied by ever larger degrees of state assistance and corporatist planning, but by the exposure of UK-based industry to the 'creative gale' of unbridled competition. Government spending was not seen as a solution to economic problems, but as part of their cause. What had gone wrong was that the UK economy was over-governed. It was insufficiently allowed to run itself. What was needed was a rolling back of the state, and a freeing of market forces from the intervention of state hierarchies and the construction of corporatist networks. The Conservative government entered office in 1979 determined to 'set the people free' — and it understood that freedom in classical liberal terms as: the freedom to buy and sell in the market-place for individual gain, unrestrained by detailed state intervention, but within a framework of strong laws and sound money guaranteed by state action of a minimalist kind. Margaret Thatcher brought Adam Smith back to government in 1979, and pushed John Maynard Keynes out.

This meant a break with much of the post-war economic and social settlement, as that had been understood by the preceding generation of Conservative and Labour politicians, and as it was still understood by the Labour

Margaret Thatcher on the steps of 10 Downing Street, May 1979

Party in the 1980s. The Conservatives denied the ability of governments to create full employment. They insisted instead that all a government could do was to create the conditions in which private initiative could create wealth and employment. These conditions — in the context of the late 1970s — were predominantly those of stable prices: but also the toleration of whatever degree of social inequality was necessary to provide the incentive for private wealth creation. The Thatcherite Conservatives were not unabashed liberals of the nineteenth century laissez-faire variety. They insisted on their commitment to the public provision of a net of welfare services to prevent absolute destitution, and to train and keep healthy the private citizens released from close state supervision. But the whole thrust of the Conservative argument was that governments governed best by governing least: by cutting direct taxation, by reducing levels of government expenditure and borrowing, and by restricting state spending to levels commensurate with the maintenance of stable prices. They were determined to squeeze inflation out of the economy — and in 1979 they were convinced they could do that best by controlling their own spending (and with it the supply of money in the economy as a whole).

The technically monetarist phase of the Conservative governments of the 1980s was a relatively brief one. By 1985 at the latest, ministers had abandoned any formal attempts to identify and restrict the growth of money in the system. The exercise had proved technically impossible, and its impact on inflation and unemployment too delayed and too limited to meet their more short-term political purposes. But the Conservative government did nonetheless persevere with reductions in public spending and in direct taxation, with cutbacks in aid to industry and the exposure of manufacturing to international competition. It also persevered with its demolition of the whole corporatist structure of the late Keynesian period. Incomes policies were abandoned. Tripartite agencies of economic intervention were shut (the NEB immediately, the MSC much later), or downgraded (the NEDC); and the unions were shackled by new and ever tougher labour laws. The Thatcherite industrial relations policy of the 1980s was held to consistently. Unemployment was allowed to rise (it peaked at 3.3 million in 1985); and against that background one group of workers after another were confronted and defeated in major industrial disputes (of which by far the longest was the miners' strike of 1984–5). Thatcherism excluded trade union leaders from the corridors of power, and — both by example and by exhortation — enabled trade unionism to be more and more excluded from industrial decision-making as well. Thatcherism exposed industry to powerful market forces, but it also ensured that managers could respond to those forces with only the minimum degree of effective resistance from any workers whose jobs and earning levels were jeopardized by the responses proposed.

The whole thrust of Conservative economic policy since 1979 has been to 'open up' the British economy to foreign competition, foreign investment and tight managerial control. Successive Conservative governments have given consistent backing to the inward investment into the UK of particularly Japanese corporate capital. They have consistently looked to the financial institutions of the City to develop their international links and to consolidate the position of London as a centre of international finance. And they have consistently encouraged the development of labour flexibility: removing barriers (like the Fair Wages resolution) to the employment of cheap and unskilled labour, supervising the replacement of the old union-controlled apprenticeship schemes with government-funded youth training programmes, and lending their weight to the reduction of working class control of the labour process. Conservative governments since 1979

> have made [strenuous] efforts to make labour markets more flexible. So far these efforts have been less concerned with re-skilling the labour force than with increasing the flexibility of wages, hours and working conditions. In addition to industrial relations, employment and social security legislation, the second Thatcher government gave a central role in this respect to the Manpower Services Commission. In its third term Thatcherism [reinforced] these policies through measures to encourage more flexible pay schemes related to regional labour markets, profit-sharing and wider share ownership.

> (Jessop, 1988, p.24)

As the Jessop quotation implies, the focus of each Thatcher government was slightly different. In the first government, the focus was on union reform and monetary control. In the second, the emphasis shifted to privatization; and in the third, to the restructuring of the welfare state. The concerns of each government were not abandoned by the next. Instead a wave of union reforms was reinforced by privatization; and welfare restructuring was accompanied by further privatization measures in the last years of the 1980s. Throughout, however, the thrust of policy was a consistent one: to reduce the reliance on *networking*, and to increase that on *markets*, as modes of allocation of resources in the contemporary UK.

Thatcherite liberalism was at its most visible in its attitude to, and policy on, the state itself. As we will see in more detail later, Thatcherism attempted to do three things to the state: to centralize and strengthen its essential functions; to return functions not seen as appropriate for state ownership to the market; and to expose any retained to strong market pressures. Certain parts of the state machine were particularly well-financed in the Thatcher years: the defence establishment until late in the 1980s (when the decline in Cold War hostility made that progressively more difficult) — and the police. Other parts of the state apparatus saw their budgets (and their powers) eroded: local government generally, big Labour-controlled metropolitan councils in particular, and local education authorities in various ways. As we mentioned in Chapter 2, large parts of the state were sold off, starting with British Aerospace and going through to the water companies, electricity supply, and potentially even coal. The public institutions which remained were increasingly exposed to market-based performance indicators and to consumer-led production tests. This was true of the civil service itself — where Margaret Thatcher's penchant for private management was evident in the appointment of Sir Derek Rayner, head of the successful retailing chain Marks & Spencer, as a temporary adviser charged with bringing commercial thinking and practice into the running of government. It is evident in the way Conservative governments 'enhanced Treasury control over all areas of government and [used] its financial powers to force restructuring' (Jessop, 1988, pp.25–6). It was also true of government policy on schools and universities — policy which left them increasingly dependent for funding on parental/student choice and private business support; and even extended to the NHS, with the 1989 White Paper on new methods of hospital and GP funding.

We will come to the detail of all that later in this chapter, when we look at the changing organization and character of the modern state. What we need to recognize now is the centrality of that state restructuring to the whole political project of Thatcherite liberalism. The Thatcherites were determined to consolidate a popular culture of self-reliance, and to break a generation's attitudes of dependence on state provision. They tried time and again to push the state back to the role of provider in the last instance/provider of last resort and to consolidate popular support for the institutions of private capitalism (by creating a society of capital-owners, in shares, houses, and businesses). Indeed they set themselves the task, no less, of breaking totally the hold of class on people's self-definitions: to get people to see themselves as owners and consumers rather than workers and producers, and to end once and for all the hold of the Labour Party, of socialism, and of social democratic assumptions on popular attitudes and expectations of politics. The Thatcherite task voluntarily adopted in 1979 was nothing less than that of shifting popular common sense to the Right, and of writing out of the political agenda the institutions and concerns of the Democratic Left. It was in this way that, as the Labour governments of the 1970s gave way to Conservative administrations under Thatcherite leadership, control of the state moved from a party keen to build corporatist *networks* of economic regulation to one determined to create the political and social space within which *markets* could play their full role in the shaping of economic life.

SUMMARY

- Thatcherism came to power with a quite new (for the post-war period — if in truth really as old as liberalism itself) argument that governments govern best by governing least. Conservative governments set out to re-introduce the market into a wide range of economic and social relationships.

- The Conservative Party under Margaret Thatcher's leadership redrew the boundaries of the state: maintaining welfare provision, but abandoning corporatist structures and confronting the industrial power of the trade unions.

- Thatcherism made a serious attempt to alter popular consciousness and to restructure the state.

3 THE RESTRUCTURING OF THE UK STATE

Behind this particular story of changing economic projects lie much deeper and longer-lasting recastings of the structure of the UK state, of the whole approach adopted by the state to the running of the UK as a whole.

One important feature of the pre-Thatcherite UK state was what Keith Middlemass called its 'corporate bias' (Middlemass, 1979, p.371). The state ran the UK, as far as it could, by the development and exploitation of what we have called a *network* mode of allocation. The term 'corporatism' has been defined in both a broad and a narrow way. Defined broadly, corporatism occurs wherever you find

> interest representation in which the constituent units are organized into a limited number of singular compulsory, non-competitive, hierarchially ordered and functionally differentiated categories, recognized or licensed (if not created) by the state and granted a deliberate representational monopoly within their respective categories in exchange for observing certain controls on their selection of leaders and articulation of demands and supports.
>
> (Schmitter, 1974, pp.93–4)

As such it is an approach to the whole structure of government. Defined narrowly, it is a strategy of economic management alone. Corporatism has been defined narrowly 'as a political structure within advanced capitalism which integrates organized socio-economic producer groups through a system of representation and co-operative mutual interaction at the leadership level and of mobilization and social control at the mass level' (Panitch, 1986, p.136).

The two definitions, as perhaps you can see, are not necessarily in tension: and certainly in the case of the post-war UK before 1979, we can see evidence of the presence of them both. The expansion in the scope and complexity of the tasks adopted by post-war British governments induced them actively to build corporatist relationships across the whole interface of their relationship with the society they were called upon to govern. Each department gathered around itself a set of 'insider' interest groups, given special access to Whitehall and Westminster in return for their participation in the implementation of policy. Where the private sector was not organized in ways which would permit this to be done with ease, governments would actively encourage the formation of private organizations, and their acquisition of monopoly rights of representation in their particular area. The classic example of this 'formation' of a corporatist network by British government lies in the narrower sphere of economic management, though no doubt other wider examples could also be found. It was a Labour government which encouraged the various employers' organizations to unite in the CBI in 1964, the better to facilitate government–business negotiations on prices and incomes; just as earlier it had been a Conservative government which had preserved the monopoly of the TUC as the representative of labour, by refusing to give a seat on the then newly-created NEDC to a non-TUC white collar federation of unions (COPPSO) in 1961 (see Coates, 1972, pp.95–100 for details). Quite contrary to what one might expect, governments of the Left reinforced the representative agencies of business, and governments of the Right those of the working class, in order to consolidate a strong corporatist structure around the British state: in order, that is, to facilitate the running of UK society by British governments through a co-operative relationship with powerful private organizations having a monopoly of representation in their particular spheres.

This penchant for a 'beer and sandwiches' approach to economic management (that is, for summoning leaders of industry and labour to No.10 for a cosy chat to fix things) has a long history in the UK — hence Middlemass's claim that British governments have had such a corporatist bias since 1918 at least. In fact the tendency goes further back still — to the days when politicians and leading members of society quietly and informally co-ordinated policy in country-house parties on Edwardian weekends. As we saw in Chapter 3, the 'old boy' network remains a tenacious one in UK society; and is still intact as a powerful mechanism for the allocation of resources and the making of policy. But as we argued before, the Establishment bonding of private capital and the state has been replaced in importance since 1945 by the proliferation, around the state, of a battery of advisory committees and semi-executive bodies (Quangos) peopled in the main by the socially-privileged, by 'the great and the good'. Active government encouragement of the formation of spokesman organizations, and the spontaneous emergence of such organizations in the face of increasing government activity, created a whole new network of institutions linking the private and the public, a new system of representation parallel to, and to a degree in tension with, Parliament itself. Initially that network was one of pressure groups lobbying an autonomous state. It has slowly transmuted itself into a network of Quangos, in which specified areas of executive power have been delegated to, and hence shared explicitly with, private organizations representative of (because generated from and sustained by) organized sections of civil society.

And if that has been a general tendency in all spheres of government activity in the post-war period, it has been at its most acute in the area of economic policy-making. Close, regular and intimate relationships have been established between leading figures in the world of business and finance and the senior administrative (and political) figures heading the departments responsible for their areas of economic activity. Business connections with the Conservative Party are particularly close, through the heavy funding of the Conservative Party for which major firms are responsible. The relationship between business and the state remains in place even with Labour in power; and their arrival in office (between 1964 and 1970, and again between 1974 and 1979) brought trade unions into a particular position of influence. The 'social contract' to which we referred earlier was in fact the high-point of trade union political influence in the post-war UK: as a Labour government returned to office in 1974 prepared to implement a whole range of union-initiated policies (on pensions, industrial relations reform, public ownership, economic expansion — even the re-negotiation of the terms of entry into the EEC) in return for wage restraint. Indeed it is not too much to say that trade union power has been in decline since because that contract broke down, or to emphasize that the general credibility of a corporatist approach to the running of the contemporary UK was one casualty of the way — between 1974 and 1979 — in which the social contract was created and was broken.

Let us be clear on a number of things here. One is that, *even* at the height of the social contract, the political power of trade unionism in the contemporary UK was very minimal. It was conventional in those years — in 1974 and 1975 in particular — to say that 'the trade unions ran the country'; and it is part of right-wing mythology that the economy is weak because, and to the degree that, unions do/did so. But even in the mid 1970s, trade union power was highly restricted. The loyalty of trade union leaders to the Labour government, and their fear of the Conservative alternative, kept them in line (if with increasing difficulty as the years passed), and made them unwilling allies in a realignment of policy (towards lower government spending, higher unemployment and tighter wage restraint) forced on the Labour government by more powerful financial and industrial pressures. The range of issues on which trade union influence on policy was maintained diminished as the Labour government succumbed to rapid inflation, an uncertain pound, balance of payments difficulties and eventually the need to borrow from the IMF. Indeed, even before the Thatcher government came in to reduce trade union legal powers and oversee mass unemployment, trade union influence in the UK was on the wane. Even with Labour in power in the late 1970s, union effectiveness as industrial bargainers was being undermined by the growth of multinational corporate ownership and the intensification of international competition; and their impact as political bargainers was slipping away because of the Labour government's failure to deliver the economic growth and full employment on which the trade union movement set so high a value (on this, see Coates, 1980, 1989a).

In the end, as we have said, the social contract broke down. Trade union leaders could no longer deliver wage restraint, and the Labour government fell after a 'winter of discontent' of mainly public sector strikes against its incomes policy. The calamitous winter of 1978–9 showed very clearly the limits and brittleness of corporatism in its narrow sense — as a strategy for running the economy in co-operation with business and the unions. For the corporatist arrangement is not one to which the representatives of business and finance are ever enthusiastic converts. They will negotiate with labour only under duress, and in times of crisis — the very time indeed in which capital finds it hard to make the concessions to labour which union leaders require to justify and sustain their own participation in corporatist structures. If unions regularly — as they did in the 1970s — agree on prices and incomes settlements which effectively cut the real living standards of their members, they will eventually lose the support of their members, and be reluctantly 'sucked out' of negotiating chambers and onto picket lines. That is certainly what happened in the winter of 1978–9: to bring into general disrepute a corporatist strategy of industrial modernization which had commanded widespread public support when first introduced in 1974–5.

Corporatism as a strategy for running the country actually *weakens* the state. It leaves politicians and civil servants dependent upon the ability of the *networks* they have built, and the private *hierarchies* which feed into them, to deliver their constituents on time, regularly and in good shape. The very building of a network precludes the possibility of major structural reform, if that reform involves a systematic diminution in the power of one of the participants to the agreement. That is why Conservative governments in the 1980s turned instead to a greater reliance on the *market*. That is why they went into a major retreat from networks and from corporatism, and that is why they effected major changes in the nature of the UK state and in its way of running the rest of the society.

The Conservative government's recasting of the UK state brought together a number of anti-corporatist changes.

- The UK state under Conservative leadership stopped doing and claiming certain things. It no longer claimed to guarantee full employment. It no longer attempted to negotiate incomes policies. It no longer gave trade unions access to the highest levels of power, or automatic representation on Quangos, training boards and the like. Conservative governments in the 1980s were not governments which emphasized the importance of consultation. They preferred to leave wage negotiation in the private sector to the ebb and flow of market forces, and to restrict themselves to stacking the gradient against trade union negotiators there — by reducing their legal powers and by tolerating high levels of unemployment.

- UK governments in the 1980s closed or downgraded the corporatist institutions of economic management they inherited from Labour. They scrapped the National Enterprise Board, and eventually the Manpower Services Commission. They downgraded the NEDC and abolished many of its sector working parties. They scrapped sixteen of the 24 tripartite industrial training boards, and replaced them with weaker institutions without trade union representation. They also kept the CBI at a distance, preferring the guidance of the more monetarist Institute of Directors and their own right-wing think-tanks, preferring to deal directly with individual firms than with trade associations and other representative bodies.

- Conservative governments after 1979 reduced the state's role as direct provider of goods and services, by privatizing large sections of the existing public sector. They also de-regulated large areas of economic life: to increase the 'freedom' of economic actors to find their own terms and conditions of service.

Table 4.3   The main privatization sales since 1979

	Company	Proceeds (£ million)		Company	Proceeds (£ million)
		Sales by share offer			
1981	Cable & Wireless (49%)	224	1986	British Gas	5,434
1982	Amersham International	71	1987	British Airways	900
	Britoil (51%)	549		Rolls Royce	1,363
1983	Associated British Ports (52%)	46		British Airports Authority	1,226
1984	Enterprise Oil	392	1989	British Steel	
	Jaguar	294		Water Authorities (10)	5,240
	British Telecom (51%)	3,916			
		Private sales			
1980	Ferranti	54	1985	Yarrow Shipbuilders	34
1982	National Freight Corporation	7	1986	Vickers Shipbuilding	60
				Royal Ordnance	201
1983	B.R. Hotels	45		National Bus Company	250
1984	Wytch Farm	80	1987	Unipart	30
	Sealink	66	1988	Rover Group	150
	INMOS	95			
		Flotations of government holdings			
1979	British Petroleum	290	1984	Associated British Ports	52
				NEB/BTG	142
1981	British Aerospace	50	1985	British Aerospace	363
1983	British Petroleum	15		Britoil	449
	British Petroleum	566		Cable & Wireless	602
	Cable & Wireless	275	1987	British Petroleum	5,727

Source: Savage and Robins (1990, p.36).

- Conservative governments re-introduced market forces and internal pricing systems into as much as they could of what public sector provision remained: obliging local authorities to tender for services, obliging universities and colleges to bid for students, and hospitals to charge for patient care. Under their leadership, the public sector was increasingly expected to model its practices on those of large private capitalist organizations and, if not to make a profit, at least to minimize costs, increase productivity, and reduce the burden of taxation on the profit-making activities of others.

- Conservative governments tried to cut down on the number and scale of Quangos, and to return much of the area of cultural provision to a reliance on private funding and corporate sponsorship. 'Here too the emphasis has been on austerity, value-for-money, the use of public money to lever private funds, getting commercial sponsorship and so forth.' (Jessop, 1988, p.38.) Though we have not seen the wholesale slaughter of Quangos promised in 1979 — 'the Thatcher government's early attempt at a substantial "cull" of quango numbers was a failure' (Harden, 1988, p.49) — we have seen 'a distinct tightening of central control … through the largely uncontrolled discretionary power of appointment, financial controls and the power simply to abolish inconvenient bodies and create more compliant ones' (ibid., p.36).

In all these ways Conservative governments attempted, wherever they could, to replace the networking of a corporatist state with the market as a key allocative device. In the process, the Conservatives under Margaret Thatcher redrew the boundaries of the state (by privatization, de-regulation and re-commodification) to leave a larger area of economic and social life free of the detailed intervention of political networks and public hierarchical controls.

But they also, wherever possible, strengthened the central state as well. If we are now exposed to a 'free market' we also face a 'strong state'. Successive Conservative governments since 1979 took every opportunity to replace the networking of local democratic control with more hierarchical modes of allocation controlled from the centre. They abolished the Metropolitan Councils and the GLC. They rate-capped local authorities, and set limits on their powers of spending and taxation. They initiated the creation of a national curriculum for schools in England and Wales. In fact there have been roughly 50 separate acts since 1979 reducing the independence of local authorities in a myriad of tiny ways, in a movement characterized by its critics as an increase in 'undemocratic centralism' (Harden, 1988, p.44) or as 'authoritarian populism' (Hall, 1989, p.150). In the process the Thatcher years brought less a full-blooded 'rolling back of the state' than a redrawing of its boundaries, and a pulling of power back towards the centre in whatever area of state regulation remained.

In other words, the state put together by more than a decade of neo-liberal Conservative policies is a stronger, more centralized and more assertive state than was the more corporatist one it replaced. Police powers have been increased, and the legal autonomy of senior police officers from local democratic control enhanced in new legislation on the policing of demonstrations. The government pressed for the greater integration of policing at national level in time of civil disobedience — as in the miners' strike — and strengthened the 'secret state' of surveillance, particularly over Northern

Confrontation between police and striking miners, Orgreave, 1984

Ireland. The government kept up intense pressure on the media, tried to erode 'the autonomy of various ideological and cultural institutions (from schools and universities through the churches to the Royal Family)' and increased 'co-ordination between the Conservative Party and the tabloid press (its "long ideological arm")' (Jessop, 1988, p.37). In a series of discrete initiatives, successive Conservative governments reduced the freedom of those who dislike Conservative policies: abolishing unions at GCHQ, restricting rights of appeal against deportation, banning interviews on the media with Sinn Fein, attempting to block publication/screening of unacceptable arguments (from *Spycatcher* to *Death on the Rock**) and resetting/stopping publication of sets of social statistics (on topics as varied as unemployment, income distribution and health inequalities). And Conservative governments lent their support to an intolerance of minorities: most notably to continuing public hostility to homosexuality.

In consequence of all this, it seems reasonable to conclude, as Ewing and Gearty do, that

> In recent years, there has been a marked decline in the level of political freedom enjoyed in Britain. It is difficult if not impossible to point to a particular turning-point. The Labour Government of the 1970s tried to stop publication of the Crossman diaries, passed the first Prevention of Terrorism Act, deported an American journalist for allegedly obtaining security secrets, and pursued two other jour-

---

* The publishers of *Spycatcher*, the memoirs of Peter Wright, an ex-MI5 officer, were hounded through the courts of the UK, the USA and Australia in an attempt to block publication. *Death on the Rock*, an investigative report by a commercial television company of the shooting of IRA suspects by UK soldiers in Gibraltar, was broadcast in spite of heavy government pressure for the programme's suppression. These were just two of a number of examples of censorship, and attempted censorship, by UK governments in the 1980s.

nalists under the Official Secrets Act 1911 (the ABC case). Repressive action, therefore, is not the preserve of any single political party. Since the first Conservative election victory in 1979, however, the process of erosion has become more pronounced. All our traditional liberties have been affected, partly by new statutory initiatives and partly by the Government and other public officials relentlessly pushing back the frontiers of the common law, the traditional guardian of the people ...

This is not to deny that the present Government is concerned with questions of liberty. These concerns have, however, an undeniable political content: the freedom to buy one's council house; to buy shares; to choose whatever hospital, doctor, lawyer, or school one wants. It is by these criteria that the Government claims to be adding to, rather than eroding, the liberty of its citizens. The traditional freedoms of the person, expression, assembly, and association come a poor second.

(Ewing and Gearty, 1990, p.v)

In the process the UK has drifted into a society which is slightly better equipped to maintain 'law and order' and to contain dissent than was the case in the pre-Thatcher years. The state created by a decade of Thatcherism expects the private world to run itself when it can: but it also uses the power of law, of administration and of ideological control to set limits on the range of ways in which that private running can occur. The state left in place by Margaret Thatcher may present itself as a limited one; but it is a state of considerable power. For even where state functions are now privatized, it is still the state which sets the boundary lines between the public and the private. It is still state initiatives that have left arts, education and even health care more dependent on commercial criteria/sponsorship than before. There was no tension — in Thatcherite liberalism — between the criteria guiding public and private funding. Thatcherite Conservatism wanted the same criteria (of profitability, commercial viability, self-reliance) to operate across the public and the private sectors. This 'rolling back of the state' was but a mechanism for enabling society to be run as the government wanted it to be run. If the 'market' rules as co-ordinator of economic/social resources now, it does so because the government willed it. This 'rolling back of the state' was in that sense a political choice, not an imperative. That is why it is possible to see the state growing in importance and power as it rolled back — to see that, even in the liberal days of the Thatcher government, the role of the state as the ultimate arbiter of how UK society functions remained firmly intact.

SUMMARY

- The British state has long had a 'corporatist bias'. This bias was accentuated during the era of social democracy by the growth in the scale and scope of government involvement in economic and social life.

- Corporatism gave enhanced power to key interest groups — particularly those representing business and labour. Even at the peak of the corporatist period, however, the power of unions was limited. But so too, in the corporatist period, was the effective power of the state.

- The Thatcher governments of the 1980s retreated from corporatism — reducing the boundaries of the state, increasing the scale of economic (and social) life regulated by market competition. The Thatcher governments strengthened the state, centralizing power to Whitehall, and setting limits on the freedom of action of key elements of the private sector.

4   POLITICAL ALLEGIANCE AND POLITICAL CULTURE

We must not create the impression that Thatcherism was unique in attempting to regulate the boundaries of the private sector, or in having a direct impact on the way in which civil society in the UK is run. Political leadership throughout the post-war years has taken to itself the task of shaping civil society. What was unique about Thatcherism was the particular direction that shaping took. Thatcherism was 'new', not in trying to run the UK, but in trying to do so by 'a retreat from politics', by shifting the weight of emphasis from networks to markets as key social allocators.

The role of Thatcherism — and previously of social democracy — as forces shaping the relationship between state and society, and as determinants of the way society in the post-war UK was organized and run — will become clearer if we focus, not on the economic policy and state organization associated with each — but on the role of political parties in the post-war UK as constructors of political alliances and as moulders of political attitudes. We need some sense of the way *ideas* help to run a country, and of the way political ideas are created, packaged and disseminated primarily by leading political parties. We need some sense, that is, of the way different *political hegemonies* have helped to shape the character of the post-war UK.

This notion of 'hegemony' is a difficult one, though very important to any understanding both of contemporary politics and of the more general origins of social stability in the post-war world. The main source for the way it is used here is the work of the Italian communist Antonio Gramsci. Gramsci emphasized — as indeed later liberal scholars like Talcott Parsons were to argue too — that societies stabilize around particular sets of ideas, values, dominant 'common senses'. We saw the importance of that in our discussion of social stability in Chapter 3. To a liberal scholar like Talcott Parsons, these core value-systems emerged as a somehow natural product of particular kinds of social development (see Femia, 1975). To a Marxist like Gramsci, there was nothing natural about them at all. These core ideas and values had to be developed, and then imposed, by ruling groups desperate to avoid class confrontation with a proletariat and peasantry exploited in capitalist social relations of production. Gramsci was aware of the key role of ideological institutions in the creation and dissemination of such ideas. In Italy in the first part of the twentieth century — as for centuries past — the key institution was the church. Today, in Britain if not in Ulster, the church is less important than are the schools and the media. But for Gramsci then, as for us now, the State itself was a vital source of dominant political ideas, and a vital institution in the consolidation around those ideas of a bloc of social classes who identified with them. Hegemonic politics — in the Gramscian sense — were the key to how a society was run: and that form of politics involved *both* the creation of a set of ideas *and* the consolidation of a bloc of classes around them.

Politics in the UK in the post-war period has definitely been hegemonic in a Gramscian sense. We can definitely see political parties running the country by establishing within it a broad bloc of social forces united around a particular set of policies and understandings of what options are available in the contemporary world. In fact we can see the shift from social democracy to neo-liberalism in precisely these terms, as a clash of hegemonic principles and their associated structures of support. The social democratic package of 'networks and markets' has given way to one of 'markets and hierarchies'. We have moved from the 'managed market and the welfare state' to 'the free market and the strong state' as hegemonic principles around which political parties have attempted to organize — not just political life and their own supporters — but also economic and social life in the years since 1945.

'Social democracy' was the first of those hegemonic projects to dominate post-war life in the UK. Its understandings were clear:

1   that we lived in a Cold War world, divided between a free society and an evil empire;

2   that, as part of the free bit, we possessed a post-capitalist mixed economy capable of being managed by the state for socially-desirable ends;

3   that it was the state's job to guarantee full employment, rising living standards and basic welfare provision; and

4   that individual citizens had a right to all three of those.

We discussed the policies associated with these understandings earlier in this chapter. What we did not discuss, and what we need to discuss now, is how these policies and understandings combined to unite a bloc of social forces in support of such a way of running the country. In the heyday of social democracy, people voted on the basis of their class. The Labour Party laid claim to the electoral loyalty of organized workers (predominantly male) and to the bulk of the votes of the women to whom they were married, plus a majority of the poor and a section of the middle class (at the start of the period, particularly the middle class with a tradition of public service — and by the end, particularly that section employed in the welfare agencies of the state). The Conservatives took the bulk of the rest — organized around a less stridently interventionist but still broadly social democratic programme — took, that is, the bulk of the traditional middle class, the new managerial strata, and deferential sections of both the industrial and agrarian proletariats.

Thatcherism offered itself as a totally different set of policies and understandings, and sought to forge and maintain a quite different bloc of electoral forces. It accepted, and indeed initially emphasized even more, the Cold War dimension of the international order (Margaret Thatcher became internationally famous first as 'the iron lady'). But it also:

1   attacked the enemy within — persuading people that the barrier to prosperity lay in the institutions and values of social democracy itself;

2   argued for greater self-reliance, defended again the superiority of the private over the public, and emphasized the inevitability and desirability of market forces as allocators of resources and rewarders of effort; and

3   downgraded the importance of state intervention, reconstituting instead an older liberal litany that equated the 'public' to the 'bureaucratic' to the 'parasitic', and the 'private' to the 'dynamic' to the 'free'.

It used that set of understandings and associated policies to forge an alliance of social forces based on their common success as consumers (of shares, wealth, law and order, national glory) to add to its traditional Conservative support (among the old and new middle class and the deferential proletariat) the votes of particularly the skilled sections of the new proletariat.

Two things happened in that process. Political attitudes altered; and voting patterns changed. Let us look at each in turn.

4.1   POLITICAL ATTITUDES

The landslide victory of the Labour Party in 1945 was an electoral reflection of the impact of inter-war depression and wartime co-operation on the attitudes of an entire generation. Strong residues of an older, more market-oriented Conservatism remained in popular attitudes — particularly in middle class circles in the post-war years — but the experience of war legitimated a substantial shift of the centre of gravity of political opinion away from liberalism towards a belief in a more egalitarian and managed society. For 25 years or more, it was axiomatic in the UK that everyone had a set of basic social rights which the state had to meet, that governments had responsibilities for full employment and rising living standards, and that there was no social justification for major inequalities of power and wealth. As Stuart Hall correctly observed, it was social democratic ideas

> to which people had become acclimatised: the taken for granted welfare state, mixed economy, incomes policy, corporatist bargaining and demand management. If you stood up at that time in a debate on the national economy and tried to justify neoclassical economics, or indeed monetarism, you would have been laughed out of court. Everyone who mattered was one kind of Keynesian or another.
>
> (Hall, 1982, p.14)

Inequalities remained, of course, but they were subdued, hidden, and thought of as largely residual, in decline. The general view was that everyone was becoming more prosperous, that the society was becoming more equal; and that the state was the critical guarantor of a new mass affluence.

With the benefit of hindsight, the fragility of these views is also now very clear: though the degree of fragility varied with the dimension of the immediate post-war consensus under review. Popular enthusiasm for public ownership, as one leg of the post-war settlement, quickly dissipated, as electorates experienced nationalized industries as bureaucratic, insensitive, as no more efficient/effective than the best of the private sector, and as governments restricted public ownership only to the bankrupt and rundown sections of the economy. By as early as 1959 there were no votes in public ownership any more. The legitimacy of private ownership of large-scale capital had been well and truly restored by then; that of state-ownership effectively eroded. Much of the communitarianism of social democracy in its radical phase had been eroded too. By the late 1950s, all the surveys of public opinion that have come down to us show a highly privatized set of concerns. Most people defined themselves in private terms (as members of isolated nuclear families), saw politics as marginal and largely irrelevant to them, and had a highly instrumental attitude to how they voted. They voted on class lines, broadly speaking, because they hardly gave voting much thought at all, and when they did, they expected a class-based vote to enhance their private prosperity and family security. Indeed by the late 1950s, expectations of politicians were already rather low. By then the UK was demonstrating a broadly apolitical and conservative political culture. Immediate post-war political radicalism had gone. The broad mass of the British electorate expected governments to oversee prosperity and guarantee full employment. They expected good health care and proper education. But otherwise there was no political mileage in major social reform, or in any further erosion of the powers/rights of private property.

Eleven years of Labour government between 1964 and 1979 then weakened the popular hold of social democratic values and definitions still further. People saw Labour governments struggling to hold incomes policies in line. They saw prosperity threatened and unemployment return. They lived through 'winters of discontent', with the visible clash of trade union and state power: and they saw (and were regularly reminded of) the way 'others abroad' were doing better, were managing things differently. They also saw and experienced the rise of a re-vitalized Conservative liberalism, offering them a different set of explanations of the UK's condition and a different specification of the role that the state should play. Even with Labour in power between 1974 and 1979, the centre of gravity of political opinion in the UK continued to shift to the Right. Of the seventeen issues which divided the main political parties in the elections of 1974 and 1979, researchers found that 'the electorate moved to a more right-wing average position on fifteen and to the left only on the questions of increasing cash to the NHS' (Kavanagh, 1985, pp.543–4). All the evidence was that Labour voters were diminishing in the intensity of their support, and declining in numbers, because of Labour's dwindling hold on their opinions and attitudes to key political issues and initiatives. By 1979, on all major issues in the election campaign other than EEC membership and the welfare services, 'the Conservative Party were more representative than the Labour Party of the views of the electorate and of the uncommitted and thus convertible Labour supporter' (Crewe, 1982, p.28). That is why Stuart Hall was right to talk of the 1970s as 'the great moving Right show' (Hall, 1983, p.19).

This shift is not altogether surprising. It tells us important things about the character of the politics of the two parties involved. The Labour Party in the post-war years has always been a party of immense moderation, prepared to leave intact the basic structures of the society it took over in 1945 and again in 1964. Labour politics are as conservative as its opponents on issues of family, nation and basic property structure. Indeed, like the Conservative Party itself through the 1950s, the Labour Party only educated its electorate in the possibility and desirability of a managed capitalism. So when that management failed to deliver either the material progress or the qualitative transformation of social experience that was promised, the ground was laid for a Thatcherite revival built on the premise that it was the management (not the capitalism) which was the problem, and the Labour Party (not the system) which was at fault. By half-heartedly 'rolling forward' the state as the answer to capitalism's crisis, Labour prepared the ground on which the Conservatives under Margaret Thatcher could claim that it was the 'rolling forward' that created the crisis, that things were going wrong not because society was still insufficiently socialist but because it had already become far too left-wing (on this, see Coates, 1989a, pp.109–10).

The Conservative Party under Margaret Thatcher was well placed to exploit all this. Conservatism had little difficulty in shedding its Keynesian-corporatist phase. That phase had been an accretion of policy for a party more basically committed to private enterprise; and as such far easier to drop than it was for a Labour Party which had found in Keynesianism its solution to the dilemma of how to run and reform capitalism simultaneously. Faced with the problems of Keynesian-corporatism in practice, the Conservative Party made an easy move back to neo-liberal politics, and set about winning the hearts and minds of a new generation of voters — one whose political memory no longer stretched back to the mass unemployment of the 1930s and to the years of common wartime sacrifice.

Thatcherism's impact on the values and belief-systems of this new generation was considerable, if in the end only partial and limited. What Thatcherism did not do was to 'change hearts and minds' totally away from all social democratic institutions and practices. On the contrary, in its basic values, a clear majority of the UK population remained throughout the 1980s wedded to the notion of a 'collectivist or welfarist society, obstinately resistant to the lure of the enterprise culture' (Jowell *et al.*, 1990, p.176). What Ivor Crewe called 'the Thatcherite preference for tax cuts over social expenditure' (Crewe, 1989, p.245) found only limited and diminishing support in the electorate as a whole: to the point at which, by 1990, surveys would regularly show more than half the electorate favouring increases in taxation to pay for better social welfare, and only tiny percentages supporting further tax cuts and public sector retrenchment (*The Times*, 15 November 1990, p.6). Throughout the 1980s the NHS in particular remained too popular for the Conservative government to privatize in any direct and frontal way; and the centre of gravity of popular opinion on core political issues — like jobs, health, education and welfare — actually shifted a little way back to the left as the 1980s closed. That is why commentators like Ivor Crewe could insist that there had been 'no Thatcherite transformation of attitude and behaviour among the British public' in spite of all the years of propaganda and power; and that even now public opinion in the UK remained 'wedded to the collectivist, welfare ethic of social democracy' (Crewe, 1989, p.243).

So it may — and the Left can draw some comfort from Crewe's view that 'a post-Thatcher Labour government will inherit an electorate as friendly to its major objectives as the 1979 electorate was to those of the Conservatives' (ibid., p.250). What is striking however is the degree to which Labour itself has shifted — in its basic thinking — in a Thatcherite way. For the Labour Party, no less than the electorate whose support it pursues, was shaped in the 1980s by the attempt of the Conservatives under Margaret Thatcher to redraw the map of British politics. Though Thatcherite domination of opinion on specific political *issues* remained patchy and uneven, the Thatcherite impact on the *general terms* within which politics and the state are now generally seen was much stronger. In that sense Norman Lamont was quite justified in his claim, made in his budget speech in 1991, that:

> The eighties were years of remarkable progress in our economy but even more striking was the change of attitude. The crucial importance of the market is now widely accepted both in this country and even in this House. It is that change of ideas and attitude that will be the lasting legacy of Mrs Thatcher.
>
> (cited in *The Times*, 20 March 1991, p.18)

Eleven years of Thatcherite government created a political climate in the UK in the early 1990s very different in its working assumptions from that prevalent 20 years before. The onus of proof is now on those who would *manage* the market. Neo-classical economists are no longer laughed out of court. The legitimacy of market methods of economic and social allocation has been effectively reinstated: and those who would challenge it are now more marginalized and defensive than at any time since 1945. Thatcherism's assault on social democratic ideas may not have captured the hearts and minds of the entire UK electorate; but it did re-establish the centrality and legitimacy of its organizing hegemonic principle — namely the market.

4.2 POLITICAL LOYALTIES

The only danger of talking in generalizations of this kind is that the existence and importance of significant minorities is obscured, and the degree of political disagreement lost in the overall statement of trends. In fact the level of consensus in post-war UK politics prior to 1979 was very high — not on support for a particular party (party competition was robust throughout the period) but on the basic terms of reference of politics itself. Ulster apart (to which we will come shortly) there has been virtually no support in the UK since 1945 for any kind of revolutionary politics. On the left, the Communist Party has long been in what has now proved to be terminal decline (its membership fell from 56,000 in 1943 to less than 16,000 in 1983; and fell further to the point, in 1990, when the Party effectively dissolved itself). The Revolutionary Left which replaced it (largely Trotskyist in inspiration) peaked at probably no more than 12,000 members in the mid 1970s and has stagnated since. On the extreme Right, the National Front had a brief period of electoral success in 1974 (it was the fourth largest political party in England that year, in terms of votes won) but was eclipsed by the rightward shift of the Conservatives under Margaret Thatcher after 1975, and subsequently disintegrated. Elsewhere, Northern Ireland apart, parliamentary politics have held total sway.

Within the loyalty to, and involvement in, a parliamentary understanding of politics, however, significant points of opposition have remained to whatever has been the dominant set of assumptions about the scope and character of state action. In the 1950s and 1960s, in the heyday of social democracy, the minority voice was largely an anti-corporatist one: associated with an opposition to government regulation of industry, to trade union power and to high taxation. The social group to whom that anti-corporatist 'package' appealed most were lower middle class groups in the private sector — the traditional petty-bourgeoisie — a constellation which was extended in the late 1960s by the revival of a 'moral majority' — particularly around Mary Whitehouse — of protest against the so-called 'moral degeneracy' associated with social democratic affluence: divorce, pre-marital sex, drugs, pornography, student protest and so on. This oppositional phalanx provided a large proportion of Conservative Party activists in the post-war period; and found itself elevated to a new dominance as part of the coalition associated with Thatcherism.

Away on the Left, the opposition to social democracy looked rather different. Through the 1950s and 1960s left-wing opposition focused almost exclusively on the foreign policy — Cold War — international alliance dimension of the dominant social democratic consensus. Unilateral nuclear disarmament became the key issue here, both important for itself and as shorthand for a more generalized desire to dissociate the UK from the American alliance and from any vestigial preoccupations with Empire. As we saw earlier, much of that same oppositional coalition was uneasy with the terms of entry into the EEC, negotiated, and then re-negotiated, between 1970 and 1975; and it broadened out in the late 1970s and early 1980s into a full set of demands for an 'alternative economic strategy' (involving extensive public ownership, import controls and state planning) as social democracy ran into difficulties with Labour in power. The social grouping to which this left alternative appealed most was the growing number of public sector white collar employees — nurses, teachers, social workers and health administrators — who also came to provide a disproportionately large percentage of party activists in the 1970s and 1980s — this time in the Labour Party. This 'middle class Left' then took Labour off in a socialist direction under Tony Benn's leadership after 1979 — giving the Labour Party in 1983 its most radical manifesto since the 1930s: and in the process leaving behind — open to recruitment by more moderate political formations — the core manual working class elements of the old Labour Party coalition.

We will come to the character, history and fate of that coalition in a moment, but before we do, we need a word about Ulster, and about Ulster exceptionalism. The story of Ulster, the way it is run, its political loyalties and history, are quite different from the rest of the UK and cannot easily be subsumed under a general argument of the kind we have developed here. That is why we have not tried. There are many histories and analyses of Northern Irish politics: and if you want to see how I explain it, please see Coates (1984, pp.183–91). The Ulster story is a different one, too long to be dealt with adequately in this chapter. Our concern here is with the way the rest of the UK has been run; and for that purpose, it is the exceptionalism of Ulster which is important: to throw into relief what is happening in the rest of the United Kingdom.

- Ulster is the one part of the UK where the legitimacy of the state itself is subject to question; and where, in consequence, the state is obliged to meet force with force. Markets, hierarchies and networks do structure Ulster life, as we will mention in a moment, but so too does coercion — state violence against terrorism, and para-military struggle against rule by London (in the case of the IRA) or the fear of rule from Dublin (with the UVF). London can only 'run' Northern Ireland by keeping an army

Parade of the Orange Order through Belfast, 12 July 1988

there: and that gives the running of Northern Ireland features which are more in common with the running of a colony than with the running of, say, Lancashire or even Scotland.

- The social networks which interlace themselves between hierarchies and markets in the rest of the UK in Ulster crystalize out into two distinct communities. Certainly in the past, and apparently still today, the allocation of housing, jobs and political power in Ulster is organized through religious communities and their supporting private networks: not just the Church, but the Orange Order and its Catholic equivalents. There is a secular middle ground in Ulster, but it is one which is continually squeezed between religious networks and divided community loyalties. The rest of the UK is a secular society. Ulster is not.

- Political loyalties in Ulster fall on either side of a quite uniquely Irish fracture — namely the border with the Republic to the south, and more recently with the Anglo–Irish agreement between London and Dublin. In Ulster people vote on religious and nationalist lines, not on class ones, and vote for parties unique to Northern Ireland. Ulster is run directly from London, but only in negotiations with local Irish political formations that have a remarkable tenacity. Parties in Northern Ireland periodically split or re-group, but they do so around an unchanging set of issues — frozen into Northern Irish politics by a border issue which will not go away. This was true in 1945, and it remains true today.

- Nonetheless things have changed dramatically in Ulster since 1968. The relative quietness and untroubled nature of post-war Protestant political domination of the province was challenged then by a campaign for Roman Catholic civil rights. That campaign triggered more than 20 years of sectarian violence. The casualty rate per head of the population is now higher in Ulster than it was in the USA during the Vietnam War: and the 'troubles' have come to be Western Europe's longest running civil war.

Elsewhere in the UK, the issues at stake are less violently contested, and the patterns of political loyalty to which they give rise have changed more slowly and less dramatically over the post-war years. In the two decades after 1945, while social democracy was the dominant political project, people voted largely by class. They identified themselves primarily in class terms, saw the two main political parties as particularly responsive to the needs of one class rather than another, and voted accordingly. Until 1970 at least 'broadly speaking the electorate was divided into two great blocs which provided reliable and stable voting support for the Conservative and Labour parties' (Denver, 1989, p.28). So, in the period of social democracy, we see

- blocs of voters organized on class lines. The organized working class largely voted Labour. The professional classes largely voted Conservative. The Conservatives also held a significant working class vote (among the non-unionized industrial and agricultural workers) and the Labour Party — in 1966 at least — was able to widen its appeal to pick up certain votes among middle management;

- there was always a third party vote for the Liberals — one which was largely regional in anchorage. Liberal support was strongest outside or on the edge of England: in Devon and Cornwall, in Wales, and in the islands of northern Scotland. Scotland otherwise voted on class lines — which, given its dependence on heavy industry, sent more Labour MPs south to Westminster than it did Conservative ones.

As social democracy ran into crisis in the 1970s and 1980s, that pattern of class voting diminished. '1970 does appear to be a convenient and sensible point from which to date a marked change in British electoral behaviour' (Denver, 1989, p.47). Class de-alignment became the order of the day. As Table 4.4 shows, the extent to which individual voters strongly identified with one particular party steadily declined.

Table 4.4 Trends in party identification[1] (%)

	Average 1964–70	February 1974	October 1974	1979	1983	1987
With party identification	90	88	88	85	86	86
With Conservative or Labour identification	81	75	74	74	67	67
'Very strong' identifiers	42	29	26	21	20	19
'Very strong' Conservative or Labour	40	27	23	19	18	16

[1] 'Identification' here refers to voters who see themselves as belonging/loyal to a particular political party. So in 1974, for example, 88% of all voters felt such a sense of identity with one particular party.
Source: Denver (1989, p.47).

In addition, new political formations came, at least briefly, to national prominence. Powerful nationalist parties rose in the 1970s in Scotland and in Wales. A new political party of moderate ex-Labourites (the SDP) broke to form a stronger political centre, and to attract voters away from the two main parties to its new Alliance with the Liberals. However, neither the nationalists nor the Alliance managed to sustain their challenge to Conservative and Labour domination into the 1990s. Of more lasting significance, perhaps, has been the way in which large numbers of skilled workers in the private sector switched allegiance to the Conservatives from 1979; and the manner in which the public sector vote consolidated around Labour as the Conservatives began to 'roll back' the state. Whether you worked in the state sector or not, and whether you owned your house or not, became the key determinants of voting patterns in the 1980s.

Through the 1980s the Labour Party struggled with increasing difficulty to hold on to the electoral loyalty of a fragmenting working class: finding it easier to hold on to its 'traditional working class [vote, from] manual workers who live in Scotland/the North, are council tenants, union members and public-sector employees' than to the electoral support of 'new working class [of] manual workers who live in the South, are owner-occupiers, private-sector employees and not union members' (Denver, 1989, pp.58–9). The Conservatives, for their part, found their electoral popularity dwindling as the 1980s closed, eroded by the persistence of economic difficulties of the kind they had faced steadily since 1979, and which they had initially blamed on the years of Labour misrule. The 'blaming of Labour' drew many ex-Labour voters to the Conservative camp in 1979 and 1983:

but the potency of such arguments diminished steadily as one Conservative administration was followed by another and another. By 1990 it was Conservative support which had begun to look as shaky as once Labour's had: and it was the Labour Party — reinvigorated by moderate political leadership and the collapse of the SDP — which headed the opinion polls by a considerable margin.

The 1990s open then with the electorate more 'up for grabs' than at any time since 1945. In 1991, the Conservative government has an enormous parliamentary majority (of over 100 seats) but still a minority of the popular vote: and lacks the edge over its Labour opponent created in 1983 and 1987 by the splitting of the anti-Conservative vote between Labour and the Alliance. In electoral terms, the battle is now on for the allegiance of the C1s — the skilled working class that Thatcher took and the Labour Party wants back. In programmatic terms, the battle is on between a revitalized, more supply-side oriented Keynesianism, and a still ascendant if slightly battered neo-liberal conservatism. In ideological terms, the battle is on between a market-driven society and a more corporately managed market capitalism. Electorally, programmatically and ideologically, the available options are not wider than this. Voices arguing for a sharper break with capitalist market systems are, temporarily at least, widely discredited. The society to be run in the 1990s will be capitalist or it will be nothing. But how it is to be run still hangs in the electoral balance. Real if limited choices remain; and it will be interesting to see, as the decade progresses, if those choices have indeed widened again to the Left — to see, that is, if liberalism's hegemonic presence in the 1980s has been sustained or replaced.

SUMMARY

- Political parties play a key role in establishing dominant 'common senses'; social democracy was one such, neo-liberal ideas another, in the post-war UK.

- The dominance of social democratic ideas in the 20 years after 1945 slowly ended, as the electorate experienced the realities of public ownership and of Labour in power. Thatcherite ideological initiatives had a big if partial impact: less on the degree of support for particular policies than on general understandings of the importance of markets as allocative devices.

- Ulster apart, class position was the prime determinant of voting in the heyday of social democracy. Class is now less important, and such class de-alignment has left the UK electorate more volatile in its political loyalties than at any time since the war.

CHAPTER 5: CONCLUSION

The patterns of change we have observed in the ways in which the UK has been run since 1945 give us a series of questions we would do well to keep before us as we watch the way in which it will be run in the decade ahead. Five questions in particular seem central to the public life of the UK in the 1990s.

1 THE SIGNIFICANCE OF EUROPE

What impact will the UK's immersion in the economic and political institutions of an enlarged European Community have on the sovereignty, character and effectiveness of UK governing institutions? What formal rights of decision-making will the UK's ruling institutions and personnel cede to European ones: governmental rights to legislate, juridical rights to decide, rights to specify terms and conditions of work by financial and industrial institutions? More difficult, what actual shifts of power will greater European integration bring? Will involvement in European governing institutions actually reduce/bring back a degree of influence — for key UK power-brokers — over important economic and social institutions and processes: give politicians and their electorates some greater leverage over, say, multinational corporations, financial flows, patterns of investment, production and trade? How far indeed will the rise of stronger European

European Parliament in session, Strasbourg

political institutions in the 1990s alter the balance between hierarchy, market and networks in the running of UK economic and social life? Are we moving towards a more managed market again, after a decade of neo-liberalism, this time under the guise of European standardization and integration? Are we moving, after decades of US domination, into a world divided regionally between orbits of economic and political power centred on the USA, Japan and a united Europe?

2 THE QUESTION OF POST-FORDISM

A second cluster of issues for the 1990s turns on the nature of the 'accumulation regime' emerging in the increasingly integrated capitalist economies of Western Europe. As we said in Chapter 1, controversy is rife in the relevant literature about whether we are moving from economies whose core areas were organized on Fordist lines to ones which are, in some sense, now post-Fordist. We saw, in Chapter 1, the argument that even to talk of Fordism was to over-generalize: that not all sectors of the UK economy in the 1950s were organized on Fordist lines, and that not all successful economies of that period (the West German, Italian and Japanese in particular) relied heavily on Keynesian methods of demand management. We are often told now not to create any impression of some equally universal shift in a post-Fordist direction. The only problem with such an instruction is that many scholars are convinced that some change of a general kind is underway.

They argue that the saturation of mass markets is leading 'to a growing differentiation of products, with a new emphasis on style and/or quality'. These more differentiated products 'require shorter runs, and thus smaller and more flexible production units' (Clarke, 1990, p.73), a flexibility made possible by new technologies. They suggest, that is, that a new economic structure is emerging, based on computerization and microchip technology, one enabling rapid gains in productivity to be achieved through full automation and computerized stock control, and one permitting more efficient small batch production. Industrial systems are emerging in which the extensive use of microelectronics allows machine tools to be re-programmed very quickly to produce 'small quantities of much more specialised products for … particular market niches' (Warde, 1989, pp.11–12). Such an industrial structure of *flexible specialization* is, they argue, no longer as dependent as Fordism on large-scale factory production by a heavily unionized male labour force. It can instead draw on green field sites, recruit non-unionized labour, and make more use of part-time workers. For it requires a flexible labour force, one free of demarcation lines, able and willing to turn its hand to a variety of tasks and prepared to work intensively for every moment of the working day. What post-Fordism represents, that is, is a shift from mass production to flexible specialization, from unionized and homogeneous labour forces to flexible and scattered ones, and from standardized products for an undifferentiated market to the servicing of highly sophisticated, affluent and discrete market niches.

That is the argument anyway — one that you need to think about. As far as I can tell, all this is still open to question. It is something to watch for, and think about, rather than to treat as unambiguously true/false right now. And if we are to think about it, we need a series of easily-accessible points of reference. So, as another question for the way the UK is being organized and run in the 1990s, ask yourself this: are the changes at play in core areas of the UK anything like the ones suggested in the set of distinctions in Table 5.1?

Table 5.1   The emergent regime of flexible accumulation

Characteristic	The post-war expansionary regime, late 1940s to early 1970s key features	The emergent regime of flexible accumulation, mid 1970s onwards key features
	Accumulation regime: monopolistic	*Accumulation regime: flexible*
Industry	Monopolistic; increasing concentration of capital; steady growth of output and productivity, especially in new consumer durable goods sectors; secular expansion of private and especially public services	Rationalization and modernization of established sectors to restore profitability and improve competitiveness; growth of high-tech and producer service activities, and small firm sector
Employment	Full employment; growth of manufacturing jobs up to mid 1960s; progressive expansion of service employment; growth of female work; marked skill divisions of labour	Persistent mass unemployment; generalized contraction of manufacturing employment, growth of private service sector jobs; partial de-feminization (in manufacturing); flexibilization of labour utilization; large part time and temporary segment
Consumption	Rise and spread of mass consumption norms for standardized household durables (especially electrical goods) and motor vehicles	Increasingly differentiated (customized) consumption patterns for new goods (especially electronics) and household services
Production	Economies of scale; volume, mechanized (Fordist-type) production processes; functional decentralization and multinationalization of production	Growing importance of economies of scope; use of post-Fordist flexible automation; small batch specialization; organizational fragmentation combined with internationalization of production

Table 5.1 The emergent regime of flexible accumulation — continued

Characteristic	The post-war expansionary regime, late 1940s to early 1970s key features	The emergent regime of flexible accumulation, mid 1970s onwards key features
	Socio-institutional structure: collective	*Socio-institutional structure: competitive-individualist*
Labour market	Collectivistic; segmented by skill; increasingly institutionalized and unionized; spread of collective wage-bargaining; employment protection	Competitive; de-unionization and de-rigidification; increasing dualism between core and peripheral workers; less collective, more localized wage determination
Social structure	Organized mainly by occupation, but tendency towards homogenization; income distribution slowly convergent	Trichotomous and increasingly hierarchical; income distribution divergent
Politics	Closely aligned with occupation and organized labour; working-class politics important; regionalist	De-alignment from socio-economic class; marked decline of working-class politics; rise of conservative individualism; localist
State intervention	Keynesian-liberal collectivist; regulation of markets; maintenance of demand; expansion of welfare state; corporatist; nationalization of capital for the state	Keynesianism replaced by free-market Conservatism; monetary and supply-side intervention rather than demand stabilization; deregulation of markets; constraints on welfare; self-help ideology; privatizing the state for capital
Space-economy	Convergent; inherited regional sectoral specialization (both old and new industries) overlaid by new spatial division of labour based on functional decentralization and specialization; regional unemployment disparities relatively stable	Divergent; decline of industrial areas (pre- and post-war); rise of new high-tech and producer services complexes; increasingly polarized spatial division of labour; widening of regional and local unemployment disparities

Source: Martin (1988, pp.213, 219).

3 THE POSSIBILITIES AND CHARACTER OF UK ECONOMIC REVIVAL

Post-Fordist or not, the UK economy in the 1990s will continue to provide a third set of problems and possibilities for those who would run the UK. The decade is beginning — as indeed the 1970s and 1980s began — with unresolved problems of balance between demand and supply, with persistent UK vulnerability — in its manufacturing base — to strong foreign competition, and with rising inflation. Standards of living for the majority of the UK population are at an all time high; but so too is UK dependence on the import of foreign manufactures, the maintenance of low wages here, and the retention in London of internationally high rates of interest. How the UK economy will be restructured in the 1990s is as yet unclear, as is the role of market forces in any restructuring that does occur. It is just intriguing to discover that, after more than a decade of neo-liberalism, the debate is still on about how best to create the conditions in which the UK economy can lift itself from a cycle of relative decline to one of broadly-based and secure international competitiveness. The playing out of that debate will be another important issue to watch for in the 1990s.

4 THE CHANGING STRUCTURE OF UK SOCIETY

The post-war years have seen both major continuities and major changes in the character of social relations and social divisions in the UK. General levels of affluence have grown, but significant pockets of poverty have remained. Class divisions have persisted: but a class structure moulded by Victorian heavy industry has given way to one reflective of Fordism — more white collar, more middle class. Gender divisions have changed only at the margin: those of ethnic discrimination have changed hardly at all. Regions have risen and fallen in prosperity. New social groups have come and gone. And through those changes the UK generally has shifted from a society united in relatively modest life styles and acceptance of traditional sources of authority and leadership to one divided by differential patterns of affluence and poverty, and unglued by the emergence of less deferential and more instrumental patterns of thought and action. The question this poses for the 1990s is one of enormous importance. Will the society be more atomized, more divided and less stable in the next ten years than it has been in the last 40? What will be the legacy of Thatcherism on the decade? Will the underclass her policies have consolidated rise in rebellion — trigger greater degrees of crime, violence and political protest? Or will the tide turn, and a society of greater compassion, social awareness and altruism rise belatedly from the ashes of social democracy?

5 COMPETING POLITICAL PROJECTS

For this is the big question of the 1990s. Will neo-liberalism continue to hold the loyalty of governments and electorates in the UK, or will new less market-oriented political philosophies rise to prominence again? How will the new international climate impinge on political attitudes and practice in the UK? Will the end of the Cold War — with its freeing of thought from a preoccupation with the choice between capitalism and communism — mark the death-knell of socialism, or open the space for its revival as a modernizing and humanizing presence in UK political life? Will the growing awareness of the shared nature of world problems (from war and poverty to global warming and ecological disaster) open the way to a new green politics of greater state intervention; or will the collapse of Russian power in Eastern Europe, and the opportunities opened up for UK business by tight labour control at home and easier markets abroad, give neo-liberalism a fresh lease of life?

No matter what answers emerge to these questions, there can be no doubt that we now live in *New Times*. The 1980s have seen changes — both in the world order and in the internal politics of the UK itself — of seismic proportions. The collapse of the Cold War abroad, and the decade-long break with the old social democratic consensus at home, mark the 1990s out as the start of a new era in the running of the contemporary UK. One era — that of global Fordism — is visibly coming to an end. What is emerging to replace it is less clear. Or rather, the new order emerging in the 1990s is still to be fixed. The kind of social and political world we and our children will face is available for negotiation. To some degree at least, its character will turn on decisions and choices we make in the years ahead: and it is to be hoped that those choices will be better made for the understanding we now have of what has gone before.

In the 1990s in the UK we face a critical choice of allocative method. It is a choice of immense importance, but not one without limit. Life in the 1990s is bound to be run by *hierarchies*. We will live, as we do now, surrounded by big institutions. But whether those hierarchies will interact with each other, and therefore with us, only through the interface of *market* competition — that is not pre-determined. The possibility remains of subordinating hierarchical structures and market forces to strong and equalitarian democratic controls. *Networks* capable of moulding social life to meet criteria which are neither unequal nor competitive can be built. Whether they are, and what form they take when they emerge, will depend in the end on us — on the political choices we make. It would be good to think that you will spend some of your time in the 1990s trying to shape those choices. It would also be good to think that any shaping you do will itself be moulded by the reading and study in which you are now engaged.

APPENDIX: A NOTE ON THE INTERNATIONAL SYSTEM OF STATES AND ECONOMIES

There is nothing new in the UK being surrounded by an international order. In one sense, of course, it has always been so: and the character of that order has often dominated local UK experience. The Roman order and Julius Caesar, the Normans and William the Conqueror, the Counter-reformation and the Spanish Armada — are key moments in the history of Britain. In modern times the international order has always made its presence felt, both politically and economically. Politically, the history of the modern UK has been coloured by an endless series of invasion threats and military confrontations — first with the French (to 1815) and then with the Germans — threats and confrontations that culminated in two periods of total war. Economically, the history of the modern UK has been coloured by a parallel series of competitive challenges: first from the Dutch, then the French, then the Germans, the Japanese and even the Americans.

The two sets of challenges have been linked, though neither can be reduced directly to the other. At the heart of the eighteenth century clash with the French was the struggle for empire and trade — a clash the British won in India and in North America. The late nineteenth century build-up of military tension was fuelled by the struggle for markets and colonies in Asia, Africa and the Middle East. So economic competition and military threats were a permanent and inter-connected feature of the pre-1945 international order. What was not so permanent was the international landscape from which those threats and that competition repeatedly emerged.

Three features of that landscape are particularly important to an understanding of how the UK has been run since 1945:

(a) the combined and uneven development of the international economic system;

(b) the shifting locus of economic and military power within this system; and

(c) the rupture of international economic and political life created within the system by the events of 1917.

The first of these three requires us to grasp the importance of 'core' and 'periphery' in the international order, the second to see the changing centre of the 'core' itself, and the third to understand the challenge to that 'core' represented this century by the Soviet Union. Let us look at each of these three in turn.

(a) 'Combined but uneven development'

There is an important sense in which capitalism* — as a way of organizing economic life — has always been international in its scope. Indeed there is a fierce dispute among economic historians about whether the origins of Western European economic development (the emergence there of capitalism out of feudalism) was triggered primarily by *internal* trends (by shifting relationships of class power between landlords and serfs) or by the *external* shock triggered by the growth of world trade (see Hilton, 1978). But the growth of trade itself is not in dispute, and Western European merchant capitalists spent more than two centuries after 1500 developing extensive trading networks with the Asian coast and with parts of the African and North American mainland.

Up to 1700 it was not obvious that Europe would win a position of world dominance from this interaction of different world empires. Initially the Ottoman, the Chinese and the Mogul empires looked better organized for domination than did the backward and fragmented system of newly-established European states. But after 1700, the non-European world empires went into decline; and the European states were left free to compete for domination between themselves: for power in Europe, for hegemony in world trade, and eventually for world leadership. That struggle for dominance between European states was played out partly in Europe, partly in North America and Asia, and left bits of the globe under direct European

---

* *Capitalism is best defined as a system of generalized commodity production based on free wage labour.* In a capitalist economy things are produced — not to be consumed by the immediate producer — but to be sold. Labour power is also a commodity in capitalism. It too has to be sold (in return for wages) if those selling it are to have access to the goods and services they do not themselves produce. It is sold — not normally to the state — but to individual enterprises, to private purchasers of labour power. For capitalism is a system driven by the pursuit of *private capital* — profit and capital that accumulate only through a competitive struggle for market advantage.

Capitalism, as a mode of organizing economic life, can be distinguished from other modes of economic organization: from feudalism, say, or from the centrally planned economies of a state-socialist kind. Indeed given our interest in modes of co-ordination, the contrast here helps the definition. The key co-ordinating mechanisms of a feudal system are primarily *political*, those of a centrally-planned economy *administrative*, those of a capitalist economy *economic*. Feudalism, that is, relied heavily on networking, state-socialism on hierarchy, capitalism on the market.

In the economic and social order of medieval feudal Europe, entitlement to productive resources was politically specified, and surpluses were extracted primarily by political means. The key productive resource was land. Individuals were allocated land — held it as a fief — ultimately at the pleasure of the central political authority. The fact that that central political authority was normally weak did not remove the centrality of political power to the entire economic and social system. It meant only that effective power was locally dispersed, within a system still bonded by networks of primarily political relationships. The producing classes did not own the land. Surplus was extracted from them by direct labour or by taxation. They were in effect coerced into supporting their non-producing military rulers, with predictably adverse effects on producer morale, initiative and loyalty. Feudalism — co-ordinated through its political networks — was economically stable but stagnant.

Centrally planned economies lately have proved to be similarly stagnant but less stable. There, economic resources are owned by the state, and the distribution of productive capital allocated administratively. People work to a plan, with goals set for them by higher levels of the central administrative structure. In such a hierarchical system, space for autonomy and initiative at the bottom is heavily circumscribed. But so too is the degree of inequality, uncertainty and commercial pressure.

colonial rule from as early as 1858 (when the UK government formally replaced the East India Company as the ruler of India). The carving up of the world between European powers was largely complete by 1914, and indeed the struggle for the few bits that were left unallocated fuelled the rush to war in the first years of this century.

People and money followed the flag. One consequence of the increasingly European domination of the world as a whole was the movement of predominantly European peoples *out* of Europe: as settlers in Australia, New Zealand, Canada, South Africa and overwhelmingly the United States — with the associated genocide or subordination of indigenous populations. Another consequence was the flow of capital out of Europe: first out of the UK into the emerging industrial systems of Western Europe and North America itself; and then later, from these industrializing economies out into Africa, Asia and South America. The cumulative effect of this uneven pattern of nineteenth century industrial development, migration and capital export was the emergence by 1914 of an integrated world system — an international economic order of *core* and *peripheral* economies.

By 1914 that system was fully in place. At its core — in a rectangle that stretched from Chicago to St. Petersburg in the north, and from Baltimore to Milan in the south — industrial economies were establishing themselves. (Japan alone, and for special reasons of its own, escaped the consequences of geographical exclusion from the core; and gave the system an alternative Asian centre of gravity that would come to full fruition only a century later.) Around the immediate perimeter of the core, agrarian economies restructured their land systems to produce the food required by the industrializing centre. (A sweep of countries were caught up in this, from Canada and the American Midwest, through Mexico, Spain, southern Italy, Hungary and the Ukraine: in the process generating a tidal wave of landless peasants whose migration into the core — and especially into the United States — provided the cheap labour vital to industrial development there.) Further afield, in the outer periphery, colonial/neo-colonial economic and political relationships locked a series of Asian, African and South American economies into a service role to the core's industrialization: providing, through processes of unequal exchange, cheap raw materials and cheap labour to protect the profit margins and living standards of the industrial classes in the system's heartland. The United Kingdom, of course, stood at the very centre of that heart.

(b) *'Loci of power'*

Power-centres within the emerging capitalist world system have also shifted over time. Capitalism initially flourished in the trading and banking networks of Renaissance Italy; and then moved north, into Germany and into Holland. Sixteenth and early seventeenth century military defeats and social turmoil permanently removed Italy, and temporarily removed Germany, from the centre of capitalist power; and left Holland, France and England to fight out the battle for initially commercial (and later industrial) supremacy. It was the English naval (and also military) victories of the 1688–1815 period, the possession of Indian wealth, and the lucrative profits of West Indian slave trading, that helped to trigger the United Kingdom into industrial take-off after 1760, and brought the UK economy and political system a century of increasing world domination (see Kennedy, 1988, p.151 for details of that dominance).

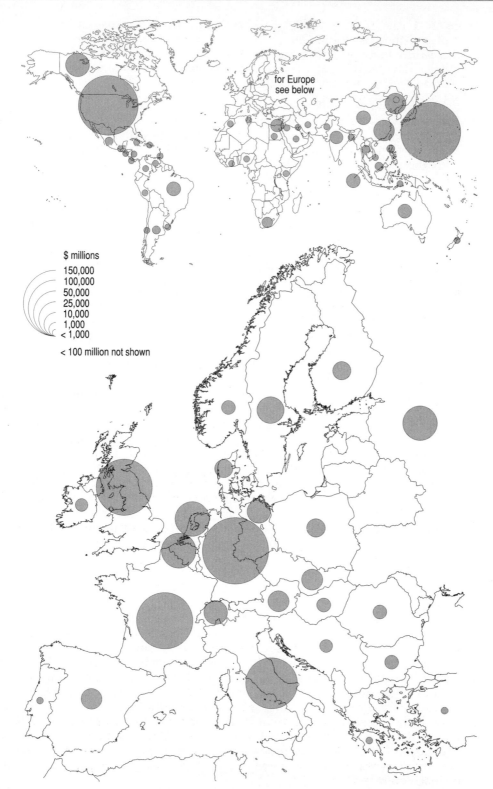

Figure A.1   *Geographical origin of world manufacturing exports, 1980*
Source: Dicken (1986, p.33).

By then it was already clear that the emerging international economic order worked best when one economy exercised a hegemonic role through the system as a whole. With one economy in dominance, its currency could lubricate the trade, its capital fuel the investment, and its military power maintain the peace, within which all the component economies of the system could flourish. The mid-nineteenth century *Pax Britannica* performed this task for the international economy in its formative years: facilitating the industrialization first of the USA, then of Germany and Japan, and later of a host of other Western European economies. After 1945 US dominance played an equivalent role.

Both UK industrializers, and much later US ones, enjoyed a brief moment of world domination — both functioned in their time as 'the workshop of the world' — only then to discover that hegemonic economic power invariably creates the conditions for its own destruction. During their brief periods of world leadership, dominant powers seem inexorably to lose the capacity to maintain their economic supremacy. Their industrialists relax in easy market conditions, and allow competitive economies to catch up and overhaul them. Trade balances whittle away into deficit, without precipitating internal economic modernization, because the currency's general acceptability throughout the international system enables those deficits to be financed by the printing of money. The cost of policing and superintending the system they dominate keeps military spending and tax burdens disproportionately high, and consolidates attitudes and political priorities unsuited to later periods of imperial decline. To quote Paul Kennedy, 'by devoting a large share of the nation's manufacturing power to expenditures upon unproductive armaments, [dominant powers] run the risk of eroding the national economic base, especially *vis-à-vis* states which are concentrating a larger share of their income upon productive investment for long term growth' (Kennedy, 1988, p.539). This certainly was the experience of the UK after 1890, and of the USA after 1973.

So there is a recognizable pattern to the distribution of power within the international capitalist order after 1760. By 1860 dominance lay with the UK, a dominance challenged after 1890 by the rise of US and German corporate strength. German and Japanese defeats in 1945 then left the United States as the hegemonic power, with the UK in a crucial but subordinate role. American policy-makers in the late 1940s looked ahead to what they anticipated would be 'the American century'. In the event, however, their period of unchallenged supremacy was to be much shorter than that. Indeed — as we discuss in more detail in the text — the post-war years have been completely over-shadowed by first the development and exercise of US leadership in international economic affairs, and then later by the emergence of a new international division of labour, and by a renewed challenge to US dominance from the economies of the Far East and Western Europe. This rise and fall of US power provides the main backcloth to the running of the UK economy in the post-war period, precisely because UK policy-makers had first to find a role for the UK in the emerging American empire and then find a new role for the UK (in a bloc of European economic powers) as the USA's hegemony began to slip away.

Table A.1 Changes in world leadership in industrial production, 1870–1980

	Percentage of world industrial output				
	1870	**1913**	**1926–9**	**1936–8**	**1980**[1]
UK	31.8	14.0	9.4	9.2	3.8
USA	23.3	35.8	42.4	32.2	29.4
Germany	13.2 ⎫	15.7 ⎫	11.6 ⎫	10.7 ⎫	12.4[2] ⎫
	⎬ 23.5	⎬ 22.1	⎬ 18.2	⎬ 15.2	⎬ 19.4
France	10.3 ⎭	6.4 ⎭	6.6 ⎭	4.5 ⎭	7.0 ⎭
Japan	—	1.2	2.5	3.5	15.7

[1] 1980 figures refer to world manufacturing output.
[2] West Germany.

Source: Dicken (1986, pp.14, 25).

(c) 'The Soviet challenge'

The detail of all this occupies much of Chapter 1. But in this Appendix we have the space to put one other component of the international context into place. We have looked so far at the emergence of an integrated world system after 1500, and at the rise and fall of particular economies within it. What we have not done is to note too the way in which the writ of that world system was restricted — for over 70 years after 1917 — by the emergence of a competing system of economic and political organization — a challenger to world capitalism triggered into existence initially by the strains involved in the uneven development of world capitalism in the nineteenth century. To grasp the *divided* nature of the post-war economic and political world, we need some understanding of the legacies left to the contemporary period by the way in which nineteenth century industrialization occurred in recognizably distinct 'waves'. It is useful to keep an image before us of 'first wave' industrializers, 'second wave' ones, and even industrializers of the 'third wave', if we are to grasp the determinants of the post-war order within which UK society and economy has been organized and run.

The European, and European-peopled, countries which most easily found their place in the capitalist 'sun', so to speak, were those with already established capitalist social relationships, a middle class, trading networks and private capital accumulation all in place well before industrial development on any scale occurred anywhere. Clearly the UK had these to excess, and had the representative political institutions within which they could flourish best. The UK had already rid itself of its peasantry, established wage–labour relationships in the countryside, and acquired a developed urban society and commerce, long before 1760. By 1800 Belgium (and to a lesser degree France, which still faced an entrenched peasantry) were similarly equipped with the prerequisites for successful capitalist industrialization. So too, in a different geographical and social context, was the United States. (The USA avoided the barriers to capitalist industrialization associated with entrenched feudal social relationships by not having any kind of feudal past, and by recruiting its proletarians from the displaced peasantries of other disintegrating feudal societies.) These 'first wave' industrializers then set the pace for the rest to follow; and they each extended their franchises slowly (making the move from representative to democratic political systems) as their industrialization generated more numerous, and eventually more self-confident, urban working classes demanding better economic, social and political conditions. These first wave industrializers reached 1945 with fully-established democratic systems in place, with well-entrenched urban societies and cultures, with extensive industrial infrastructures, and with the beginnings of comprehensive welfare systems.

In Table A.2 Rostow gives 'tentative and approximate take-off dates for industrialization'.

Table A.2 'Waves' of industrialization

First wave:	Great Britain	1783–1802
	France	1830–60
	Belgium	1833–60
	USA	1843–60
Second wave:	Germany	1850–73
	Japan	1878–90
Third wave:	Russia	1890–1914

'Take-off' here involves productive investment reaching 10% of GNP, the development of one/more manufacturing sectors with growth potential, and the emergence of institutions able to mobilize credit.

Source: Rostow (1961, pp.15, 38).

The next wave of societies to undergo industrialization came on stream later, in part because they lacked the full set of prerequisites which had triggered industrialization in the UK and USA. In consequence, they had to modernize their economic structures in the face of already existing industrial competition. They were initially behind in the capitalist race (Germany and Japan particularly) because their land-owning classes were less commercially-minded, their peasantries less proletarianized, and their middle classes less developed and self-confident than in the UK and the USA. These societies industrialized under the leadership of traditional aristocratic castes, with their middle classes subordinate to autocratic political regimes. But at least they did industrialize, and they did so without major peasant and worker rebellion (although Germany lost a Kaiser in such a rebellion in 1918); and by the 1930s both Germany and Japan were engaged in expansionist military adventures made possible by the heavy industrial development they had by then achieved. If these 'second wave' industrializers arrived in the post-war world as liberal democracies, they did so only through the route of military defeat by other capitalist powers (and in the German case, by the Soviet Union as well, to which we will come). Yet at least they remained *within* the capitalist bloc by 1945, as Russia by then did not; and indeed in 1945 actually began the post-war years *under* the direct political control of the leading capitalist power, namely the United States.

The Soviet Union is the great exception to all this in the West (as China was later to be in the East). The inexorable spread of an international capitalist world order, in wave upon wave of capitalist industrialization, faltered at the borders of Russia in 1917. Pre-Soviet Russia had also lacked an extensive

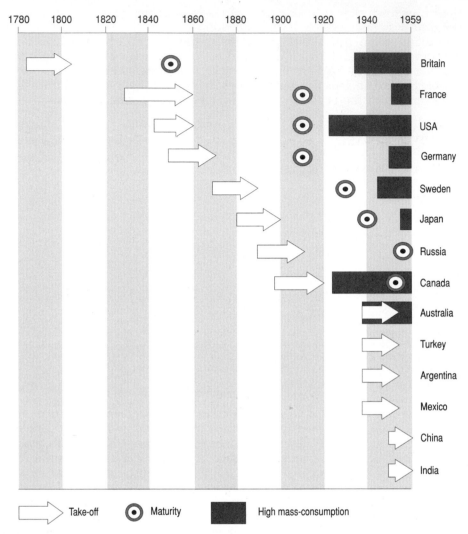

Figure A.2 *Chart of the stages of economic growth*
Source: Rostow (1961, p.1).

middle class urban society, extensive private capital accumulation and a developed trading network. It also — like Japan and Germany — was aristocratically dominated and peasant based. But so restricted was its middle class, so plentiful its peasantry and so retarded its industrial base, that state-induced industrialization in the Russian case did not break through to sustained economic growth. Instead the severity of the economic and social upheaval involved in rapid industrialization in so backward a society — and its military defeat by more advanced capitalist powers in 1905 and after 1914 — precipitated working class and peasant revolutions in 1917, and the creation of a communist alternative to the capitalist West.

Capitalist power failed to destroy that revolution by invasion in both 1918 and in 1941; and Russian-inspired proletarian revolt failed to spread into the centres of capitalism in the same period. Instead, after 1917, the Soviet

Union was cut off (and cut out) of the international capitalist order, a peasant society isolated in its own bunker, and forced to industrialize on its own resources. The cost paid by Russian peasants and workers for forced industrialization by Stalin in the 1930s and 1940s was truly appalling, and laid the seeds for what — more than 50 years later — would be a generalized crisis of legitimacy of Soviet communism. But between 1945 and the outbreak of that crisis in Eastern Europe in 1989, the Soviet empire stood solid and stood alone: as an apparently impregnable bloc of states built around a Stalinized Soviet Union, a bloc put together partly by Russian conquests in 1944–5 and partly by peasant revolutions in China and Vietnam in the late 1940s.

That is why, between 1945 and 1989, the international context within which the UK operated was not just the capitalist one over which the UK had presided in the nineteenth century. It was instead an international context divided into mutually antagonistic blocs of states organized on incompatible social principles. It was moreover one in which the UK occupied a key place in the capitalist half of that divided world order.

SUMMARY

- The emergence of an international capitalist order divided the world by 1914 into core industrial areas and subordinate peripheral regions of agrarian and other forms of primary production.

- The centre of power — the hegemonic core — of the system shifted over time — from Italy to the UK to the USA — and is now in dispute again.

- Industrialization occurred in 'waves', with each 'wave' more traumatic for its participants than the one before; and after 1917 produced an alternative industrial system organized on state-socialist lines.

BIBLIOGRAPHY

Aaronovitch, S., Smith, R., Gardner, J. and Moore, R. (1981) *The Political Economy of British Capitalism*, London, McGraw-Hill.

Abercrombie, N., Hill, S. and Turner, B.S. (1980) *The Dominant Ideology Thesis*, London, Allen & Unwin.

Abercrombie, N., Warde, A., Soothill, K., Urry, J. and Walby, S. (1988) *Contemporary British Society*, Cambridge, Polity Press.

Aglietta, M. (1979) *A Theory of Capitalist Regulation*, London, New Left Books.

Allen, J. (1988a) 'Towards a post-industrial economy', in Allen, J. and Massey, D. (eds) *The Economy in Question*, pp.91–135.

Allen, J. (1988b) 'Fragmented firms, disorganized labour', in Allen, J. and Massey, D. (eds) *The Economy in Question*, pp.184–228.

Allen, J. and Massey, D. (eds) (1988) *The Economy in Question*, London, Sage.

Anderson, J. (1991) 'Traditions in contemporary society', Unit 27, in D103 *Society and Social Science: a Foundation Course*, Milton Keynes, The Open University.

Anderson, P. (1987) 'Figures of descent', *New Left Review*, no.161, pp.20–77.

Anell, L. (1981) *Recession, the Western Economies and the Changing World Order*, London, Francis Pinter.

Armstrong, P., Glyn, A. and Harrison, J. (1984) *Capitalism Since World War II: the Making and Break Up of the Great Boom*, London, Fontana.

Atkinson, J. (1984) 'Manpower strategies for flexible organizations', *Personnel Management*, August.

Auerbach, P. (1989) 'Multinationals and the British economy', in Green, F. (ed.) *The Restructuring of the UK Economy*, pp.263–80.

Barbrook, J. (1990) 'The two souls of post-Fordism', *Catalyst*, no.3, pp.28–9.

Barnett, C. (1984) *The Collapse of British Power*, London, Alan Sutton.

Barnett, C. (1986) *The Audit of War*, London, Macmillan.

Barratt Brown, M. (1972) *What Really Happened to the Coal Industry?*, Nottingham, Institute for Workers Control.

Barry, N.P. (1979) *Hayek's Social and Economic Philosophy*, London, Macmillan.

Beetham, D. (1987) *Bureaucracy*, Milton Keynes, The Open University Press.

Beynon, H. and Nichols, T. (1977) *Living with Capitalism*, London, Routledge & Kegan Paul.

Blank, S. (1985) 'The impact of foreign economic policy', in Coates, D. and Hillard, J. (eds) *The Economic Decline of Modern Britain: the Debate Between Left and Right*.

Bottomore, T. and Brym, R.J. (eds) (1989) *The Capitalist Class: an International Study*, Hemel Hempstead, Harvester-Wheatsheaf.

Breitenbach, H., Burden, T. and Coates, D. (1990) *Features of a Viable Socialism*, London, Harvester-Wheatsheaf.

Brett, E.A. (1985) *The World Economy Since the War: the Politics of Uneven Development*, London, Macmillan.

Brett, E.A., Gilliatt, S. and Pople, A. (1982) 'Planned trade, Labour Party policy and US intervention: the successes and failures of post-war reconstruction', *History Workshop*, Issue 13, pp.130–42.

Burnham, J. (1945) *The Managerial Revolution*, Harmondsworth, Penguin.

Bush, R., Johnston, G. and Coates, D. (eds) (1987) *The World Order: Socialist Perspectives*, Cambridge, Polity Press.

Calder, A. (1981) *Revolutionary Empire*, New York, Dutton.

Cashmore, E.E. (1989) *United Kingdom? Class, Race and Gender Since the War*, London, Unwin Hyman.

Castles, S. and Kosack, G. (1973) *Immigrant Workers and Class Structure in Western Europe*, Oxford, Oxford University Press.

Central Statistical Office, *Social Trends*, London, HMSO.

Childs, D. (1986) *Britain Since 1945: a Political History*, London, Methuen.

Clarke, S. (1990) 'The crisis of Fordism or the crisis of social democracy', *Telos*, Spring, no.83, pp.71–98.

Coates, D. (1972) *Teacher's Unions and Interest Group Politics*, Cambridge, Cambridge University Press.

Coates, D. (1980) *Labour in Power?*, London, Longman.

Coates, D. (1984) *The Context of British Politics*, London, Hutchinson.

Coates, D. (1989a) *The Crisis of Labour*, London, Philip Allan.

Coates, D. (1989b) 'Britain', in Bottomore, T. and Brym, R.J. (eds) *The Capitalist Class: an International Study*, pp.19–45.

Coates, D. and Hillard, J. (eds) (1985) *The Economic Decline of Modern Britain: the Debate Between Left and Right*, Brighton, Wheatsheaf.

Coates, D., Johnston, G. and Bush, R. (eds) (1985) *A Socialist Anatomy of Britain*, Cambridge, Polity Press.

Cook, C. and Ramsden, J. (eds) (1978) *Trends in British Politics Since 1945*, London, Macmillan.

Coote, A. and Campbell, B. (1982) *Sweet Freedom: the Struggle for Women's Liberation*, London, Picador.

Coote, A. and Pattullo, P. (1990) *Power and Prejudice: Women and Politics*, London, Weidenfeld & Nicolson.

Cox, A. (ed.) (1982) *Politics, Policy and the European Recession*, London, Macmillan.

Cox, M. (1990) 'From the Truman doctrine to the second superpower détente: the rise and fall of the Cold War', *Journal of Peace Research*, vol.27, no.1, pp.25–41.

Crewe, I. (1982) 'The Labour Party and the electorate', in Kavanagh, D. (ed.) *The Politics of the Labour Party*, London, Allen & Unwin, pp.9–49.

Crewe, I. (1989) 'Values: the crusade that failed', in Kavanagh, D. and Selsdon, A. (eds) *The Thatcher Effect*, Oxford, Clarendon Press, pp.239–50.

Crosland, A. (1956) *The Future of Socialism*, London, Cape.

Davis, M. (1986) *Prisoners of the American Dream*, London, Verso.

Davis, M. (1987) 'From Fordism to Reagonism: the crisis of American hegemony in the 1980s', in Bush, R., Johnston, G. and Coates, D. (eds) *The World Order: Socialist Perspectives*, pp.7–25.

Denver, D. (1989) *Elections and Voting Behaviour in Britain*, London, Philip Allan.

Department of Employment, *Employment Gazette*, London, HMSO.

Dicken, P. (1986) *Global Shift*, London, Harper & Row.

Ewing, K.D. and Gearty, C.A. (1990) *Freedom under Thatcher*, Oxford, Clarendon Press.

Femia, J. (1975) 'Hegemony and consciousness in the thought of Antonio Gramsci', *Political Studies*, vol.23, pp.29–48.

Ford, J. (1988) *The Indebted Society: Credit and Default in the 1980s*, London, Routledge.

Gamble, A. (1981) *Britain in Decline*, London, Macmillan.

Garton Ash, T. (1990) 'Hold tight, old John Bull', *The Independent*, 2 August.

Glendinning, C. and Miller, J. (eds) (1987) *Women and Poverty in Britain*, Hemel Hempstead, Wheatsheaf.

Glyn, A. (1989) 'The macro-anatomy of the Thatcher years', in Green, F. (ed.) *The Restructuring of the UK Economy*, pp.65–79.

Glyn, A. and Sutcliffe, B. (1972) *British Capitalism, Workers and the Profits Squeeze*, Harmondsworth, Penguin.

Graham, C. and Prosser, T. (eds) (1988) *Waiving the Rules*, Milton Keynes, The Open University Press.

Grant, W. and Sargent, J. (1987) *Business and Politics in Britain*, London, Macmillan.

Green, F. (ed.) (1989) *The Restructuring of the UK Economy*, Hemel Hempstead, Harvester.

Hall, S. (1982) 'The battle for socialist ideas in the 1980s', in Eve, M. and Musson, D. (eds) *The Socialist Register 1982*, London, Merlin, pp.1–20.

Hall, S. (1983) 'The great moving Right show', in Hall, S. and Jacques, M. (eds) *The Politics of Thatcherism*, London, Lawrence & Wishart.

Hall, S. (1989) *The Hard Road to Renewal*, London, Verso.

Hall, S. and Jacques, M. (eds) (1989) *New Times*, London, Lawrence & Wishart.

Hall, S., Chritcher, C., Jefferson, T., Clarke, J. and Roberts, B. (1978) *Policing the Crisis*, London, Macmillan.

Halliday, F. (1983) *The Making of the Second Cold War*, London, Verso.

Halsey, A.H. (ed.) (1988) *British Social Trends Since 1900*, London, Macmillan.

Harden, T. (1988) 'Corporatism without labour: the British version', in Graham, C. and Prosser, T. (eds) *Waiving the Rules*, pp.36–55.

Harris, L. (1985) 'British capital: manufacturing, finance and multinational corporations', in Coates, D., Johnston, G. and Bush, R. (eds) *A Socialist Anatomy of Britain*, pp.7–28.

Harris, L. (1988) 'The economy at the cross roads', in Allen, J. and Massey, D. (eds) *The Economy in Question*.

Harrison, J. and Bavar, D. (1987) 'Ups and downs: the fortunes of the West European and Japanese economies since 1945', in Bush, R., Johnston, G. and Coates, D. (eds) *The World Order: Socialist Perspectives*, pp.43–64.

Hill, S. (1989) 'Britain: the dominant ideology thesis after a decade', in Abercrombie, N. (ed.) *Dominant Ideologies*, London, Allen & Unwin, pp.1–37.

Hilton, R. (1978) *The Transition from Feudalism to Capitalism*, London, Verso.

Hirst, P. and Zeitlin, J. (1991) 'Flexible specialisation versus post-Fordism: theory, evidence and policy implications', *Economy and Society*, vol.20, no.1, pp.1–56.

Hoogvelt, A. (1987) 'The new international division of labour', in Bush, R., Johnston, G. and Coates, D. (eds) *The World Order: Socialist Perspectives*, pp.65–86.

House of Lords Select Committee on Overseas Trade (1985) *Report*, House of Lords, Session 1984–5, 238-I, London, HMSO.

Hudson, R. and Williams, A.M. (1989) *Divided Britain*, London, Bellhaven Press.

Hyman, H. (1988) 'Privatization: the facts', in Veljanovski, C. (ed.) *Privatization and Competition: a Market Perspective*, London, Institute of Economic Affairs.

Jessop, B. (1988) *Conservative Regimes and the Transition to Post-Fordism: the Case of Britain and West Germany*, Essex Papers in Politics and Government, no.47.

Jowell, R. *et al.* (1984–90) *British Social Attitudes: Annual Reports*, London, Gower.

Kavanagh, D. (1985) 'Whatever happened to consensus politics', *Political Studies*, vol.XXXIII, pp.529–46.

Kennedy, P. (1988) *The Rise and Fall of the Great Powers: Economic Change and Military Conflict from 1500 to 2000*, London, Unwin Hyman.

Lewis, J. and Piachaud, D. (1987) 'Women and poverty in the twentieth century', in Glendinning, C. and Miller, J. (eds) *Women and Poverty in Britain*, pp.28–52.

Mann, M. (1982) 'The social cohesion of liberal democracies', in Held, D. and Giddens, A. (eds) *Classes, Power and Conflict*, London, Macmillan, pp.373–95.

Marshall, G., Rose, D., Newby, H. and Vogler, C. (1988) *Social Class in Modern Britain*, London, Unwin Hyman.

Martin, R. (1988) 'Industrial capitalism in transition: the contemporary re-organization of the British space-economy', in Massey, D. and Allen, J. (eds) *Uneven Development: Cities and Regions in Transition*, pp.202–31.

Martin, R. (1989) 'Regional imbalance as consequence and constraint in national economic renewal', in Green, F. (ed.) *The Restructuring of the UK Economy*, pp.80–100.

Martin, R. and Rowthorn, B. (eds) (1986) *The Geography of De-industrialization*, London, Macmillan.

Marwick, A. (1990) *British Society Since 1945*, Harmondsworth, Penguin.

Marx, K. (1852) *The Eighteenth Breumaire of Louis Bonaparte*.

Massey, D. (1986) 'The legacy lingers on: the impact of Britain's international role on its internal geography', in Martin, R. and Rowthorn, B. (eds) *The Geography of De-industrialization*, pp.31–52.

Massey, D. and Allen, J. (eds) (1988) *Uneven Development: Cities and Regions in Transition*, London, Hodder & Stoughton.

Maynard, G.K. (1988) *The Economy Under Threat*, Oxford, Blackwell.

McCormick, B.J. (1988) *The World Economy: Patterns of Growth and Change*, London, Philip Allan.

Meegan, R. (1988) 'A crisis of mass production?', in Allen, J. and Massey, D. (eds) *The Economy in Question*, pp.136–83.

Middlemass, K. (1979) *Politics in Industrial Society*, London, André Deutsch.

Morgan, K.O. (1990) *The People's Peace: British History 1945–1989*, Oxford, Oxford University Press.

Murray, R. (1989) 'Fordism and post-Fordism', in Hall, S. and Jacques, M. (eds) *New Times*, pp.38–53.

Noble, T. (1975) *Modern Britain: Structure and Change*, London, Batsford.

Nolan, P. (1989) 'The productivity miracle?', in Green, F. (ed.) *The Restructuring of the UK Economy*, pp.101–30.

O'Connor, J. (1973) *The Fiscal Crisis of the State*, New York, St. Martin's Press.

Overbeek, H. (1990) *Global Capitalism and National Decline*, London, Unwin Hyman.

Panitch, L. (1986) *Working Class Politics in Crisis*, London, Verso.

Parboni, R. (1981) *The Dollar and its Rivals*, London, New Left Books.

Paxman, J. (1990) *Friends in High Places: Who Runs Britain?*, London, Michael Joseph.

Reddaway, W.B. (1983) 'Problems and prospects for the UK economy', *Economic Record*, vol.59, pp.220–31.

Reid, I. and Strata, E. (eds) (1989) *Sex Differences in Britain*, London, Gower.

Rostow, W. (1961) *Stages of Economic Growth*, London, Cambridge University Press.

Rowthorn, B. (1986) 'De-industrialization in Britain', in Martin, R. and Rowthorn, B. (eds) *The Geography of De-industrialization*, pp.1–30.

Rowthorn, B. (1989) 'The Thatcher revolution', in Green, F. (ed.) *The Restructuring of the UK Economy*, pp.281–98.

Rubery, J. (1986) 'Trade unions in the 1980s: the case of the United Kingdom', in Edwardes, R. *et al.* (eds) *Unions in Crisis and Beyond*, Dover, Mass., Auburn House.

Salaman, G. and Thompson, K. (1978) 'Class culture and the persistence of an élite: the case of Army Officer selection', *Sociological Review*, vol.26, no.2 pp.283–303.

Savage, S.P. and Robins, L. (1990) *Public Policy under Thatcher*, London, Macmillan.

Schmitter, P.C. (1974) 'Still the century of corporatism', *The Review of Politics*, vol.36, no.1, pp.85–131.

Scott, J. (1985) 'The British upper class', in Coates, D., Johnston, G. and Bush, R. (eds) *A Socialist Anatomy of Britain*, pp.29–54.

Scott, J. (1991) *Who Rules Britain?*, Cambridge, Polity Press.

Smith, A. (1776) *The Wealth of Nations*, reprinted by Penguin Books (1970).

Smith, C. (1990) 'Flexible specialisation, automation and mass production', *Work, Employment and Society*, vol.3, no.2, pp.203–20.

Smith, D. (1987) 'The arms race and the Cold War', in Bush, R., Johnston, G. and Coates, D. (eds) *The World Order: Socialist Perspectives*, pp.141–68.

Smith, D. (1990) 'Work still needed to close productivity gap', *The Sunday Times*, 2 September.

Spence, M. (1985) 'Imperialism in decline: Britain in the 1980s', *Capital and Class*, Spring, pp.117–39.

Szeftel, M. (1987) 'The crisis in the Third World', in Bush, R., Johnston, G. and Coates, D. (eds) *The World Order: Socialist Perspectives*, pp.89–140.

Theakston, K. and Fry, G. (1989) 'Britain's administrative élite: Permanent Secretaries 1900–1986', *Public Administration*, vol.67, no.2, pp.129–47.

Thompson, E.P. (1961) *The Making of the English Working Class*, London, Gollancz.

Thompson, E.P. (1979) 'The peculiarities of the English', in his *The Poverty of Theory and Other Essays*, London, Merlin, pp.35–91.

Thompson, E.P. (1980) 'The logic of exterminism', *New Left Review*, no.121, pp.3–32.

Toporowski, J. (1989) 'The financial system and capital accumulation in the 1980s', in Green, F. (ed.) *The Restructuring of the UK Economy*, pp.242–62.

Urry, J. (1985) 'The class structure', in Coates, D., Johnston, G. and Bush, R. (eds) *A Socialist Anatomy of Britain*, pp.55–75.

Urry, J. (1989) 'The end of organized capitalism', in Hall, S. and Jacques, M. (eds) *New Times*, pp.94–103.

Warde, A. (1989) 'The future of work', *Social Studies Review*, vol.5, no.1, pp.11–15.

Webb, M. (1989) 'Sex and gender in the labour market', in Reid, I. and Strata, E. (eds) *Sex Differences in Britain*, pp.133–91.

Wells, J. (1989) 'Uneven development and de-industrialization in the UK since 1979', in Green, F. (ed.) *The Restructuring of the UK Economy*, pp.25–64.

Westergaard, J. and Resler, H. (1975) *Class in a Capitalist Society*, London, Heinemann.

INDEX

(Note: the alphabetical arrangement of this index is in word-by-word order. Prepositions, etc. at the beginning of subheadings have been ignored in determining the alphabetical order of subheadings. The word *passim* means that the subject so annotated is referred to in scattered passages throughout the pages indicated.)